The City Centre

PATTERNS AND PROBLEMS

Oblique view of Perth central area 1972. The core boundary is shown by the dotted lines: note the strong contrast of building height and form across this boundary. (Aerial Photographs Pty. Ltd.)

The City Centre

PATTERNS AND PROBLEMS

IAN C. ALEXANDER

M.A.(W.A.), M.Phil.(Lond.)

UNIVERSITY OF WESTERN AUSTRALIA PRESS

1974

First published in 1974 by
University of Western Australia Press
Nedlands, Western Australia

Eastern states of Australia, New Zealand, Papua and New Guinea, and Hawaii:
Melbourne University Press, P.O. Box 278, Carlton South, Vic. 3053

U.K., Europe, the Middle East, Africa and the Caribbean:
Prentice-Hall International, International Book Distributors Ltd,
66 Wood Lane End, Hemel Hempstead, Hertfordshire, England

USA, its territories and possessions, Canada:
International Scholarly Book Services Inc., P.O. Box 4347,
Portland, Oregon 97208, USA

Singapore, Thailand, Malaysia, Hong Kong, Philippines:
Angus & Robertson (S.E. Asia) Pty Ltd, 159, block 2, ground floor
Boon Keng Road, Singapore 12

ISBN 0 85564 075 8

Text set in 10/12 pt Baskerville

Printed in Western Australia
by Frank Daniels Pty Ltd, Perth
Western Australia

TO HELEN

Contents

	Page
Acknowledgements	xix
Introduction	xxi

1 The city centre in perspective

1-1 What's in a name?   1

    1-1.1 The CBD—catchword or misnomer? 1
    1-1.2 Central functions 3
    1-1.3 Towards a more comprehensive concept 8
    1-1.4 The need for further investigation 12

1-2 The explanation and evolution of central-area structure   13

    1-2.1 The theory of the land market 13
    1-2.2 The importance of linkages 15
    1-2.3 Models of city structure 16
    1-2.4 Transition and change 19
    1-2.5 The planning response—a comment 21

1-3 Synthesis   22

2 Central-area processes, activity patterns and problems I: the frame

2-1 Character and definition   23

2-2 Composition   29

2-3 Activity patterns in the frame: analysis and explanation   32

    2-3.1 An analytical framework? 32
    2-3.2 Public and organizational activities 33
    2-3.3 Residential premises 33
    2-3.4 Automotive-oriented activities 36
    2-3.5 Manufacturing activities 39
    2-3.6 Wholesaling and storage activities 44
    2-3.7 Activities which occupy offices 46
    2-3.8 Other activities 47

Page

2-4   Planning problems in the frame   49
    2-4.1   Blight   49
    2-4.2   Freeway impact   50

2-5   Conclusion   57

3   Central-area processes, activity patterns and problems II: the core

3-1   Character   59

3-2   Composition and contents   59

3-3   Office location   66
    3-3.1   The general pattern   66
    3-3.2   Financial offices   68
    3-3.3   Professional offices   75
    3-3.4   Government offices   78
    3-3.5   General offices   81
    3-3.6   Offices—summary   81

3-4   Location of retail and service activities   82
    3-4.1   Introductory remarks   82
    3-4.2   Inner elements: specialist retailing   85
    3-4.3   Inner elements: personal services   89
    3-4.4   Outer elements: household-goods retailing   91
    3-4.5   Miscellaneous and dispersed elements   92
    3-4.6   Summary   94

3-5   Wholesaling and other activities   97

3-6   Conclusion   99

4   Synthesis of activity patterns: perspectives on regionalization

4-1   Overall structure: a conventional approach   101
    4-1.1   Functional zones   101
    4-1.2   Vertical differentiation   111
    4-1.3   The need for alternative strategies   116

4-2   Classificatory techniques: the taxonomist's dilemma   119
    4-2.1   Choice of strategy   119
    4-2.2   Information analysis   121

4-3   Overall structure: new perspectives   123
    4-3.1   Analysis at the general level   123
    4-3.2   Detailed analyses: the core area   124
    4-3.3   Concluding comments   129

Page

5 Central-area dynamics

5-1 Change: the dynamic element   130

5-2 Boundary movement   133

5-3 Building activity and changing land use   133

    5-3.1 Overall change 133
    5-3.2 Office development 144
    5-3.3 Retail-service development 149
    5-3.4 Wholesaling development 154
    5-3.5 Manufacturing development 155
    5-3.6 Development of public and cultural facilities 156
    5-3.7 Residential development 158
    5-3.8 The patterns synthesised 160

5-4 Planning for central-area change and redevelopment   165

    5-4.1 The need for planning 165
    5-4.2 The limitations of conventional planning controls 166
    5-4.3 Comprehensive redevelopment as an answer? 167

6 Central-area structure and dynamics: a synthesis

6-1 Towards a model?   172

    6-1.1 Parallels and precedents 172
    6-1.2 The core 175
    6-1.3 The frame 178
    6-1.4 Overall considerations 180

6-2 Implications for planning   181

6-3 Conclusion: directions for further research   184

Appendices

I   Central-area delimitation   187

II The land-use code   190

IIIA Retail and service establishments: vertical location, Perth core 200

IIIB Retail and service establishments: changes in numbers, Perth core
    1957-68   202

IV Retail-sales trends and regional significance, Perth inner city area
    1957-69 (by commodity)   203

Bibliography   205

Index   213

Tables

		Page
1-1	General types of land use considered by Murphy and Vance to be non-central business in character	2
1-2	Percentage by value of Australian capital city retail trade transacted in CBD, 1962	4
1-3	Percentage of central-area floorspace devoted to wholesaling and warehousing activities in selected cities	6
1-4	Industrial activities found in the central areas of various cities (in descending order of frequency)	7
2-1	Properties of the central-area frame (according to Horwood & Boyce)	24
2-2	Criteria adopted for classification of activities into core and frame types	27
2-3	Classification of activity types into 'core' and 'frame' categories for purposes of delimiting the Perth central-area core	28
2-4	Comparison of the internal composition of the frame areas of five cities (by floorspace occupance)	31
2-5	Numbers and area of various classes of manufacturing plants within the Perth frame	40
2-6	Increases in vacant space: freeway path and environs, Perth frame area 1968-72	53
3-1	General properties of the CBD core	60
3-2	Composition of core areas of selected cities	61
3-3	Relative rank order of core uses according to amount of space occupied on separate floor levels	65
3-4	Concentration indices and numbers of office activities in Perth's core at 1968	69
3-5	Percentage (by number and floor area) of various office types at all floor levels: Perth core	73
3-6	Locational classification of retail-service elements, Perth core 1957 and 1968	84
3-7	Dispersal indices and numbers of retail-services activities, Perth core 1968	85

Tables

Page

4-1 Percentages of floor area occupied by major uses within functional zones, Perth core   110

4-2 Activity groupings resulting from inverse analysis of ground-floor grid (block-oriented)   125

5-1 Floorspace changes: Perth and London central areas 1953-68, 1957-66, respectively   138

5-2 Building construction, Perth central area 1954-72 (inclusive)   140

Figures

		Page
1-1	*The Horwood/Boyce core/frame concept (1959)*	9
1-2	*The Murphy/Vance CBD (1954)*	11
1-3	*Land values and location in an urban area*	14
1-4	*Three models of city structure*	17
1-5	*The Preston/Griffin transition zone framework (1966)*	20
2-1	*Definitions of the Perth central area, three views*	26
2-2	*Definition of Perth core 1968*	26
2-3	*Height indices of frame blocks, Perth central area 1968*	30
2-4	*Distribution of public and civic facilities, Perth central area 1968*	30
2-5	*Predominantly residential areas, Perth central area 1968*	35
2-6	*Distribution of parking facilities and automotive-oriented activities, Perth central area 1968*	35
2-7	*Zoning ordinances for central area, adopted by Perth City Council 1963*	38
2-8	*Distribution of manufacturing floorspace, Perth central area 1968*	38
2-9	*Distribution of wholesaling and storage premises, Perth central area 1968 (2 figs: A, B)*	43
2-10	*Distribution of profesional offices, West Perth 1968*	48
2-11	*Vacancies in Perth frame 1968*	51
2-12	*Development of ring road concept*	51, 52

      2-12a   The Stephenson central-area road plan 1955
      2-12b   The 1963 MRPA central-area road plan
      2-12c   The modified central-area road plan 1968

| 2-13 | *Changes in vacancy in freeway area 1968-72* | 54 |

      2-13a   Pattern of vacancy 1968
      2-13b   Pattern of vacancy 1972

| 2-14 | *Distribution of vacancy and resumed property in freeway path, Perth frame 1972* | 55 |

Page

2-15 *Frame floorspace to be absorbed by the proposed freeway, Perth central area* 56

3-1 *Variation of office and retail floorspace with city size* 62

3-2 *Distribution of Perth core space by floor (1968 data)* 64

3-3 *Distribution of office space, Perth core 1968* 67

3-4 *Market land values, Perth core 1968* 67

3-5 *Distribution of financial offices, Perth core 1968* 70, 71
    3-5a Stockbrokers
    3-5b Estate agents
    3-5c Insurance offices
    3-5d Banks and finance companies

3-6 *Distribution of professional offices, Perth core 1968* 76, 77
    3-6a Accountants
    3-6b Lawyers
    3-6c Doctors
    3-6d Dentists

3-7 *Distribution of governmental offices, Perth core 1968* 79

3-8 *Distribution of general offices, Perth core 1968* 79, 80
    3-8a The wholesale-production group
    3-8b Business services
    3-8c Travel agents and travel companies

3-9 *Distribution of inner retail elements, Perth core 1968* 86
    3-9a Department, variety and clothing stores
    3-9b Footwear and jewellery stores

3-10 *Pedestrian flows within Perth's core 1968* 88

3-11 *Distribution of Personal-service elements, Perth core 1968* 90

3-12 *Distribution of household-goods stores, Perth core 1968* 92

3-13 *Distribution of miscellaneous retail elements, Perth core 1968* 93
    3-13a Banks, hotels, restaurants
    3-13b Food stores

3-14 *Diagrammatic representation of core structure* 96
    3-14a Activity arrangement
    3-14b Idealized model

3-15 *Distribution of wholesaling outlets, Perth core 1968* 98

3-16 *Plans for central Hay Street mall* 98

4-1 *Functional zones within Perth's central area 1968* 103

4-2 *Space use within functional zones, Perth frame 1968* 103

Page

4-3 *Comparison of functional zoning in central areas of eight cities* 105-8
    4-3a Perth 1973
    4-3b Adelaide 1973
    4-3c Hobart 1968
    4-3d London 1966
    4-3e Manchester 1966
    4-3f Cardiff 1966
    4-3g Model of U.S.A. city
    4-3h Capetown 1965

4-4 *Functional zones, by floor, Perth core 1968* 112-15
    4-4a Ground floor
    4-4b First floor
    4-4c Second floor
    4-4d Third floor
    4-4e Fourth floor
    4-4f Fifth floor
    4-4g Sixth floor
    4-4h All floors combined

4-5 *Space use by floor, Perth core 1968* 117

4-6 *Agglomerative* vs *divisive strategies for classification: linkage trees* 122

4-7 *Regionalization of Perth central area by information analysis at the general level (1968 data)* 122

4-8 *Regionalization of Perth core by information analysis at the micro level (1968 data)* 126, 127
    4-8a Ground floor
    4-8b First floor
    4-8c Second floor
    4-8d All floors

5-1 *Land use, Perth central area 1953* 132

5-2 *Changing structure of Perth central area* 134-6
    5-2a Land use, Perth central area 1968
    5-2b Internal boundary changes in Perth core 1959-72
    5-2c Boundary changes, Perth central area 1968-72

5-3 *Proposed zoning ordinances for Perth central area 1971* 137

5-4 *Construction activity, Perth central area 1954-72* 141

5-5 *Office construction, Perth* vs *Sydney 1954-70* 143

5-6 *Land value changes, Perth central area 1954-68* 145

5-7 *Construction of professional offices, West Perth 1954-72* 148

Page

5-8 *Classification of renewal activity in retail segments of Perth core 1954-72* 152

5-9 *Spatial movement of wholesaling construction, Perth central area 1954-72* 152

5-10 *Distribution of construction activity, Perth central area 1954-72* 162

5-11 *Classification of change, Perth central area 1954-72* 162

5-12 *The concept of comprehensive redevelopment* 169, 170
      5-12a   The general concept of multi-level development
      5-12b   Plans for Covent Garden, London

6-1 *Conceptual model of the central area* 173
6-2 *Cross-section through conceptual model* 174

Plates

Frontispiece
Oblique view of Perth central area 1972

Between 88 and 89

I   Residential premises in the frame: traditional style

II   Residential premises in the frame: modern style

III   Transitory residential premises in the frame

IV   The significance of parking areas within the frame

V   'Automobile row', frame area

VI   Blight in the frame

VIIa, b   Wholesaling premises in the frame

Between 104 and 105

VIII   Land-use succession in the frame

IX   Freeway interchange

X   Offices in the core hub area

XI   Retail-services premises in Perth's core

XII   Perth's skyline 1955

XIII   Perth's skyline 1973

XIV   High-status housing

XV   Foreshore activities, Perth central area

Acknowledgements

This book is a revised and expanded version of an M.A. thesis presented to the University of Western Australia in 1970. I am grateful to professor Martyn Webb for his assistance in negotiations with the University of Western Australia Press Board that led to the acceptance of the manuscript for publication. I am also indebted to Professor Webb for allowing me the opportunity to prepare the book whilst teaching in the Department of Geography, and for his helpful comments on the successive drafts. My colleagues within the department also deserve thanks for their forbearance of an initiate author.

Many people assisted this study with the furnishing of data and preparation of material for publication. I must express sincere thanks to the Perth City Council and officers of the Planning and Building Surveyor's Departments for allowing me access to data on which most of the analysis is based. The Commonwealth Department of Works, the Bureau of Census and Statistics and various state government departments were also extremely helpful in providing statistical data.

Words are not really sufficient to thank the many who slaved over hot typewriters, drawing boards and developing machines; in particular I would like to thank Geoff Ward for cartographic advice, Gaye Roberts for patiently producing the skilfully composed maps and diagrams, and Anne Howell, Lynette Dalziell and Enid Thomas for typing my illegible handwriting. Roger Webber undertook development of photographs; and produced the excellent oblique shots that form Plates IV and VIIb. Officers of the University Press, in particular Vic Greaves, deserve, thanks for ready assistance and guidance. Florian Brodalka must be accorded special thanks for his expert editorial advice and his adept patchwork on my grammatical construction.

Thanks are also due to the Editors of E. J. Brill & Co., Washington University Press and the journal *Economic Geography* for permission to reproduce certain copyright material.

Introduction

The city centre has always attracted special attention. One reason for this is the concentration of taller buildings that is invariably found in the centre. This characteristic immediately separates the area out from the complex urban mosaic and gives it a distinct image (see frontispiece). More than this, however, the centre impinges directly on the life of a large proportion of the city's population whether they be employers or employees, shopkeepers or shoppers, artists or entertainment seekers, harried pedestrians or simply frustrated motorists attempting to cross the congested city. The centre plays an important rôle in the life and economy of the city by providing goods and services for people over an area that often extends well beyond the limits of the immediate built-up space.

Over the last twenty years, particularly in western Europe, North America and Australasia, where affluence and car ownership have become more widespread than ever before, a gradual change in the function and status of the central area has been observed. Problems have arisen and the future of the centre has come under close scrutiny from urban analysts and planners. The most common problem that is perceived stems from the changing structure of the city as a whole. Many activities, once found only in the centre, have joined the outward movement of population and housing, and thus lessened the dominance of the centre over the city. This has raised fears, particularly in the United States, where the trends are most marked, that the area is gradually being drained of life. It is suggested that the city centre has been progressively strangled by mounting traffic congestion, lack of parking space, competition from new suburban centres and a declining population. So widespread has the outward movement of activities become in certain cities that central-area functions have recently been wryly defined as those 'that have not yet left the central area [sic]' (Allpass *et al.* 1966:1).

This movement has not always been viewed darkly, however, but rather as an inevitable and desirable consequence of city growth and the growing dependence on the car as a means of transport (see e.g. Webber 1964). Moreover in cities in Britain and Australia, if not in North America, the centres have not died as a result of these trends; indeed, demand for land has sent land prices soaring and made many a speculator rich. Central redevelopment has continued apace despite the decentralization—in fact there is evidence to suggest that the rebuilding has encouraged the outward movement of less-profitable activities.

But whatever the causes and desirability of these trends, there is no doubt that they have focused attention upon the future composition and function of the centre. Grandiose schemes involving the complete remodelling of the area have been proposed by architects and others as a means of revivifying the centre (see Gruen 1965, Crosby 1968). Superficially such schemes seem attractive; yet all too often they take little account of the present structure, character and dynamics of the central area. Such aspects have been examined in great detail by many researchers in recent years, and a number of background surveys of individual centres have been undertaken by planning authorities. But these reports often pay little more than lip service to the need for integration of survey and plan. Hence many plans produced are not in accord with the area's present character or future needs. Meanwhile, the proliferation of research into the nature of the city centre has been characterized by a dearth of generalizations and coherent theories. Furthermore, those that have been developed manifest considerable discrepancies over the area's nature and composition—this is noticeable even in the latest monograph on the area (Murphy 1972).

It has been suggested by Carter (1972) that much geographical research into the central area has become sidetracked into the sterile avenues of argument over definitions. Be this as it may, it is also true that there exists considerable confusion in the literature over the meaning and usage of basic terminology. Such confusion and the discrepancies referred to above may be thought to arise from differences between cities studied, yet a closer examination of data suggests that this is not so. As long ago as 1962 it was suggested that the similarities in the structure of the central area of cities outweigh the differences (Diamond 1962:533).

This book sets out to resolve these confusions and discrepancies and to develop a clearer picture of the land-use arrangement and changing structure of the city centre than that which currently exists. This objective is pursued through a detailed examination and analysis of land use and activity patterns within the city centre and an analysis of the ways in which these patterns are changing. The analysis draws heavily upon the results of a recent survey and field-work carried out in Perth, Western Australia;* wherever possible, however, comparisons are made with cities elsewhere in order to broaden the study base and to enable development of generalizations. The analysis lays the groundwork for the construction of a conceptual model of central-area structure that incorporates reference to processes of organization and change in order to overcome the inherent static nature of a conventional land-use analysis. The model, furthermore, is based on a rigorous and wide-ranging exploration of analytical techniques.

The analysis of structure and change also points to certain problems of planning the central area, and solutions to these problems are proposed and discussed. Many

* The survey was carried out in 1968 by the Perth City Council and the results can be found summarized in a recent council publication (1971a). The analysis was effected on the detailed records of the survey, supplemented by field surveys in 1969 and 1972. All data were transferred on to computer tapes to facilitate analysis. The study of change (Chapter 5) was based on building permits data collected by the Perth City Council Building Surveyor's Department.

current approaches to the planning of the area are seriously questioned and alternatives proposed. In this way, the planning of the area's spatial structure is viewed
as a logical response to the analysis of its current characteristics and patterns of
evolution.

1

The city centre in perspective

1-1 WHAT'S IN A NAME?

'Tis but thy name that is my enemy . . .
What's in a name? That which we call a rose
By any other name would smell as sweet.
[Shakespeare: *Romeo and Juliet*]

1-1.1 THE CBD—CATCHWORD OR MISNOMER?

The upsurge of scientific research that has occurred this century has considerably broadened man's knowledge of his relationships with the environment. But one of the by-products of this occurrence has been the rise of a large amount of specialized terminology and jargon which can be most confusing to the uninitiated observer. The study of cities is no exception in this regard: the literature bristles with what Chadwick (1971) has aptly described as 'meaningless horrors' such as transportation, functional relationship, space linkage, component behaviour and nested hierarchies. The term CBD (Central Business District) can also be added to this list, for in recent years it has become widely accepted as a short-hand description of the concentration of activities found in the centres of most cities. Despite its popularity, however, it has no standard meaning: as Horwood and Boyce (1959:8) have pointed out, to some it corresponds with the entire 'inner city' area (or downtown in the United States jargon), whilst to others it implies only the central core of shops and offices. Furthermore, it seems in many ways an inappropriate term to use as a description for the gamut of activities that typify the modern city centre. The term has enjoyed the apparently uncritical adoption of urban analysts and planners particularly since American geographers Murphy and Vance (1954a, 1954b, 1955) carried out what were probably the first detailed studies of the nature and content of the city centre. One of their objectives was to derive a definition for the term CBD, and as a starting point they suggested that

> the really essential central business functions appear to be the retailing of goods and services for a profit and the performance of various office functions.
> [Murphy & Vance 1954a:203]

Activities other than these, for example public halls, churches, hotels, hospitals, wholesaling and industrial establishments are regarded by these authors as non-

1

central business in character and as having no rightful place within the CBD (see Table 1-1). It can be argued that if the area is a *business* district (as the term CBD implies), then non-business activities have no place there. Rose (1967:117) suggests that this type of argument arises from the 'pervasiveness of the commercial ethos even among academics in the U.S.'. Whether or not this is the case (and, if so, it may not only apply to American academics), the reasoning of Murphy and Vance is somewhat narrow. This is very evident in a recent statement by Murphy (1972:25):

> there may be a common central park, a public garden, an architecturally distinguished city hall, a church spire or two, or the state capitol. But these . . . add to the crowding and hence to the problems of the CBD without having the qualities that give the area its essential character.

Business activities are cetrainly important in the city centre in terms of space occupancy and income-earning capacity, and offices, at least, appear to be increasing in importance at the expense of less-intensive and non-commercial uses. But it is too categorical to classify all other uses as 'non-central' on the grounds of their failure to generate a sufficient level of profit.

Table 1-1

GENERAL TYPES OF LAND USE CONSIDERED BY MURPHY AND VANCE
TO BE NON-CENTRAL BUSINESS IN CHARACTER

1 Permanent residences (including apartments and rooming houses)
2 Government and public (including parks and public schools as well as establishments carrying out city, county, state and federal govt. functions)
3 Organizational establishments (churches, fraternal orders, colleges, etc.)
4 Industrial establishments (excepting newspaper publishing)
5 Wholesaling
6 Vacant buildings
7 Vacant lots
8 Commercial storage

Source: Murphy and Vance 1954a:204

This classification is at odds with the functional nature of the city's central area and it implies a depressing sterility. As Jane Jacobs (1964:177) has commented: 'A CBD that lives up to its name and is truly described by it is a dud.' This brings to light the inappropriateness of the term 'CBD' and the narrowness of the implications it carries (Gruen 1965:47). As a result, the term will be avoided in the body of this book and the less ambiguous and more suitable term 'central area' will be employed.

1-1.2 CENTRAL FUNCTIONS

Apart from the inappropriateness of the term, however, it is worth noting that the classification of activities into CBD and non-CBD categories has been widely accepted as a part of a delimitation technique for the area. The technique devised by Murphy and Vance (1954a) has been adopted and used extensively by many workers and planning agencies (see e.g. Scott 1959, Davies 1959 and 1965, City of Hobart 1968, City of Adelaide 1968). This is fortunate in one sense for as Murphy (1972:12) has noted, the use of a common delimitation technique is essential to rigorous comparative CBD study. Yet it is unfortunate in another sense, since the classification of activities on which the technique is based does not conform with the true function of the central area: that is, as Murphy and Vance themselves state (1954a:203), to serve the entire city and its region rather than any section of it. Several studies have confirmed that the central area occupies the peak position within the hierarchy of metropolitan activity centres (see Carol 1960, Berry *et al.* 1963). There is no reason to believe that retailing and office activities are the only ones of importance within this hierarchy. Furthermore, as Bowden (1971) has noted, a number of activities typical of the city centre are not specifically 'central' in their function, but are nonetheless an integral part of the area since they are closely linked to the central activities. The centre appears, therefore, to have both basic components that serve the entire city and region and non-basic activities that serve the basic sector.

Thus to use the Murphy/Vance classification of activities as a starting point for the analysis of the central area would be seriously misleading and would cause the study to concentrate on only a segment of the centre's activity. The classification needs a complete overhaul that takes into account the true nature and worth of all activities that seek a location in the centre.

With regard to retailing, there is little doubt that the city's major retail area invariably occurs in the centre. The mixture of large department stores and specialist retail outlets gives the central retailing district a range and depth of merchandise unmatched even by the largest modern suburban centres. Although in many cities the proportion of total city trade and even the absolute amount of trade transacted within CBDs is declining (see e.g. Taeuber 1964), the area still tends to retain the largest share of any metropolitan retail centre (Berry *et al.* 1963:25). The percentage of city trade accounted for by the CBD varies with city size, but the Australian city CBD continues to account for a large proportion particularly in specialist retail lines (Table 1-2). However, this proportion has dropped significantly in recent years.

The increasing emphasis upon information storage and transaction in Western society over the last 100 years has led to considerable office development in most modern cities. Although the actual growth rate of offices varies with the economic characteristics and function of the individual city and its region, a universal trend appears to have been the concentration of such development in city centres (Hall 1966:26). The vast number of 'white-collar' workers employed in these offices has

Table 1-2

PERCENTAGE BY VALUE OF AUSTRALIAN CAPITAL CITY RETAIL TRADE

TRANSACTED IN CBD, 1962*

Item	CBD % of total city trade				
	Perth	Adelaide	Brisbane	Melbourne	Sydney
Groceries	10.3	10.7	8.8	2.5	8.8
Meat	5.3	13.1	13.1	1.9	13.1
Hardware	62.5	not published	53.7	33.5	32.1
Furniture	45.3	,, ,,	57.8	41.8	43.4
Men's clothing	69.4	81.6	81.9	49.9	53.1
Women's clothing	73.7	82.6	84.6	54.4	51.7
Jewellery	80.4	85.9	85.1	65.0	63.2
Population (1961)	420 133	587 957	621 550	1 911 895	2 183 388

* Figures are for 'inner city retail areas' defined by the Bureau of Census and Statistics; these cover in general an area embracing the city's major retail districts within the CBD.

Sources: Retail data: Commonwealth Bureau of Census and Statistics, *Census of Retail establishments and Other Services, 1962,* bull. 2-6; population: Commonwealth Bureau of Census and Statistics, *Census of the Commonwealth of Australia, 1961,* viii.

aggravated peak-hour transportation and congestion problems a great deal, particularly in larger cities. It has recently been observed that certain types of office are beginning to decentralize (Hoyt 1964, Location of Offices Bureau 1964, Goddard 1971), but on the whole the trend appears only gradual, and generally has involved routine and clerical types of activity. In many cities central office development continues unabated, forcing the characteristically vertically-developed skyline it produces even higher (see e.g. Beajeau-Garnier 1965, Archer 1967).

Many of those responsible for office location decisions seem unwilling to abandon the external economies such as prestige or functional advantages of the city centre. Recent surveys have shown that there is a close network of personal contact patterns amongst many offices in the centre and that relocation would mean the reorganization of these contacts and probably increases in operating costs despite savings on office rentals (see Goddard 1971). Nonetheless the relative importance of the centre as an office concentration will probably decrease in the future as communication techniques improve and the advantages of a suburban location for certain office types become more widely recognized. But it will take many years for the centre's dominance to disappear.

Thus in the light of current progressive development, it seems reasonable to include retailing and office activities as typical although the diminishing status of the central area must be recognized. However, as hinted earlier, the major flaw in the Murphy/Vance classification is its complete rejection of all non-economic activities; this feature, whilst often applauded, has also been subject to considerable criticism from various workers. For example, Weiss (1957:18) has contended that the major weakness of the Murphy/Vance system is its exclusion of certain functions, such as public and organizational land uses, which should be considered central in character. She points out that such land-use activities often occupy considerable space within the central area—consider city halls, government offices, central churches and other central public facilities, all of which need and benefit from a central location. Murphy and Vance (1954a:203) do admit the presence of such structures, but still consider them as 'non-CBD' uses. This seems illogical and one cannot help but agree with Weiss's judgment that there is clear evidence in favour of including such uses as typical of the city centre.

This contention has been backed by other workers. Mabogunje (1964:310, citing Murphy & Vance 1954a) states that their admission that some 'non-CBD' uses perform necessary functions is sufficient justification for including these establishments as a part of the central area. In similar vein, Weber (1958:84) has pointed out that civic and cultural institutions should be considered an integral part of the city's central area since they are just as important functionally as are commercial activities.* It is on similar grounds that Dickinson (1964:223) finds the Murphy and Vance definition 'too narrow'. There would seem, therefore, to be strong grounds for a revision of the Murphy/Vance classification so as to include central civic and cultural facilities which serve the city and region.

Governmental offices are also included in the 'government and public' category that is classified as non-central in character (Table 1-1). This classification seems somewhat unrealistic considering the increasingly important rôle that government agencies are playing in the economy and in the everyday life of the city's inhabitants. The relative significance of government offices will no doubt be dependent to a certain extent on the importance of the administration function of the cities in question. In this respect it should be noted that of the nine CBDs that Murphy and Vance (1954a:313-16, 318) studied, only one (Sacramento) is functionally prominent in government administration activities. Even so, Horwood and Boyce (1959) believe that regardless of the functional bias of a city, government offices are 'endemic' to the central area. In the Australian city, particularly the administrative capitals, this certainly seems true: in Perth, for example, almost 30% of all office space within the central area is occupied by government departments (see Chapter 3), with the comparable figure for Adelaide being 29% (City of Adelaide 1968:67).

Even in respect of business establishments, however, the Murphy/Vance classification seems inconsistent since certain types of commercial activities listed as 'non-central business' (Table 1-1) in character seem to be either linked functionally to

* It is of some significance that both Weber's (1958) and Weiss's (1957) comments on the Murphy/Vance classification are based upon observation of the United States cities. The exclusion of civic facilities by Murphy and Vance cannot therefore, as some workers suggest, be regarded as a result of the peculiarities of the United States cities.

other activities within the central area, or to be definitely 'central' in character
(i.e. serving the entire city and region). Wholesaling is excluded by Murphy and
Vance (1954a:203) on the grounds that it is localized more by the presence of rail-
roads and other transport media than by the pull of centrality. Since wholesaling
is dependent for its livelihood upon the collection and distribution of goods, it is
clear that proximity to efficient transport will be an important location factor (the
strength of this factor will vary with the type of good concerned). However, in the
case of wholesalers located within a city's central area, apart from other possible
advantages such as convenience for metropolitan-wide distribution, the presence of
the city's major retailing area close by, must also be an important location factor for
certain wholesalers. Admittedly, evidence on this point is somewhat limited, owing
to a lack of research into wholesaling location, yet what is available supports the
contention. Rannells (1957) concluded from a study of central Philadelphia that
functional linkages probably exist between central wholesalers and retailing activities.
This hypothesis has been recently confirmed by local research, which has shown that
by far the most important locational criterion for wholesalers close to the city's major
retail district was 'proximity to a concentration of buyers' (Wolinski 1970:53).

Even a cursory analysis of data from the Perth central area and from other cities
shows that there is a considerable amount of space occupied by wholesaling activities)
(Table 1-3).

Table 1-3

PERCENTAGE OF CENTRAL-AREA FLOORSPACE DEVOTED TO WHOLESALING AND
WAREHOUSING ACTIVITIES IN SELECTED CITIES*

City	%CA devoted to wholesaling
1 Perth, W.A.	7.07
2 Glasgow, Scotland	11.93
3 Richmond, Va., U.S.A.†	13.50
4 Worcester, Mass., U.S.A.†	13.40
5 Youngstown, Ohio, U.S.A.†	5.30
6 Rockford, Illinois, U.S.A.†	19.50
7 Adelaide, S.A.	12.12
8 Capetown, South Africa	22.13

* It is appreciated that these percentages depend upon the criteria used to delimit the 'central
area'. In the above cases an area corresponding with the CBD core and frame (Horwood &
Boyce 1959) has been used (see § 1-1.2).
† Includes frame area only.

Sources: 1, Perth City Council, land-use survey data (see footnote in Introduction, p. xxii);
2, Diamond 1962:526; 3-5, Preston 1968:477; 6, Griffin 1963:44; 7, City of Adelaide 1968:59;
8, Davies 1965:101.

It is true that the actual location of wholesaling activities within the central area is not akin to that of retailing or offices—this point is expanded later—but its undoubted presence and functional linkages seem to justify its inclusion as a 'central' activity, which has a rightful place within the area. This is not to suggest that the city's wholesaling is concentrated within the central area alone, or to deny that certain types of wholesaling—notably those handling goods with a low value-to-weight ratio (Wolinski 1970:91)—are at present in the process of 'decentralizing' from the area; rather it gives recognition to the linkages between wholesaling and other central-area activities. As Dickinson (1964:223) points out, Murphy and Vance do admit that some wholesaling activities benefit from a central location. In addition they include newspaper publishing and certain office activities only on the grounds of linkages to other functions (Murphy & Vance 1954a:204). To exclude wholesaling, therefore, is an unjustifiable inconsistency.

Another questionable aspect of the classification is the rendering of all industrial establishments, with the exception of newspaper publishing, as 'non-central' (Table 1-1). Decentralization of manufacturing activity from the inner city area has become increasingly apparent in recent years, owing largely to increasing congestion and associated dis-economies, and lack of room for expansion (Colby 1933, Kenyon 1967). Yet certain types of manufacturing remain and recent surveys have shown that in many cases this is due to close functional links to other central-area activities (see Pred 1964, Kerr & Spelt 1967, Perth City Council 1968). Cooper (1960) has asserted that the industrial function of the city's central area has been over-

Table 1-4

INDUSTRIAL ACTIVITIES FOUND IN THE CENTRAL AREAS OF VARIOUS CITIES
(IN DESCENDING ORDER OF FREQUENCY)*

1 Common to 40 U.S. city centres	2 Toronto, Canada	3 Perth, W.A.	4 Glasgow, Scotland
Printing	Printing	Engineering	Jewellery
Apparel	Jewellery	Printing	Printing
Jewellery	Food processing	Clothing	Clothing
Food processing	Furniture	Furniture	Food processing
Leather goods	Industrial machinery	Food processing	Engineering
Cosmetics	Clothing	Chemical products	
Paper	Metal stamping		
Drugs			
Toys			
Electrical goods			

* Only categories with over ten establishments are shown. Central area defined as for Table 1-3.

Sources: 1, Cooper 1960:14; 2, Kerr and Spelt 1958:8; 3, Perth City Council, land-use survey results; 4, Diamond 1962:528.

looked, for he found that many industries were common to some forty United States cities (Table 1-4). As may be seen, this list compares favourably with separate findings from surveys of other cities. The presence of certain types of semi-intensive industries appears typical of many city centres.

Residential premises are also classified by Murphy and Vance as non-central business in character on the grounds that they are 'antagonistic to true central business uses' (1954*a*:204). Whatever this statement means, it seems to be a rather dogmatic one which reflects their narrow concept of the function of the centre. It is certainly true that the permanent residential population of city centres in Europe, America and Australasia has been falling for sometime—for example the resident population of London's central area fell by 20% between 1951 and 1966 (General Register Office 1966). Central-area population is now at a low level in most cities compared with the suburbs; indeed, few would maintain that one of the centre's major functions was to house people. Residences are still present on the periphery of city centres, but these are disappearing fast. However, multi-storey residential establishments are not disappearing so fast; indeed they appear to be increasing in certain cities as the demand for such accommodation rises amongst certain minority sections of the community, such as retired people and single businessmen (see Rapkin & Grigsby 1959). This trend is seen by some as a means of bolstering the decline of the city centre and of reintroducing twenty-four-hour 'life' into the area that is now typified by a huge contrast between daytime and night population. Its occurrence suggests that this type of residence at least should not be regarded as antagonistic to the balance of the area; on the contrary it would seem to be complementary and might well save congestion costs arising from commuting to the city centre and assist the trade of retail establishments. But whatever its merits (and this will receive more attention in following chapters) there are strong grounds for including these in the revised roster of appropriate central-area activities.

In summary, it is difficult to avoid the conclusion that the adoption of the Murphy/Vance classification of land-use types into 'central-business' and 'non-central-business' categories will result in the delineation of an area so restricted that it would have little validity as the city's central region. There are strong grounds for expanding the 'central-business' activities to include all central civic and cultural facilities, certain types of wholesaling and manufacturing, and residential establishments. In addition there seems little justification for excluding vacant lots or buildings, or at least for regarding these as non-central business in nature, since vacancy appears to be present to a greater or lesser extent throughout the city area as a result of the normal processes of the land and business markets.

1-1.3 TOWARDS A MORE COMPREHENSIVE CONCEPT

The term 'central area' has been suggested to be more suitable as a fundamental tag for the city centre than 'CBD'. Without wishing to become involved in semantics, it is clear that there is some confusion over the use and relative meaning of the two terms, since, while some workers have used them interchangeably, it has

Fig. 1-1 *The Horwood/Boyce core/frame concept (1959).* After Horwood and Boyce 1959. Reproduced with permission of Washington Uni. Press.

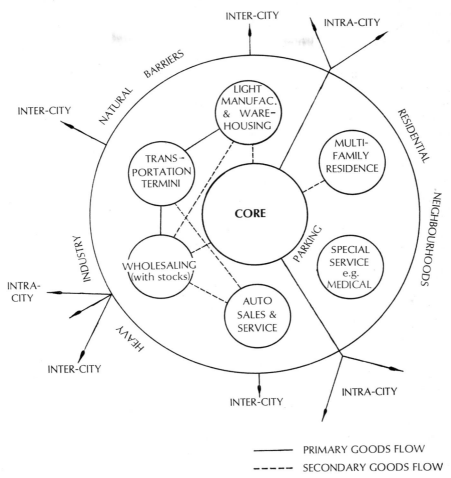

been claimed that they represent different concepts. According to Johnston (1968: 105) the CBD represents that area of the city, where retailing, services and offices are dominant; the central area, on the other hand, includes this area as well as surrounding industrial and residential zones. This may be the case if one adopts the Murphy/Vance definition of the CBD, which, whilst having a considerable 'following', has been shown to be inconsistent. To suggest that it is 'the' concept of the CBD is to overlook other concepts such as the 'core-frame' hypothesis proposed by Horwood and Boyce (1959:9-22).

It is true, as suggested above, that the term 'central area' has always implied a larger part of the inner city than has the term 'CBD' (see also Edwards 1962.

Carter & Rowley 1966). Certainly the former is less ambiguous than the latter. Regardless of what ambiguities exist, however, our study will focus attention upon the total assemblage of all types of activitiy found within the city centre.

In this respect the Horwood/Boyce concept has relevance. According to them, the city centre possesses an inner 'core', characterized by vertical development and an extreme concentration of intensive activities. The extent of this area is correlated with the pedestrian scale. Typical activities are retailing and offices (including governmental). The area is encircled by an outer 'frame' (see Fig. 1-1) which is seen as a zone of less-intensive land use dominated by nucleations of such activities as wholesaling, light manufacturing, high-density residences, transport depots and institutional uses; in contrast to the core it has extended horizontal scale (Horwood & Boyce 1959:15-22). Together, the core and the frame constitute the total central business district. Such definition of the CBD is, therefore, more akin to the central area concept cited above than it is to the Murphy/Vance CBD notion.

The Horwood/Boyce hypothesis has been criticized by Murphy (1962: 529), who claims that

> the core and the frame together include considerably more of the downtown area than it seems reasonable to include in the CBD.

The comment highlights the wide variance of opinion that exists as to just what constitutes the CBD. The major disagreement is over the place and function of Horwood and Boyce's frame area. Murphy (1972:116) asserts that 'to include the frame as conceived by Horwood and Boyce as part of the CBD would leave a CBD with little semblance of unity'. A comparison of the content of the frame area (Fig. 1-1) with Murphy and Vance's 'non-central-business' activities (Table 1-1) shows a high degree of similarity. Murphy and Vance do not deny the existence of such activities within close proximity to the centre—this is confirmed by their diagrammatic representations which depict the CBD abutting on to frame-type uses (Fig. 1-2). Rather they do not regard these activities as a part of the CBD; their CBD in fact bears strong resemblances to Horwood and Boyce's core. Horwood and Boyce, on the other hand, make the point that while the core and the frame are distinctive zones with differing properties, together they form one unit 'because of the many linkages and complementary functions they perform for each other' (Horwood & Boyce 1959:21).

The basis of the frame area in the Horwood/Boyce interpretation is the 'zone of transition' identifed by Burgess (1925) in his theory on the city's concentric growth and structure. The core appears to correspond in some ways to the area Burgess designates as the CBD. Of the land-use characteristics of the two areas, Burgess (1925:38, 40) says the following:

> In the CBD . . . we expect to find the department stores, the skyscraper office buildings, the railroad stations, the great hotels, the theaters . . . and the city hall. . . . Encircling the downtown area is . . . an area of transition which is being invaded by business and light manufacture.

Fig. 1-2   *The Murphy/Vance CBD (1954)*. Reproduced with permission of the editors of *Econ. Geogr.*

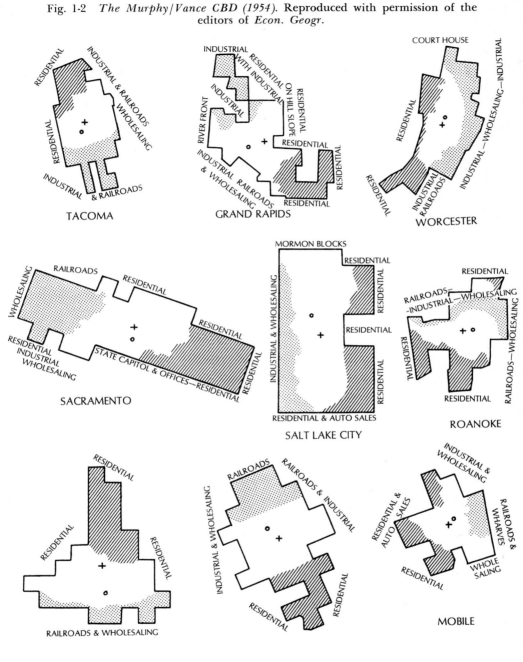

It is clear that Burgess regarded the transition zone as a distinct area of the city rather than as a part of the CBD (see also Fig. 1-4). This viewpoint has also been adopted in some recent studies. Preston (1966:236) talks of the transition zone as something 'peripheral' to the CBD (the latter being defined by the Murphy/Vance delimitation technique). Davies (1965:27) regards the frame area in Capetown as part of the city's central area, yet he claims it to be separate from the CBD (which is again based on Murphy/Vance). He further asserts that 'most geographers' agree with this viewpoint. Be this as it may, the Horwood/Boyce concept appears to present a much more realistic picture of central-area structure than does any previously discussed. Analysis of data collected for this study supports, in the main, both the broad core-frame concept and the postulates concerning land-use arrangement within the area. Certain features of the theory are taken issue with, in particular its failure to recognize the importance of central civic and public facilities, which as pointed out earlier, are just as much a part of the area as are business functions, and tend to gravitate towards a core location. In addition, Horwood and Boyce's contention that the subregions within the CBD are in general 'unlinked' (see Fig. 1-1) will be challenged.

However, the general assertions of the core-frame concept stand. One of its authors (in Horwood & McNair 1961) has claimed that it has been validated by subsequent findings. This judgment has subsequently been backed by other workers (e.g. Hartenstein & Stack 1967) and the concept has recently been described as the most important contribution to CBD literature yet made by geographers (Archer 1969:64).

Thus, the available evidence points favourably to the core-frame concept and it will be utilized, with some modifications, as a basic analytical framework for land-use patterns in the study. And since it is the function of the central area to serve the entire city, any establishment fulfilling this rôle (or any activity functionally linked to or dependent upon such establishments) will be treated as a valid and integral part of the area. This is not to deny that certain activities are inappropriate to the central area, but rather to recognize its real character.

1-1.4   THE NEED FOR FURTHER INVESTIGATION

Disagreements and conflict over the structure and content of the city centre discussed in preceding sections point to the need for further investigation. However, the value of previous studies of the centre cannot be overlooked. Particularly important are the investigations of Scott (1959), which present a comparison of land use within each of the Australian capital city centres, Perth included. In the light of such an apparently comprehensive study, the need for further investigation may be queried. Nevertheless, as already pointed out, Scott's study, and many others, were based upon the Murphy/Vance concept of the CBD, which at best covers the core of the central area and presents, therefore, a somewhat incomplete picture of the city centre. Moreover, Scott's study is based on ground-floor patterns, and given the considerable vertical extension of the core leads to a distorted view of what is essentially a three-dimensional structure.

Other recent examinations of central-area land use (e.g. Preston 1966, 1968) have concentrated only on the frame and thus clearly provide no answers to questions concerning total central-area structure. Nevertheless, data presented in these and other studies can be utilized for comparative purposes in order to resolve conceptual conflicts and make some progress towards a deeper understanding of the city centre.

1·2 THE EXPLANATION AND EVOLUTION OF CENTRAL-AREA STRUCTURE

In the previous section, various concepts concerning central-area land-use arrangement or structure were discussed. Although they are of considerable assistance in interpreting the composition and character of the city centre, the concepts themselves offer little in the way of explanation of the centre's structure and are furthermore inherently static, thus giving little guide to the evolution of the area. These two aspects are of critical importance to the planning of the area, for unless the contemporary processes are understood, plans cannot hope to be successful in solving the problems of the area. This lesson has only been learnt by bitter experience in certain cities.

1-2.1 THE THEORY OF THE LAND MARKET

The theory of the urban land market as conceptualized by Haig (1926) and Ratcliff (1949) and formalized by Alonso (1960), suggests that the land-use pattern in a city is determined primarily by the competition between and the relative rent-paying ability of the various functions wishing to locate in the area. As was noted in the previous section, the city's central area is characterized by a large number of activities, all competing for space: thus the theory appears to have some relevance to an explanation of the pattern of land use.

According to the theory, there is a hierarchy of rent-paying abilities amongst activities seeking a location in an urban area. The rent-paying ability will vary according to the nature and accessibility requirements of the activities concerned. Central sites are seen as most desirable since they are theoretically the most accessible and thus command the highest prices; for that reason these sites will be occupied by activities that can afford to pay the highest rent. It is claimed that such competition between activities results in an orderly pattern of land use, where each activity is located in accordance to its position in the hierarchy of rent-paying ability with respect to the city centre (as illustrated in Fig. 1-3). But despite the competition between land uses, the theory's assumption of a hierarchy of bid-rent levels with respect to location suggests that except where these levels actually conflict (where lines cross in the diagram), each activity occupies an optimum position owing to different accessibility requirements or profit levels. Rent-paying ability is held to be commensurate with the 'utility', an activity gains from a particular location. And since in economic terms the market is said to reflect the preference patterns of the community, the resulting distribution of functions can be held to be fair and right.

Fig. 1-3 *Land values and location in an urban area—the theoretical model.*
After Alonso 1960.

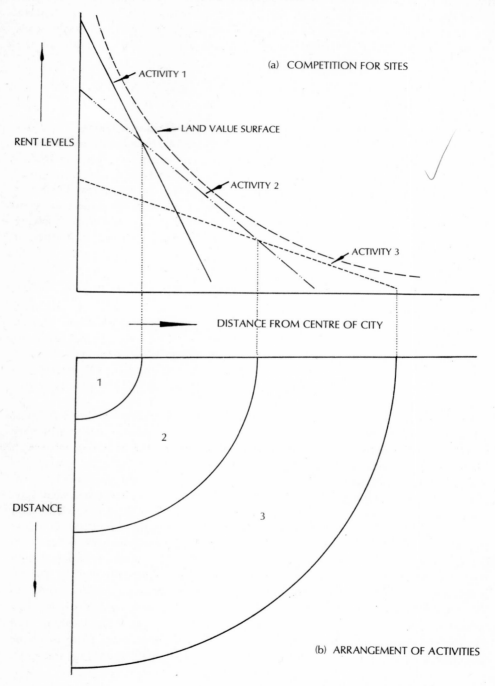

RENT LEVELS

ACTIVITY 1

(a) COMPETITION FOR SITES

LAND VALUE SURFACE

ACTIVITY 2

ACTIVITY 3

DISTANCE FROM CENTRE OF CITY

DISTANCE

1

2

3

(b) ARRANGEMENT OF ACTIVITIES

Such arguments, however, take no account of the fact that there is no reason why utility should be measured in purely monetary terms, particularly where non-economic activities are concerned. Moreover, the theory fails to recognize that the differing revenue-earning capacities of economic activities in the urban market will constrain rent-paying abilities. Thus the level of the bid-rent curve of a particular activity does not necessarily reflect its true preference pattern. What is more, the theory assumes that the operation of the land market is based on perfect competition, thus ignoring the significant amount of external costs which distort considerably the operation of the market. For example, the continued concentration of a function of high rent-paying ability in the city centre (say offices) is regarded as a natural trend in terms of the theory; however, those responsible for the location of offices will take no account of the external costs of traffic congestion that are foisted on the entire community as a result of the location decision (except insofar as they affect the individual making the decision).

In any case, the fact that the theory is framed in purely economic terms is to deny the importance of non-economic activities within the city centre; yet the failure of an activity to generate a profit should not necessarily disqualify it from central location. The city centre acts as both a social and economic focus; hence to suggest that its activity content should be decided on purely economic criteria is somewhat extreme. Nevertheless, unless planners act to reverse or control such trends, it is clear that the city centre will become increasingly dominated by functions of high rent-paying ability. The theory can be used to rationalize and explain such trends, but to use it as a justification is to ignore reality. Even so, there is no doubt that the theory has some relevance to an explanation of the relative location of activities within the central area.

1-2.2 THE IMPORTANCE OF LINKAGES

The operation of the land market impinges on most activities in the central area (apart from those protected by governmental ownership or by zoning ordinances), but it cannot necessarily be invoked as an explanation of the location pattern of all activities. The significance of linkages (or in non-jargon terms, connections) between activities for purposes of their operation has already been pointed to as a general location factor which draws activities to the city centre. But linkages may also be important on a more detailed level as they appear to affect the specific location of certain activities within the central area.

The importance of these factors was first analysed in conceptual terms by Rannells (1957) in his classic study of central Philadelphia. Rannells suggested that the location of certain groups of activities such as offices and business services in proximity to one another was influenced by linkages between them, with accessibility requirements also being important. However, his analysis was not based on any actual study of connections, and it was not until the studies of Goddard (1971, 1973) and Thorngren (1970) that these hypotheses received confirmation. These studies were based on surveys of office contact patterns, and as noted earlier, they established the importance of contact between and within office types. Goddard's survey results emphasize the significance particularly of personal contacts between managerial staff of different firms, although they also show that telephone contacts are very important. This latter factor suggests that proximity of offices to one another may not be so significant as is sometimes suggested. Thus the studies have not yet established the precise importance of these contact patterns in the location of the activities concerned, and have only covered a small proportion of central-area activities. Nonetheless, they emphasize the general significance of linkages. The fact that they have only been recently investigated stresses the point that our knowledge of the forces operating in the central area is far from complete; but it is these forces that are of the utmost importance to an explanation of the structure of the city centre.

1-2.3   MODELS OF CITY STRUCTURE

The operation of economic forces within the central-area land market as outlined in §1-2.1 leads to a concentric zonation of activities about the point of maximum land value (as shown in Fig. 1-3). Interestingly, such a model was devised for the whole city by Burgess (1925) whose diagrammatic representation of the city (Fig. 1-4) suggests that land use tends to arrange itself in rings about the central area. This arrangement is reminiscent of that suggested for agricultural activities in the isolated state of von Thünen (1826); however, it should be noted that whilst Thünen specifically set out to construct an economic model, Burgess was mainly concerned with the sociological structure of the city and did not seek to explain the arrangement of land use in economic terms. Furthermore, the major emphasis in Burgess's explanation is on process rather than structure: he suggests (1925:38) that the model 'represents an ideal construction of the tendency of any town or district to *expand radially* from its business district'.* Of course there is a close relationship between process and structure, and such a tendency to radial expansion will give rise to the zonal structure.

In a study of central Capetown, Davies (1965:2 to 6) suggests that a structure similar to Burgess's zonation for the entire city can be seen in the centre. Away from the point of maximum land value, bands of decreasing specialization of activity and intensity of space occupance correlate with declining land values and accessibility, giving rise, it is claimed, to a concentrically-zoned structure. Other studies of central-area structure have provided some evidence that such a zoning does exist (see e.g. Murphy & Vance 1955), although in general to represent the structure in terms of a simple concentric zonation seems rather facile in view of the apparent complexity of processes operating within the area. It is on these grounds that the Burgess's theory has been discounted as a completely adequate representation of the structure of the entire city (see e.g. Carter 1972). In any case, as hinted above, although Burgess's theory may imply the operation of certain economic processes, it does not deal with them explicitly, and thus it is incorrect to suggest that

* My italics

Fig. 1-4   *Three models of city structure: Burgess 1925, Hoyt 1939, Harris and Ullman 1945.* After Harris and Ullman 1945.

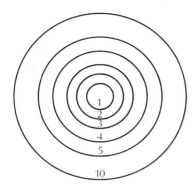

Burgess: Concentric Zonation

Hoyt: Sectoral

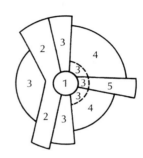

Harris & Ullman: Multiple Nuclei

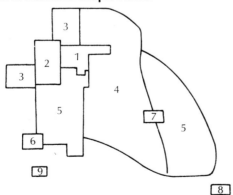

1   CBD
2   Wholesale Light Manufacturing
3   Low-Class Residential
4   Medium-Class Residential
5   High-Class Residential
6   Heavy Manufacturing
7   Outlying Business District
8   Residential Suburb
9   Industrial Suburb
10 Commuter's Zone

Three Models of City Growth and Structure

Burgess was concerned to create an urban equivalent to von Thünen's theory of agricultural land use. The observation of land-use patterns within the central area should be used as a basis for seeking an explanation of process rather than for purposes of drawing dubious analogies.

Nevertheless Burgess's theory does draw attention to the relevance of change and expansion to an explanation of present structure. But as first pointed out by Hoyt (1939), it places too great an emphasis on the principle of radial (or central) growth, and disregards the effect that transport links have on the city's physical pattern. According to Hoyt, such links distort any concentric zonation since they encourage axial rather than radial growth, which produces a sectoral as opposed to a zonal pattern of land use within the city (as illustrated in Fig. 1-4). This idealized city form has again been criticized by a number of later workers, but they failed to note that Hoyt himself recognized the danger of applying set principles arbitrarily to any city, and stressed that no two cities will have an exactly similar form.

This point was taken up by Harris and Ullman (1945) who suggested that even in combination the theories of Burgess and Hoyt are insufficient to explain the diverse structure of the modern city. They were mainly concerned with the structural implications of the theories, and hypothesized that most cities are poly rather than monocentric, leading to a multinuclear pattern of land use as shown in Fig. 1-4.

However, the authors do recognize that this pattern of land use is the result of certain principles:

(1) Certain activities require specialised facilities
(2) Certain activities group together because they benefit from cohesion . . .
(3) Certain unlike activities are detrimental to each other . . .
(4) Certain activities are unable to afford the high rents of the most desirable sites. [Harris & Ullman 1945:14]

The principles are clearly relevant factors for the activities that seek a location in the central area. They may be applicable in explaining the clusters of land use observed in Capetown by Davies (1965) and in the United States city frame areas by Preston (1966), and those hypothesized by Horwood and Boyce (1959; see Fig. 1-1) and since investigated by such workers as McNair (1960). Harris and Ullman also noted that in the final analysis most cities will exhibit a combination of both the multinuclear pattern (Fig. 1-4) and the pattern produced by the processes of radial and axial growth.

The applicability of Burgess theory to the central area has already received attention. According to Davies (1965) a parallel can also be drawn between ribbon development occurring along major traffic arteries leading to and from the heart of the centre and Hoyt's sectoral pattern of land use. This would seem plausible, yet the main point to note is not the similarity of observable pattern but the applicability of the principle of axial development to patterns of growth within the centre. This applies equally to all three theories of land-use arrangement and it emphasizes the need for study of patterns of change as opposed to mere observation of static patterns. (This point is taken up in Chapter 5.) In the meantime one cannot help but agree with Carter (1972) who has stressed that geographers have become obsessed with the study of patterns within the central area at the expense of considering processes of change.

1-2.4 TRANSITION AND CHANGE

The contention that process has been overlooked in city-centre studies is amply illustrated by the 'transition-zone concept' put forward by Preston and Griffin (1966), based on their study of patterns of land use in three United States cities (see Preston 1966, Griffin 1963). The concept rests on the principle of a sectoral framework within the transition zone (frame): they identify zones of 'active assimilation', 'passive assimilation' and 'general activity' (see Fig. 1-5). Such a classification is an attempt to describe processes of transition and change that are seen as a major characteristic of the zone. However, it arises from a study of patterns at one date only and is therefore a completely subjective assessment. As Bourne (1968:314) has forcefully pointed out, there was no analysis of the actual process at work; in this respect Bourne's own work on changing patterns of land use and redevelopment in central city areas is of relevance (Bourne 1967, 1971). Bourne was able to establish through a study of private redevelopment in Toronto that such a process is a major cause of the continuing intensification of land use within the central area. According to the analysis land-intensive functions (e.g offices) have tended to replace space-extensive activities (such as manufacturing and whole-saling). This is seen to be due to the fact that it is 'generally uneconomic' to replace an existing structure 'with anything but a more intensive use' (Bourne 1967:3). In a more recent study, the same author suggests that the changing pattern of land use in an area could be predicted by the incorporation of the results of such analyses into probability matrices (Bourne 1971).

Other analysts have shown that they are aware of the importance of formalizing the study of change and of devising explanations, but often fail to pursue this in their research. For example, in an introduction to a study of changing patterns of land use in Melbourne's central area Johnston (1967) noted that it should be possible to apply the principles of Burgess and Hoyt to the analysis, but unfortunately, he does not follow the matter further, with the result that the analysis is largely descriptive and throws little light upon the causes of land-use change or their relationship to theories. This is not to say that such studies have no value, for as Carter and Rowley (1966) have shown, the historical development of a city centre is often an important clue to its present form. Murphy and Vance (1955) have pointed to the ever-changing nature of the centre by suggesting the presence of a 'zone of assimilation' on the advancing front, and a 'zone of discard' on the receding front of the area (see Fig. 1-2). They fail, however, to tie these observations (which are in any case rather subjective) with existing theories, or to offer any possible explanations of process; their analysis of the dynamic nature of the

Fig. 1-5   *The Preston/Griffin transition zone framework (1966).* Source: Preston and Griffin 1966. Reproduced with permission of the editors of *Econ. Geogr.*

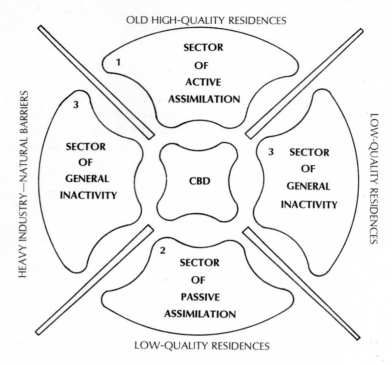

central area suffers accordingly. Bowden's (1971) study of the expansion and growth of San Francisco's central area confirmed the hypotheses of Murphy and Vance. This is a start in the right direction, although the work still lacks a firm theoretical base. This topic seems worthy of further investigation.

In this respect the notions of Colby (1933) appear to be relevant. Although his work is by now somewhat dated, the principles he enunciated cannot be ignored in a discussion of patterns of growth and change within the city.

Colby claimed that two opposing forces are constantly at work within the city, affecting both its physical form and its functional pattern: the first of these, *centrifugal forces,* result from a combination of adverse conditions in the central zones of the city and attractive conditions of the peripheral areas, and are seen in action through the migration of activities (e.g. manufacturing) from the former to the latter area; *centripetal forces,* on the other hand, due to attractive qualities of the central zones of the city, produce an opposite movement, or increased concentration of certain activities (e.g. offices) within this area. The operation of these forces led Colby (1933:288) to the conclusion that 'the city is a dynamic organism constantly in process of evolution.' Thus, it was argued, centrifugal and centripetal forces affect the central area by altering its composition with respect to the hinterland. As will be shown in the course of this study, they are also of assistance in explaining the changing patterns of land use within the central-area's core and frame.

1-2.5 THE PLANNING RESPONSE—A COMMENT

The changing nature of the city centre has not unexpectedly attracted the attention of city architects and planners. In general terms the trend towards increasing specialization of the city centre in activities of high rent-paying ability has been viewed with disapproval, as it is seen to be robbing the centre of vitality and character. Meanwhile, concern has also mounted over the increasing congestion evident in many city centres, and in many instances massive freeway programmes have been launched in an attempt to ease this problem; but although they appear to offer certain benefits in terms of time savings and reduced delays on the traffic network, they have often encouraged even greater use of the car which has offset the supposed gains. Moreover, the impact of the freeways upon the land-use pattern of the city centre and its inevitable displacement of many activities has aroused much criticism. Even so, these effects remain largely undocumented and as Murphy (1966: 314) has noted, there is considerable scope for research into these matters. This subject is taken up in Chapter 2, and some of the adverse effects of freeway development upon the central-area frame (through which they generally pass) are investigated.

Returning to redevelopment, the criticism of the processes of private action in this respect has been coupled with the promulgation of the concept of comprehensive redevelopment which is proposed as a cure for the centre's problems. This idea (as described, for example, by Gruen 1965 & Crosby 1968) envisages the total reconstruction of large tracts of the central area along futuristic lines, with complete vertical segregation of pedestrian and vehicular traffic and the incorporation of activities that would not otherwise be able to compete for space within the centre. Such action, it is suggested, will not only solve the congestion and pedestrian/vehicular conflict, but will also bring back life into the supposedly dying city centre and will overcome the adverse effects of continued private redevelopment of the centre. Furthermore the comprehensive approach is designed to overcome the fragmented nature and design of most modern privately-sponsored redevelopment projects. The benefits appear tangible and attractive at first sight; however, it is also true that comprehensive schemes can, owing to their intensity, cause the disruption of the existing fabric and activities on an unprecedented scale and also the generation of higher than normal external costs. Such points are broached in more detail later, but here it should be noted that these costs may well outweigh the apparent benefits of comprehensive redevelopment. Thus the planners' conventional response that arises from a grand design rather than from a study of the centre's needs may not necessarily be the answer to the structural ills of the central area.

1-3 SYNTHESIS

In this chapter attention has been drawn to the conflicts and inconsistencies that characterize much of the literature on city centre and urban land use. It has been suggested that a broader approach to the study of the central area is necessary both in terms of concepts and terminology, and the appropriate rôle of the centre. The criticism of current theory has not been made from a negative standpoint, but in the belief that these inconsistencies must be resolved if the level of understanding of the structure of the city centre is to improve.

It has also been noted that many studies of the centre have been biased in their emphasis on a description of patterns at the expense of considering processes of change and other forces. If planning of the city centre is to have any relevance, it must be based upon a firmer comprehension of the complex processes at work within the area. A stronger attempt must be made to integrate existing knowledge of the patterns of land utilization in the central area with theories concerning land-use arrangement, change and linkage patterns. These tasks will be attempted in the chapters that follow in the hope that at least the foundations of a more adequate, than at present existing, model of central-area structure can be laid.

2

Central-area processes, activity patterns
and problems

I: THE FRAME

2-1 CHARACTER AND DEFINITION

The recent upsurge of interest in the city's central area has not been matched by a similar increase in the state of knowledge of the patterns and processes occurring within. This applies particularly to the peripheral portions (the transition zone or frame), where the problems of blight and deterioration cause much concern but attract few solutions. Preston (1966:236) suggests that this is symptomatic of the neglect of the area by both private and public sectors; and further notes: 'Although it is the object of dramatic concern in the form of abundant public lip-service, the transition zone is perhaps the least understood of the major sub-regions of the city.'

Despite this, the general nature of the frame has been the subject of some analytical attention. As seen in Chapter 1, the core-frame concept (Horwood & Boyce 1959) provides a valid framework within which to view the area. The general characteristics of the frame area have been listed by Horwood and Boyce and are presented in Table 2-1. Some of these, such as the extended horizontal scale and semi-intensive land use are obvious from a glance at an aerial view of the area (see frontispiece); others are less obvious, and stem from the domination of the area by vehicular- (as opposed to pedestrian-) oriented (or generating) activities such as wholesaling, light manufacturing, transport termini and parking lots. These activities are depicted as clustering in foci or subregions throughout the frame (Fig. 1-1). In broad terms such a structure has been verified by subsequent studies in several countries including Britain (Diamond 1962, Carter & Rowley 1966, Goddard 1967); South Africa (Davies 1965, Davies and Rajah 1965); New Zealand (Robinson 1965, Pain 1967, Merriman 1967); and the United States (Preston and Griffin 1966). The latter study, in fact led to the formulation of the 'transition zone concept' (Fig. 1-5) which sees the frame area as having a similar 'poly-nuclear' structure to that proposed in the core-frame concept. This chapter will generally add credence to these findings concerning the content and structure of the frame area through a comparison of available material and an examination of pattern in Perth. However,

23

Table 2-1

PROPERTIES OF THE CENTRAL-AREA FRAME

Property	Definition	General characteristics
Semi-intensive land use	Area of most intensive non-retail land use outside CBD core	Building height geared to walk-up scale Site only partially built on
Prominent functional subregions	Area of observable nodes of land utilization surrounding CBD core	Subfoci characterized mainly by wholesaling with stocks, warehousing, off-street parking, automobile sales and services, multifamily dwellings, intercity transportation terminals and facilities, light manufacturing, and some institutional uses
Extended horizontal scale	Horizontal scale geared to accommodation of motor vehicles and to handling of goods	Most establishments have off-street parking and docking facilities Movements between establishments vehicular
Unlinked functional subregions	Activity nodes essentially linked to areas outside CBD frame, except transportation terminals	Important establishments linkages to CBD core (e.g. intercity transportation terminals, warehousing) and to outlying urban regions (e.g. wholesale distribution to suburban shopping areas and to service industries)
Externally conditioned boundaries	Boundaries affected by natural barriers and presence of large homogeneous areas with distinguishable internal linkages (e.g. residential areas with schools, shopping, and community facilities)	Commercial uses generally limited to flat land Growth tends to extend into areas of dilapidated housing. CBD frame uses fill in interstices of central focus of highway and rail transportation routes

Source: Horwood and Boyce 1959:20. Reproduced with permission of Washington University Press.

it will also throw some light on the neglected question of linkages in order to elucidate the rationale of the location patterns evident. Furthermore, an attempt will be made to remove the traditional sterility from the study of land-use patterns by concentrating as much on process as on structure; this approach will be elaborated in later chapters when attention is turned to the analysis of change and redevelopment within the area.

The general characteristics of the frame distinguish it both from the inner core (with its extended vertical scale and intensive uses) and the inner residential zones of the city. The transition zone, by definition, contains remnant residential areas. Its mixed-use nature contrasts sharply with the homogeneity of the city's inner suburbs, and yet the boundary between these two areas is not itself sharp, which gives rise to problems of delimitation. Some authors such as Preston (1966) and Davies (1965) have attempted to overcome this problem through the establishment of limiting 'indices' of land-use content, which are then used to define the outer boundary of the area (after the procedure established by Murphy & Vance 1954a). However, it is clear that such indices will be of arbitrary value and for this reason misleading, since the establishment of a 'limiting value' gives the spurious impression of accuracy and 'scientific' methodology. Even so, as Rannells (1957) points out, the boundary must be drawn somewhere, and thus it is worthwhile to consider briefly the question of the delimiting criteria.

According to Horwood and Boyce (1959) the outer boundaries of the frame are 'externally conditioned' by natural barriers and large tracts of homogeneous land use (see Table 2-1). This seems reasonable in the case of physical barriers which will clearly limit the expansion of the frame—the river serves this function in Perth (see frontispiece). Thus the nature of the site of the central area will affect both its form and extent. However, it is misleading to suggest that adjoining areas of homogeneous land use act also as similar barriers. The transition zone is dynamic in nature and therefore likely to expand into these very areas, particularly residential zones which find it increasingly difficult to compete for space unless protected by zoning legislation. Nonetheless, the commencement of the city's inner residential areas marks the outer limits of the frame area. Whilst, as noted, this boundary is not likely to be sharp, it seems reasonable to delimit the frame by circumscribing all land occupied by central activities in whole or part.

Delimitation procedures, however, must also pay attention to previously drawn boundaries. In Perth, Scott (1959) adopted the Murphy/Vance CBD concept to define the area. As previously noted, this concept is based on extremely narrow premises and thus has no validity for the city's central area. In fact, the CBD (illustrated in Fig. 2-1) does not even provide a suitable definition of the core, owing to its exclusion of areas of core-oriented government offices and public facilities.

Another delineation of the city's central area was carried out in connection with the drawing up of proposals for a metropolitan plan (Stephenson & Hepburn 1955) —the boundary arrived at is also shown in Fig. 2-1. It appears to have been based on the commencement of the inner residential zones along the lines suggested above. However, some expansion of central-area activities has occurred in intervening years and thus the 1953 boundary cannot be regarded as suitable for present purposes; it will however be utilized later as a basis for assessing changing patterns of space use in the area (see Chapter 5).

A more recent definition is that adopted by the Perth City Council for purposes of the activity survey upon which this study leans heavily for basic data. (The results of the survey are reported in Perth City Council 1971a.) This boundary seems rational in many respects (see Fig. 2-1), yet it was drawn arbitrarily and

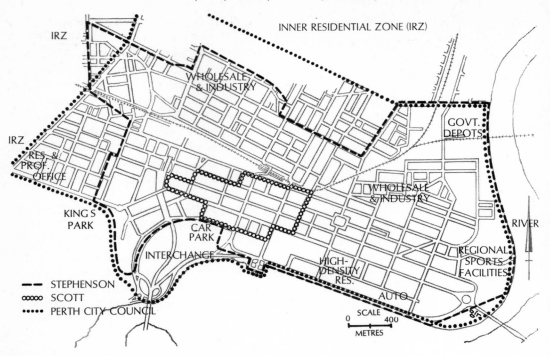

Fig. 2-1   *Definitions of the Perth central area, three views: 1955 (Stephenson),*
1959 (Scott), 1968 (Perth City Council).

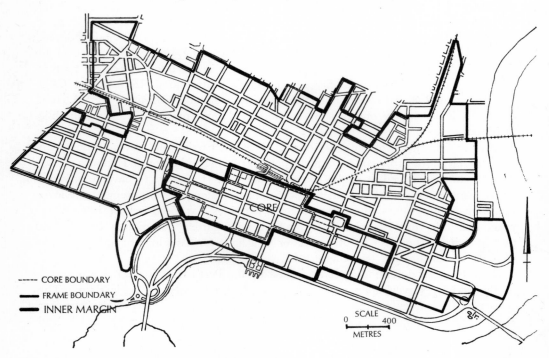

Fig. 2-2   *Definition of Perth core 1968*

includes large tracts of the city's inner residential zones whilst excluding some areas that differ little in character from the mixed-use areas within the boundary. As an initial step towards the more accurate definition of the central area, this boundary was re-drawn to exclude these residential areas (which were identified from personal survey and examination of aerial photography) and made to include the mixed-use areas regarded as central in character. In addition, areas of ribbon development were excluded on the margins in the belief that they form a component distinct from the central area (see Berry *et al.* 1963:20); as Outwater (1967:43) points out, such areas have been included incorrectly in studies of other central areas (see Davies 1965, Preston 1966). Finally, areas of non-residential but con-central use (such as local sports facilities), or of central uses that developed as separate units from the balance of the area but now abut it, were also excluded. These criteria are elaborated in Appendix I and need not concern us further here, except to state that it is believed that the boundary produced (see Fig. 2-1) is consistent in terms of the essential character of the frame.

The *inner* boundary of the frame area corresponds, naturally, with the outer limits of the core. Since the core differs markedly from the frame in character and appearance, with its high-rise development and intensive space-use (see Table 3-1), its approximate boundaries can be defined from an inspection of aerial photographs (see frontispiece). However, it would be hazardous to rely on such a method entirely and thus other possibilities were investigated. It was finally decided that most activities within the central area could be classified as either 'core' or 'frame' in character (after Merriman 1967). A similar method was used by Outwater (1967) in defining the extent of the CBD core and CBD edge or frame in three cities in the United States state of Oklahoma. This stems from the essentially contrasting character of the core and the frame as identified by Horwood and Boyce (1959); core activities are more intensive in nature, in terms of their space occupancy and productivity, than the frame activities, and are generally pedestrian rather than vehicular oriented (see Table 2-2).

Table 2-2

CRITERIA ADOPTED FOR CLASSIFICATION OF ACTIVITIES
INTO CORE AND FRAME TYPES

Core activities	*Frame activities*
1 Predominantly central location with respect to central area boundaries	1 Predominantly peripheral location pattern
2 Intensive occupier of space given to vertical rather than horizontal extension	2 Extensive occupier of space, given to horizontal rather than vertical extension
3 Customer-oriented activity or one having direct contact with the public; pedestrian generating	3 Minimal contact with public; vehicular rather than pedestrian-generating activities

Following an examination of the location pattern of the various sets of activities within the area it also became clear that some of them were predominantly concentrated in the inner sections of the area and others in peripheral areas; in general the latter coincided with frame activities in terms of the the other criteria (listed in Table 2-2), and the former with core activities.

Thus most activities could be classified as either 'core' or 'frame' on this basis (see Table 2-3); the balance that exhibited a dual location pattern were treated

Table 2-3

CLASSIFICATION OF ACTIVITY TYPES INTO 'CORE' AND 'FRAME' CATEGORIES
FOR PURPOSES OF DELIMITING THE PERTH CENTRAL-AREA CORE*

Core activities		*'Frame' activities*		*Core and frame*	
Retail:	Use code†	*Residential:*	Use Code	*Residential:*	Use code
Clothing	12	Houses	00	Hotels, transient	02
Department	13	Flats	01, 03		
Variety	14			*Retail:*	
Household goods	15	*Retail:*		Food shops	10
Miscellaneous	16	Motor vehicles,		Supermarkets	11
		machinery	18	Liquor, bars	17
Service:		Builders' hardware	19		
Personal	20			*Other:*	
Personal business	21	*Service:*		Vacant premises	26
Business	22	Contractors	24	Professional offices	31
Banks	23	Vehicle, machinery			
		repair	25		
Office:		Repair services	27	*'Frame' activities*	
Business	30			(contd)	
Governmental	32	*Wholesale:*			
Business advisory	33	Wholesaling		*Public:*	
		(with stock)	41, 42	Utilities	70
Manufacturing:		Storage (closed)	43, 44	Govt. service	71-76
Jewellery	642	Open storage	45-48	Car parks (public)	79
Women's clothing	569			Transport depots	78
Newspaper publishing	620	*Manufacturing:*		Indoor amusement	84, 86
		Mineral processing	50	Clubs	85
Public:		Chemicals	51	Parks	89
General post office	722	Engineering &		Open recreation	87, 88
		metalworking	53, 54		
Cultural:		Textiles & clothing			
Recreational school	81	(excl. 569)	55, 56		
Central churches	83	Food	57, 58		
Cinema	847	Leather goods	59		
Lottery sales	854	Furniture	60, 61		
		Printing (excl. 620)	62		
Other:					
Offices under		*Other:*			
construction	293	Vacant land	28		

* Based on criteria listed in Table 2-2.
† See Appendix II for an elaboration of the code.

as a part of the area within which they were finally included. The classification of individual activities is pursued further in Appendix I. It is recognized that the classification, being based largely on location patterns in Perth, will not be valid for other cities in entirety. However, the basic procedure should be utilizable elsewhere and in any case (as will soon become evident) the location pattern of central-area activities is remarkably consistent from city to city.

The classification lays the groundwork for the delimitation of the core. The first step in this direction is the identification of those areas dominated by either core or frame uses.* The extent of the core defined in these terms is shown in Fig. 2-2. However, since vertical extension is a typical characteristic of the core, a further criterion was adopted before an area was finally included: that is, a 'core height index' of 1.00 or over (Fig. 2-3). This index, based on the Murphy/Vance central-business height index (see Murphy & Vance 1954a:206), relates the amount of core space (as defined in terms of Table 2-3) to the ground-floor space. Although this index appears arbitrary, it ensures that the areas included within the core are truly characteristic of it not only in terms of overall content but also in respect of use intensity and vertical extension. The adoption of the frontage unit for the delimitation allows the well-known variation of land use by street rather than by block (see Murphy & Vance 1954a, Jacobs 1958) to be taken into account. The change of character across the core boundary is well illustrated in frontispiece.

The resulting frame area is, as expected, one of marked horizontal as opposed to vertical extension; in general the height index of most blocks is low, with an average of 1.4 (see Fig. 2-3). This value compares fairly closely with the 1.8 average Preston (1966:478) discovered for three United States cities (Worcester, Massachusetts; Youngstown, Ohio; Richmond, Virginia). The only areas of marked vertical extension in Perth's frame are provided by multi-storey car parks, high-density residential development, hospitals and occasional high-rise offices on the expanding fringes of the core (see frontispiece). Thus the character of the frame is derived from the form of the structures and the activities housed in the area.

2-2 COMPOSITION

It has already been noted that the activities that are located predominantly in the central-area frame tend to be space-extensive in nature and oriented to vehicular rather than pedestrian traffic. A comparison of the relative amounts of space occupied by different activities in the frame areas of five cities (Table 2-4) allows some investigation of these hypotheses. Of course, such comparisons must be viewed with caution, owing to the small number of cities involved and because the composition of a city's central area will probably vary to some extent with both the size and the function of the city. Nonetheless, although the proportions of total space occupied by each category of activity vary markedly from city to city, the relative rank order shows a high degree of correlation.

---

* For these purposes areal domination is taken to mean 50% or more of a block's floorspace as deduced from 1968 data. Changes in boundaries between 1968 and 1972 are discussed in Chapter 5.

Fig. 2-3 *Height indices of frame blocks, Perth central area 1968*

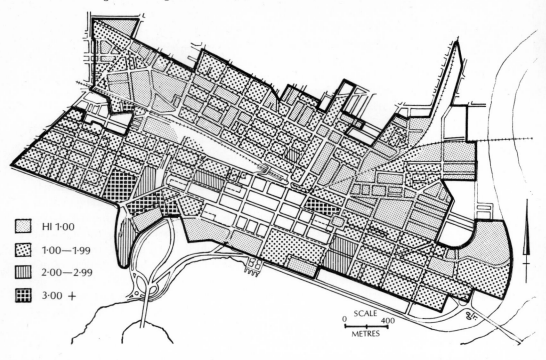

HI 1·00

1·00—1·99

2·00—2·99

3·00 +

SCALE
0   400
METRES

Fig. 2-4 *Distribution of public and civic facilities, Perth central area 1968*

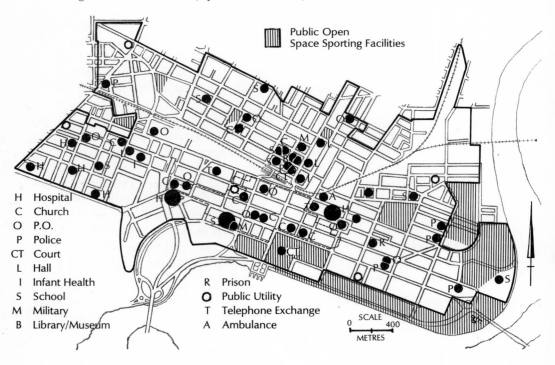

Public Open
Space Sporting Facilities

H   Hospital
C   Church
O   P.O.
P   Police
CT   Court
L   Hall
I   Infant Health
S   School
M   Military
B   Library/Museum

R   Prison
O   Public Utility
T   Telephone Exchange
A   Ambulance

SCALE
0   400
METRES

Table 2-4

COMPARISON OF THE INTERNAL COMPOSITION OF THE FRAME
AREAS OF FIVE CITIES

	Floorspace proportions and rank order											
	Perth		Richmond		Worcester		Youngstown		Capetown		Mean	
Activity	%	*rank*	%	*rank*	%	*rank*	%	*rank*	%	*rank*	%	*rank*
Public and organiz-ational	27.8	1	29.7	1	19.8	2	23.4	2	41.3	1	28.4	1
Automotive, transport-ational, parking	26.3	2	11.1	5	9.0	5	12.5	3	5.5	5	12.9	3
Residential (permanent)	9.9	3	16.0	2	16.4	3	26.8	1	11.8*	3	16.2	2
Manufacturing	9.8	4	12.7	4	24.5	1	6.6	5	7.8	4	12.3	5
Wholesaling and storage	8.0	5	13.5	3	13.4	4	5.3	6	22.8	2	12.6	4
Vacancy	7.8	6	7.1	6	6.8	6	9.4	4	3.1	7	6.8	6
Offices	5.8	7	2.3	7	1.7	10	2.1	10	3.1	7	3.0	8
Residential (transient)	2.4	8	1.9	9	1.8	9	3.2	9	—	—	1.9	10
Retail (excluding automotive)	2.1	9	1.7	10	3.9	7	4.6	7	3.3	6	3.2	7
Service (excluding automotive)	2.1	9	2.1	8	2.5	8	3.5	8	1.1	9	2.3	9
Totals (errors due to rounding)	100.0		100.0		100.0		100.0		100.0			
Populations	*c.* 600 000				*c.* 300 000				*c.* 807 000			

* Including transient

Note: The land-use classification code used elsewhere in this study (Appendix II) has been revised here to coincide with that used by Preston and Davies.

Sources: Perth: Perth City Council, land-use survey data; U.S. cities: Preston, 1968:475; Capetown: Davies 1965:101.

Thus it is noticeable that the first- or second-ranking activity in each city are public and organizational uses (comprising such facilities as recreation spaces, public halls, churches and government service establishments). This trend is not, in fact, predictable from the Horwood and Boyce concept; they do not mention such activities as being typical of the frame. This is a serious omission in view of significance of public and institutional activities guaged from the figures in Table 2-4, where the percentage occupancy varies from 19.8 in Youngstown to 41.3 in Capetown. However, the activities that rank between second and fifth in significance

—automotive and transportational, residential, manufacturing and wholesaling—
are all noted by Horwood and Boyce as significant space occupiers in the frame
area (see Fig. 1-1). The other uses specifically referred to (special services) are,
although not important in terms of space occupance, a feature typical of many
city frame areas as will be shown in § 2-3.6. Other uses are generally of minor
significance, although it is worthy of note that in four of the five frame areas under
consideration, over 6% of total space is vacant; this reaches a peak of 9.4% in
Youngstown and 7.8% in Perth, and in each city exceeds space devoted to several
other activities. The phenomenon is indicative of the relative lack of demand for
land in the frame area of many cities, but is also due to pressures of external factors
such as freeway systems.

This examination of space occupancy in the frame is a fair indicator of its
general composition; however, it gives little indication of spatial structure. The
latter can only be revealed through an examination of the location patterns of the
different types of activity characteristic of the area.

2-3 ACTIVITY PATTERNS IN THE FRAME: ANALYSIS AND EXPLANATION

2-3.1 AN ANALYTICAL FRAMEWORK?

The analysis of the distributional patterns of the activities that characterize the
central area has often been undertaken within a framework of zones; this has the
advantage of pointing to contrasts between different sections of the area. Thus
Murphy and Vance (1955) followed by Mika (1965) and Davies (1965), by
adopting a framework of concentric zones around the point of maximum value
in the CBD, were able to show that the character of space utilization of the area
changed and became generally less intense towards the peripheries. However, such
an imposition of zones tends to camouflage the distribution of individual activities
and also implies that there is something significant in the shape and area of the
zones. As Davies (1965:31) points out, this is undoubtedly distorting reality.

Such weaknesses led Davies (1965:37) to the conclusion that the Murphy/Vance
type of analytical framework is 'at best inadequate . . . at worst positively misleading'. For this reason Davies devised an alternative framework of zones based
on the tendency of certain activities to cluster; these clusters were delimited by a
somewhat tedious and arbitrary procedure, and land use analysed within each one
of them (see Carter 1972).

Although this enables some of the salient features of central-area structure to
emerge, it tends to obscure the detailed distribution patterns of individual activities,
and hence any explanation of the patterns is overlooked. Furthermore the zones
themselves are of doubtful validity as meaningful units within the central area.

In order to avoid such pitfalls, our study will commence with an analysis of
individual activity patterns within the frame, and attempt an explanation in the
light of various evidence. This is not to suggest that distinctive subregions are not

identifiable within the frame; however it is believed that these emerge more naturally from a detailed analysis of individual patterns than from the imposition of an arbitrary framework over the area. This chapter and next therefore, will concentrate on individual activity distributions, whilst attention will be turned to a synthesis of patterns in Chapter 4.

2-3.2 PUBLIC AND ORGANIZATIONAL ACTIVITIES

The importance of these activities in terms of their space occupance emerged in the previous section. As far as their location pattern is concerned a common feature is the tendency of certain public facilities, government services and open spaces to concentrate in areas adjoining the core boundary. According to Davies (1965:57) this trend has been 'widely observed'; he finds it also occurs in Capetown and cites Sydney as another example. Preston (1966:251) notes a similar tendency in the three United States cities (listed in Table 2-4), Robinson (1965:44) in Hamilton, and Pain (1967:91) in Auckland. In Perth there are strong concentrations of buildings and open spaces given over to public or government-service activities (such as hospitals, libraries and museums, court houses and fire stations) to the immediate north and south of the core (see Fig. 2-4). Such concentrations form very effective barriers to the expansion of the core since the land involved is generally in public ownership and hence not subject to the normal pressures of the land market.

This common location pattern seems logical in terms of the nature of these activities: they are in many instances desirous of location accessible to the public (e.g. court houses and hospitals) (see Preston 1966:253), and yet their extensive nature and hence lack of rent-paying ability rules out a core location. Close proximity to the core thus becomes a suitable compromise. Not all such facilities show a clustering tendency, however: elements such as local churches and halls and public open spaces tend to be scattered throughout the frame area (see Fig. 2-4; Davies 1965: Fig. 33, Preston 1966:252), in response to demand from nearby residential areas and availability of land. Those on the fringe of the core tend to serve the entire city rather than any local area. However, in certain cases, where the frame houses concentrations of ethnic groups, such locational pulls may outweigh considerations of centrality, giving rise to a more peripheral location.* Thus in general it appears that the location of these facilities is determined both by their nature and space-occupancy characteristics, and the types of links they have with the city population.

2-3.3 RESIDENTIAL PREMISES

The tendency of the population of inner city and central areas to decline over the years has been observed throughout the world (see Carter 1972) and, as will be seen later, is at the root of many of the processes of change and transition that

---

* Unlike those cases cited above, churches and privately-owned halls are subject to land market pressures, and this may influence their location. See also § 2-4.

are currently affecting the centre. Its implications for the future of residential premises within the frame are clear: a declining number of housing units *in toto* and a declining proportion of those that remain and are given over to residential purposes.

Nonetheless, residential premises still form an important component of the land-use patterns of most frame areas. As illustrated in Table 2-4, they rank as second most important use (on average) in that particular sample of cities. The location pattern of single family dwellings in several cities is characterized by arcuate distribution around the outer margin of the area, with isolated clusters remaining in other segments of the frame—a phenomenon apparent in Capetown (Davies 1965: Fig. 32), the United States cities studied by Preston (1966:258) and in Perth (see Fig. 2-5).

These clusters are often the heart of 'reception areas' for groups of migrants reaching the city for the first time. Economic and racial discrimination may ensure the perpetuation of such areas (see e.g. Berry & Horton 1970) although the internal social links often mitigate against their 'natural' disintegration in any case. The result is a concentration of minority ethnic groups in these areas of the frame, and it is also these groups who will suffer most from the gradual replacement of such residential structures within the area by uses of higher rent-paying ability that are widely regarded as being more desirable. Certainly some of the residential premises in the frame are in poor physical condition and are lacking in basic amenities (as illustrated in Plate I), but whether the structures that replace them are necessarily an improvement seems open to doubt.

This applies particularly to newer high-density residential structures within the frame, which, in contrast to the general trend, are on the increase (see Chapter 5) and are developing into distinct nodes as hypothesized in the core-frame concept. Such development is noticeable within most Australian city central areas, and according to Rose (1972:72) is a 'logical response' to the relatively high land values that prevail in the frame in comparison to outer areas of the city. In Perth, two nodes of high-density housing have developed: one to the east and one to the west of the core (Fig. 2-5; their appearance [Plate II] reflects that 'logical response').

Again, as Rose notes, the provision of such facilities has often formed part of publicly-sponsored slum-clearance programmes in inner city areas, although this 'bulldozer approach' to redevelopment is coming under increasing criticism as its impact upon the social structure of the areas becomes evident (see e.g. Jones 1970). Such issues receive further attention in Chapter 5. In the meantime it can be noted that desirable or not, the development of nodes of high-rise residential premises close to the core of the city is becoming an increasingly typical feature of many frame areas.

The other component of the residential premises in the frame are transient facilities, including boarding houses, hotels and motels. Although these uses are not important in terms of the space they occupy in comparison to other activities (see Table 2-4), they are a feature that in many ways typifies the general atmosphere

Fig. 2-5 *Predominantly residential areas, Perth central area 1968*

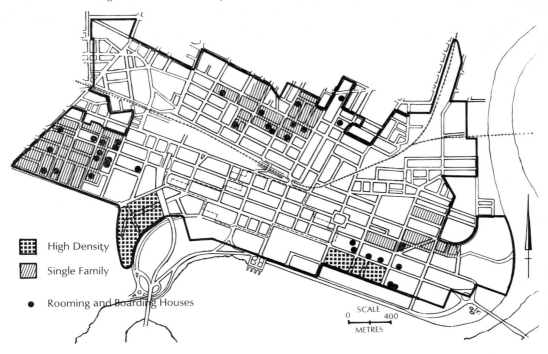

High Density

Single Family

Rooming and Boarding Houses

SCALE
0   400
METRES

Fig. 2-6 *Distribution of parking facilities and automotive-oriented activities, Perth central area 1968*

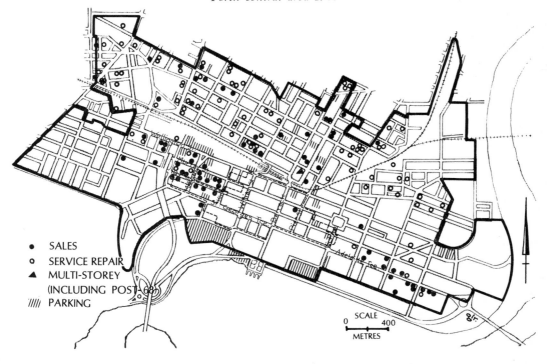

• SALES
○ SERVICE REPAIR
▲ MULTI-STOREY
  (INCLUDING POST 68)
///// PARKING

SCALE
0   400
METRES

of many sections of the frame. The boarding-houses and private hotels in particular are often of a dilapidated nature (see Plate III) and are found in association with the more run-down areas (and often, population), where demand for land appears to be least (or in some way artificially constrained) and blight the worst. This pattern of blight is not aided by impending freeway construction programmes that often cut through the areas (see §2-4).

2-3.4 AUTOMOTIVE-ORIENTED ACTIVITIES

The impact of the motor vehicle upon cities has long caused concern amongst urban analysts and planners; the motor car is often regarded as public enemy number one, whilst also being a cherished friend to a large section of the community. People pay lip service to the need for better public-transport systems and abhor the amount of public funds spent on new road and freeway construction; yet for the most part appear unwilling to part with their beloved machines. Hence the use of the car becomes more widespread, congestion worse and public transport forced further along its downward spiral. Of course there are some benefits for the car-owning sections of the community such as increased mobility and ease of access to the city and to what remains of the countryside surrounding the cities; but an inevitable by-product of the rising mobility is a dispersed city or what Webber (1964) has aptly called the 'non-place urban realm'. Such an environment can be extremely isolated for the non-car owner, and it forces future generations to accept dispersal and increased travel time as a part of life (see Buchanan 1964).

Whatever the answer to this dilemma, one thing is certain: the city centre, being traditionally located at the focus of the city's transport system, will feel the impact of the motor vehicle more than any other area. The apparent universal trend towards increasing dependance upon the motor vehicle has obvious adverse effects upon the environment close to and within the central area as congestion builds up. Such congestion often leads to the launching of ambitious freeway programmes in an attempt to ease the situation, but whether the benefits of such programmes exceed their costs seems open to doubt. (This theme is pursued further in §2-4.)

Another aspect of the impact of the motor vehicle on the central area is the rising amount of land given over to parking: concrete deserts, rarely occupied for more than a third of the day, tend to form a ring around the core. This tendency noted in the United States (Preston 1966:253), the United Kingdom (Masser 1967:56) and also observable in Perth (Fig. 2-6), results from demands of employees concentrated in the core. In Perth, for example, there is a string of council-owned parking areas along the southern perimeter of the central area in close proximity to the main office zone to serve the needs of commuters (see Fig. 2-6). Individual cities will vary in the amount of land given over to parking, depending both on local policies and the proportion of workers commuting by car,* but the location patterns are nonetheless likely to be similar.

---

* In Perth the population of the central workforce arriving by car had reached 60% by 1966 (Perth Regional Transport Study Group 1970), a much higher proportion than in many cities.

Apart from the publicly-owned parking areas many of Perth's smaller parking lots are commercially owned and appear to be only temporary uses occupying sites earmarked for redevelopment projects. A similar tendency has been noted in the United States study by Preston (1966:253) who suggests that the owners are awaiting rises in land values and meanwhile provide themselves with a 'highly remunerative' source of income. Whether or not such rises in value will occur seems doubtful in many cases, as the areas are often located in currently stagnating segments of the frame. In the meantime these activities are having the unfortunate effect of fragmenting the land-use pattern in these areas (see Plate IV), and thus further loosening the structure and possibly contributing to the stagnation. This pattern is likely to be reinforced by the current policy of the Perth City Council to provide a number of short-term shopper car parks close to the core in an effort to bolster declining retail trade. This policy may have considerable long term benefits for the core, but the immediate impact on links with the frame should be set against this.

Apart from parking areas, another important component of the activities derived from the base of increasing car ownership are sales, service and repair establishments. The areal association of such activities is a well-recognized feature of the retail structure of the American city at least; Berry (1963:20) suggests that such 'automobile rows' form along major arteries within the city as one of the distinctive 'specialised areas' within ribbon developments. Subsequent investigations elsewhere have shown that such features are also noticeable within Australasian and British cities (see May 1967, Pain 1967, Carter & Rowley 1966). The location of the frame area and the fact that many of the city's major arterial routes pass through it help explain the replication of these automobile-oriented nodes of activity throughout the frame areas of many cities. Thus they are evident along major arteries close to the core in Capetown (Davies 1965:52), Johannesburg (City of Johannesburg 1967), Auckland (Pain 1967:72), Cardiff (Carter & Rowley 1966:127), as well as in Perth (See Fig. 2-6), and in the United States cities studied by Preston (1966) and Johnson (1954). Whilst Preston (1966:254) maintains that these clusters are not true 'automobile rows', there is no doubt that they benefit both the entrepreneur and the customer by facilitating comparison shopping, and their location along major arteries ensures both accessibility and advertising to the passing potential market. The visual character of these areas, however, often leaves much to be desired (Plate V). The need for these establishments to occupy relatively large areas precludes a core location for most and makes them particularly susceptible to changes in the land values (see Chapter 5, §5-3.8).

The clusters of sales establishments are apparently complemented by associated clusters of service and repair facilities in many cities (see Tacoma City Planning Commission 1959:43, Preston 1966:253); yet in Perth the two sets of activities tend to separate. This apparent quirk is explicable by the nature of the Perth City Council (1963) zoning regulations (Fig. 2-7) that classify motor-repair establishments as 'industrial' in character. Hence they are excluded from the major 'automotive clusters' that are generally located within areas zoned for retail purposes (as shown by a comparison of Figs 2-6, 2-7).

Fig. 2-7 *Zoning ordinances for central area, adopted by Perth City Council 1963*

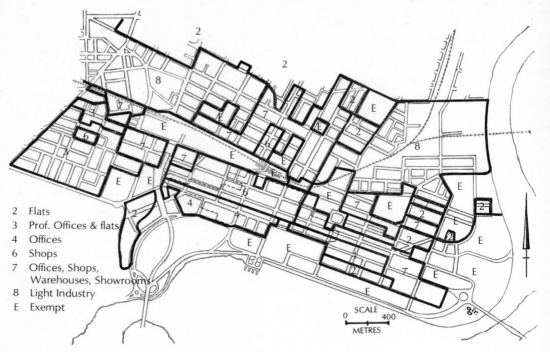

2   Flats
3   Prof. Offices & flats
4   Offices
6   Shops
7   Offices, Shops,
    Warehouses, Showrooms
8   Light Industry
E   Exempt

SCALE
0   400
METRES

Fig. 2-8 *Distribution of manufacturing floorspace, Perth central area 1968*

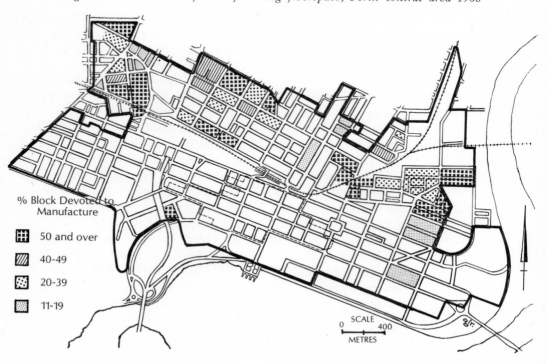

% Block Devoted to
Manufacture

50 and over

40-49

20-39

11-19

SCALE
0   400
METRES

An exception to the clustering tendency of automotive and associated activities occurs in the case of petrol stations, which in Perth are scattered along the major arteries running through the frame, as in the case in Capetown, and in Youngstown, Worcester and Richmond (U.S.A.). This is to be expected in view of the spatial competition occurring between these establishments.

2-3.5 MANUFACTURING ACTIVITIES

The location of manufacturing activity is a topic that has received a good deal of attention in recent years, following the pioneering work of Weber (1929) and Lösch (1933). It has been suggested that whether on the macro or the micro scale, the location process is particularly sensitive to the balance of costs and returns over space, although there has been some dichotomy between those stressing the significance of supply factors and those emphasizing the rôle of demand. Recently it has been realized that neither supply nor demand factors, alone or in combination, are sufficient to explain locational behaviour, and thus attention has been focussed on the development of behavioural models (see Stafford 1972: 200-7), and on the integration of non-economic factors into the traditional models. Yet it appears that manufacturing plants are nonetheless sensitive to differing pressures of cost over space. This implies a dynamic location pattern, a phenomenon readily evident within the city.

Land close to the original focus of the city became the logical location for early urban industrial development and this caused the concentration of manufacturing in inner city areas. Time was to alter these patterns as the competition for space within these areas became more intense, and led to the widespread trend towards the dispersal of manufacturing activity to suburban locations. The increasing orientation of such activities towards horizontal as opposed to vertical arrangement, and hence their increasing space demands, together with the rising importance of motor transport, compounded and accelerated these trends. The extensive types of manufacturing plants were at the forefront of the movement (see e.g. Scott 1963, Logan 1966, Pred 1964). Such trends have been responsible for weakening the dominance of the central area as the prime location for manufacturing within the metropolis (Rimmer 1969), yet as demonstrated in the previous chapter the area remains a significant industrial location, the strength of its pull depending on the nature of the manufacturing activity involved and the extent of linkages with other central-area activities. The forces of industrial inertia also cause certain activities to remain in the area despite the disappearance of their original locational advantage.

The frame is the home of the majority of the central-area's manufacturing since it provides relatively spacious sites at relatively cheap prices, and yet a location accessible both to the core and to the remainder of the metropolitan area. Some smaller plants can afford locations in the core, but these tend to manufacture products with a high value-to-bulk ratio that have a ready market within the core (e.g. women's clothing and jewellery). Otherwise, the industrial content of the central area can be judged in terms of the frame; according to Horwood and Boyce (1959:21) 'light manufacturing' concerns are typical. This term is particularly vague in connotation despite its popularity—Pred (1964:172) ascribes it to 'fuzzy thinking'—yet it is usually taken to mean small-scale activities that have minimum nuisance value. If this is so, one could expect such activities as small printing works and clothing manufacturers to dominate the area's industrial structure. Referring back to Table 1-4, however, it is clear that many other types of activity that would not normally be regarded as 'light' industry abound within the frame. Thus, whilst printing, jewellery and clothing figure importantly, more extensive and/or potential nuisance plants such as food processing, furniture, leather goods and engineering concerns are also common. As already hinted these plants are becoming relatively less significant over time and with city growth (see also Chapter 5), but their presence cannot be overlooked.

It is thus no doubt more profitable to classify the industries concerned according to likely locational criteria rather than by some arbitrary system of 'light' and 'heavy'. Pred (1964) has worked along these lines in proposing that industries near the city centre find it advantageous either because of accessibility to a city-wide market, or because of external economies derived from linkages to other central activities, or alternatively as a convenient transhipment point for raw materials. In this context, the industrial composition of the frame becomes more logical.

Table 2-5

NUMBERS AND AREA OF VARIOUS CLASSES OF MANUFACTURING
PLANTS WITHIN THE PERTH FRAME

Class	*Use code**	*No.*	*Rank*	*Area* (m^2)	*Rank*	*Mean size* (m^2)
Engineering and metalworking	530 to 549	56	1	74 100	3	1 300
Printing and allied trades	620 to 629	48	2	28 500	5	600
Sawmilling and furniture	600 to 615	28	3	36 700	4	1 300
Food and drink processing	570 to 589	23	4	91 000	1	4 000
Clothing and textiles	560 to 569	19	5	17 100	6	900
Mineral processing	500 to 509	12	6	84 700	2	7 100
Chemical products	510 to 518	11	7	14 000	7	1 300
Leather goods	590 to 596	6	8	2 600	8	400

* See Appendix II for details of uses included in these classes.

Source: Data from Perth City Council and personal land-use surveys. (Figures refer to *nett* floorspace.)

In Perth the leading industrial activity in terms of the number of plants present is engineering and metal working (Table 2-5); in view of its nature and the comparative size of plants it might be thought that such an activity is 'anachronistic' in the central area. Yet its presence has been noted in other cities such as Capetown

(Davies 1965:59) and Auckland (Pain 1967:83). Reference to the results of a recent questionnaire survey of firms in Perth's frame area shows that a major factor keeping the engineering firms there was accessibility to a metropolitan-wide market (Perth City Council 1968).

The survey also revealed, however, that over half of the existing plants (at 1968) planned a shift within the near future, thus continuing the trend originally detected by Scott (1963:199). Such factors help explain the fact that many of the remaining industries are housed in ageing and seemingly obsolescent premises; with a move pending, further investment in existing plant is clearly not an economic proposition. Indeed, many firms are probably only remaining in the area to take full advantage of the plant run-down period. This helps contribute to the general air of stagnation prevalent in many segments of the frame (Plate VI).

Similar considerations apply to the mineral processing and chemical manufacturing plants that remain in the frame. In general these industries either utilize local raw materials or attach a particular significance to a location at the hub of the city's transport network. However, the space they occupy in Perth (an average of between 1 300 and 7 100 m^2: Table 2-5) will make it increasingly difficult for them to compete for space in the central area in the future; such competition will test the real strength of these location factors. Food processing plants (with their average space occupancy of 4 000 m^2 in Perth: see Table 2-5) will also come under increasing pressure, although in this case the linkages to the nearby metropolitan produce markets may prove a more potent factor (Scott 1963:208). It has been suggested by Pain (1967:89) that such plants are anomalous within the city centre, but evidence from other studies (Cooper 1960, Pred 1964, Logan 1966) suggests otherwise.

Linkages to other activities within the city centre also rate as significant location factors for most of the remaining manufacturing activities within the frame. In contrast to those just discussed, these tend to be labour intensive and of smaller scale. Clothing factories, furniture manufacturers, leather-goods makers and printing works are typical examples found in many cities (Davies 1965:58, Cooper 1960:14, Pred 1964:175). In Perth's frame these activities occupy an average floorspace of 800 m^2 (see Table 2-5). The clothing manufacturers are in an excellent location to supply the nearby concentration of clothing stores in the core. The fact that some plants of this type are also located in the core has already been mentioned; however those in the frame are larger concerns of a general rather than a specialized nature. This renders a core location an uneconomic proposition, whilst the frame is also closer to a major source of female labour in the inner city residential areas.

Manufacturers of furniture find a ready market for their products in the nearby retail outlets; however the current trend to decentralization of both these outlets and the suppliers (sawmills) may invoke a locational shift on the part of the manufacturers. In contrast, such a move is unlikely in the case of printing works which are intimately linked to the burgeoning office sector of the core—in the Perth survey (Perth City Council 1968) none of the printers expressed a desire to relocate away from the centre. Moreover, many new printing plants have been erected within the frame in recent years (see Chapter 5). In general terms, therefore, the industries that are gaining increasing prominence within the frame have strong linkages to the core, and are of a semi-intensive nature; those without such linkages and whose nature is extensive are, on the other hand, becoming a less significant part of the frame's industrial structure.

Previous paragraphs have referred to general location factors influencing central-area manufacturing activities; but little has been said of the location patterns of the activities within the frame. Indeed this aspect has not received a great deal of attention in the literature except in very general terms. Preston (1966:251), for example, has noted that in the United States cities he studied 'light industry is located mainly near railway lines', whilst Davies (1965:59) notes that the industrial premises in Capetown's frame area are 'comparatively widely spaced'. These workers also noted, however, that there was a marked tendency for wholesaling and industrial activities to cluster together in particular segments of the frame. A similar pattern has also been observed in Philadelphia by Rannells (1957:154), where in fact the two activities exhibited the strongest pattern of association of any pair within the central area. Such locational association has been explained in terms of the similar locational and site requirements of the two activities.

Some similar degree of locational association is observable in Perth, yet there is a tendency for wholesaling activities to be located closer to the core than manufacturing plants (compare Figs 2-8, 2-9). The three main concentrations of manufacturing activity observable within the area are all located to the north of the railway, whilst a good deal of wholesaling is found to the south of this axis. Thus the patterns exhibit marked spatial separation rather than association; however, examination of past land-use maps of the area (see Fig. 5-1) shows that much manufacturing activity was in fact located closer to the core in proximity to the major wholesaling cluster in the 1950s. The shift since that time has no doubt been partly due to the rising diseconomies of central locations (see Scott 1963:133-5), but zoning ordinances (Fig. 2-7) that have precluded industrial activities from this area since 1963 have also played a part in breaking the locational ties between the two activity-sets.

Further reference to Fig. 2-8 shows also that the major clusters of manufacturing activity are confined to the north-east and north-west sectors of the frame in areas that have now been specifically zoned for the purpose (see Fig. 2-7). As will be seen in §2-4, the stability of both these industrial clusters is seriously threatened by the proposed inner ring freeway.

As far as the individual manufacturing activity types are concerned there is a relatively even scatter throughout these areas. Food manufacturers, however, favour the north-western sector in proximity to the nearby metropolitan markets (Fig. 2-9b) and the rail yards (now defunct). Printing works are predominantly clustered in the north-east sector in apparent response to the pull of nearby electroplating and photoengraving premises (Perth City Council 1968). Furniture factories, although scattered throughout the manufacturing areas tend to concentrate around their sawmill suppliers.

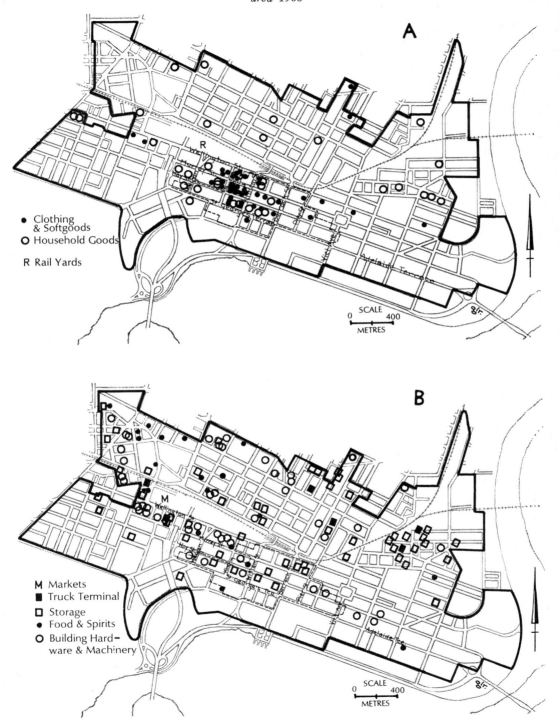

Fig. 2-9 *Distribution of wholesaling and storage premises, Perth central area 1968*

A

R

• Clothing
  & Softgoods
O Household Goods

R Rail Yards

SCALE
0   400
METRES

B

M

M Markets
■ Truck Terminal
□ Storage
• Food & Spirits
O Building Hard–
  ware & Machinery

SCALE
0   400
METRES

In general terms, therefore, the industrial activities with the most definite and clustered location patterns are those with strong linkages to anchors or to other sets of central-area activity. The significance and arrangement of these linkages is a factor that should receive more attention in planning the structure of the region.

2-3.6   WHOLESALING AND STORAGE ACTIVITIES

Unlike the location of manufacturing activities, that of wholesaling premises has received little attention from urban analysts. With the exception of a few specific studies (such as that of Simons 1966), even less has been said of the location of central-area wholesalers. However, following the observations of Horwood and Boyce (1959), the major studies of specific central areas (already referred to: Preston 1966, Griffin 1963, Rannells 1957, Davies 1965, Pain 1967, Goddard 1967, Carter & Rowley 1966) have demonstrated that wholesaling facilities are typically located in concentrations close to the central-area core and to transportation termini in the frame. Similarly Simons (1966) identified a 'wholesale district' immediately adjacent to Sydney's core and the nearby port.

In Perth, concentrations of wholesaling activities occur to the north-west of the core close to the original rail termini, and storage facilities show some areal correlation with the distribution of trucking termini in the north-east of the frame (these patterns are illustrated in Fig. 2-9). It would seem that they are a response both to linkages to the core and to the dependance on transportation facilities.

Closer examination of the distribution patterns, however, shows that although some wholesalers strongly clustered in particular areas, others are more widely distributed. In general terms in fact, wholesaling in the Perth frame showed a more widely scattered pattern than manufacturing activity; this may in part be due to lessening dependance on rail transport, but is also attributable to zoning influences, since the ordinances allow wholesaling to locate over much wider segments of the frame than manufacturing (see Fig. 2-7). On the other hand they exclude new wholesaling premises from locating in the major cluster area to the north-west of the core. The possible adverse effects of this zoning will be discussed further in Chapter 5, but it can be noted here that notwithstanding the obsolescent nature of some of the premises in this area in terms of the wholesaling function (Plate VIIa), the zoning has certainly encouraged the continued dispersal of wholesalers from this locality. This dispersal is altering the balance of the frame's wholesaling mix, since those firms dealing with low-value bulky goods (such as machinery and certain household goods) are at the forefront of the movement (Wolinski 1970:90-8). Thus the point made in the previous section concerning the increasing pressure placed on the most extensive activities in the frame is reinforced. As was the case with manufacturing activities, it appears that those wholesalers that are becoming less significant within the central area are also less cohesive as a group; the distribution of machinery, building and hardware wholesalers appears to reflect weak intra-group linkages. Their decentralization tendencies are probably also connected with the concomitant decline of heavy retailing activities within the central area.

This process provides an example of the competition between land use as outlined in the theory of the land market. As we have seen, these processes are having their effect upon many of the activities that have traditionally located in the frame, that is, activities of an extensive nature and/or of low rent-paying ability. The hierarchy of activities will be a critical factor in shaping the processes of land-use succession in the frame.

Turning to the location pattern of individual activities within the storage-wholesaling sector, it is clear from Fig. 2-9 that in Perth, the strongest cluster is formed by the clothing and soft-goods set: two-thirds of their total central area numbers are located in the area immediately to the north-west of the core bounded by Milligan (west), Wellington (north), William (east) and Hay (south) Streets. In fact the cluster overlaps the core-frame boundary, but those within the core are almost exclusively located on upper-floor levels, whereas a good proportion of the balance are located at ground level. If wholesaling is to be regarded as a function typical of the frame, then this distribution pattern suggests that the core-frame boundary ought to be regarded, strictly speaking, as multi-level (cf. Simons 1966:11). On the other hand the concentration of wholesalers in this area is partly a response to the proximity of a concentration of clothing retailers in the core nearby (Wolinski 1970:82). A similar concentration is observable in Sydney (Simons 1966:12) for apparently the same reasons. The strength of links between core and frame and the overlapping of the cluster provides grounds for suggesting that a core-frame boundary in this area is completely arbitrary. Evidence to substantiate this point is discussed further in Chapter 4, where resort has been made to multivariate techniques to establish the components of total core structure.

Firms dealing with household goods also concentrate in the zone close to the core (Fig. 2-9) and in upper-floor premises in the core itself, in apparent response to the nearby concentration of household-goods retailers in western Hay Street (see Fig. 3-12). However under 50% of the total numbers represented in the central area are found in this cluster, with the balance scattered widely over the frame.

The pattern of food and spirit wholesale establishments in Perth's frame parallels that of analogous manufacturing plants to some extent, with a definite concentration observable around the produce markets in the western frame (Fig. 2-9). Functional linkages clearly exert a dominant influence on location. Simons (1966:14) finds a similar concentration in Sydney's wholesale district, and one is certainly evident in the Covent Garden district in central London around the famous fruit, vegetable and flower market.

The clusters of storage premises in the northern segments of Perth's frame are to some extent focussed on the transportation termini nearby, with a cluster also being noticeable around the since abandoned rail-goods yards (Fig. 2-9). The fact that the former cluster has strengthened over recent years at the expense of the latter is another indication of the growing significance of road transport. A similar areal correlation of these facilities has been observed in the United States cities by Preston (1966:249). However, it should be noted that many of the storage premises in the north-western cluster in Perth's frame are occupied by government departmental works and transport depots, and warehouses of core-located department stores—apparently as a response not so much to the proximity of termini as to the availability of extensive sites in this relatively peripheral location. A similar situation has been identified in Tacoma in the United States (Tacoma City Planning Commission 1962). In Perth, the proposed freeway will cause the abandonment of many of the premises in this area: indeed its blighting effects are already noticeable (see §2-4).

2-3.7 ACTIVITIES WHICH OCCUPY OFFICES

In terms of their space occupance, offices are a relatively insignificant component of frame structure, accounting for an average of only 3.0% of the floorspace in the five cities compared earlier (Table 2-4). Yet evidence suggests that the activities seeking accommodation in offices in the frame are steadily growing in significance, in contrast to many of the other activities so far examined. This has resulted from two trends: (1) the tendency for certain offices traditionally located in the core to migrate to former residential areas of the frame; and (2) the lateral extension of the core.

These matters are elaborated in Chapter 5, but it can be noted here that the former trend has resulted from a combination of adverse conditions in the core along with attractions in the nearby frame; the latter area has been seen by a number of activities as a suitable alternative but nonetheless still as a central location. Professional services have commonly been prominent among the activities involved (see e.g. McNair 1960, Merriman 1967, Kemp 1972).

The second trend has been noted in several cities including Sydney (Whipple 1970), Melbourne (Johnston 1967) and London (Goddard 1967). It can eventually lead to an extension of core boundaries as has occurred in Perth between 1968 and 1972 (see Fig. 5-2c), but initially it results in the inner segments of the frame being invaded by a variety of offices on a fragmentary basis. In Perth, the segment of the frame involved was marked initially by a predominance of general offices (such as those of manufacturers, wholesalers and import-export agents) which are a relatively footloose element within the core. This suggests that such elements place less importance on a core location than others, such as financial offices which remained strongly clustered in the core (see Chapter 3). However, a field check of the area in 1972 showed that a wider cross-section of typical core-office activities has occupied premises in the intervening period.

The movement of professional offices has led to the development of a definite node of such premises in the western sector of Perth's frame, considerably fragmenting the former pattern of residential land use (Fig. 2-10). This phenomenon has also occurred in other cities—such as Christchurch, Auckland (Merriman

1967:122, Pain 1967:79) and Seattle (McNair 1960)—which tends to confirm the original hypothesis of Horwood and Boyce (1959). In 1968 over 80% of the office premises in the West Perth area were professional chambers, mainly in the form of doctors (50%), engineers and surveyors (33%), and accountants (15%). A more recent survey undertaken (Kemp 1972) showed that while the total numbers increased considerably between 1968 and 1972, the proportions remained fairly constant.

In 1968 over 70% of the central-area medical premises and those of architects, surveyors and engineers were located in the frame; on the other hand only 40% of accountants were found in the frame. The continued drift of professional offices to the area since that time would have boosted both these proportions.

The general tendency for professional offices to cluster in the frame is complemented, in Perth at least, by further sub-clustering of the various types of offices. This is most apparent with medical offices: several nodes are observable within an overall cluster to the south of Hay Street (as shown in Fig. 2-10). The nodes consist of groupings of specialists' consulting rooms within the same buildings. In observing a similar phenomenon in Hamilton, New Zealand, Robinson (1965:48) suggests that this is due to doctor's needs for specific accommodation facilities (such as plumbing, small consulting and waiting rooms): purpose-built premises (or houses adapted for the purpose) are a logical answer to these requirements. Another explanation proferred by Morris (1966:120) in discussing the concentration of medical offices observed in several United States city centres is that it is the consequence of 'the growing practice of referring patients'. In discussing the evolution of the West Perth area Lister (1972:73) agrees with this explanation, pointing to nodes of closely-related specialists premises. Such arguments, however, are only based on inference; a recent survey of locational criteria of the professional offices in West Perth has shown that although intra-group linkages *are* an important locational factor, other less tangible factors of perception and psychology are also significantly encouraging the grouping tendency (Kemp 1972:117).

Other professional activities in the area display weaker grouping tendencies, which the investigations of Kemp (1972) have shown to be directly related to the lesser strength of intra-groups linkages. Thus accountants, which are fairly widely distributed over the area (see Fig. 2-10), prefer not to share premises, and display a low degree of intra-group linkages. Similar considerations apply to the architect-surveying-engineering group, although their internal linkages are stronger than those of accountants and hence their location more concentrated. But regardless of such factors, the general professional cluster in the area has been an important location factor for many of the offices in all groups.

2-3.8 OTHER ACTIVITIES

The only other activities of importance that tend to locate in the frame area are clusters of retail and personal-service premises. In Perth these clusters are linear

Fig. 2-10 *Distribution of professional offices, West Perth 1968*

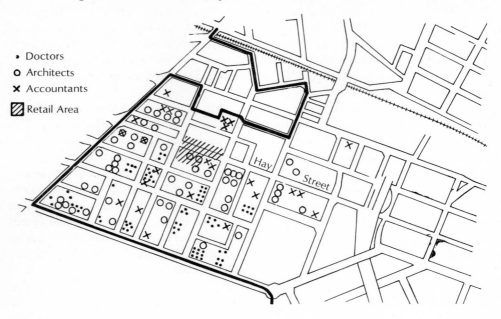

in nature and are situated along major traffic arteries to the north, west and east of the core. This arrangement parallels that in Youngstown, Worcester and Richmond (U.S.A.) and reflects the partial reliance of the premises on passing trade (Preston 1966:256). However, an examination of the content of the 'centres' shows that food stores, delicatessens, snack bars, clothing outlets, bars, personal-service establishments (such as hairdressers, tailors and dressmakers), and banks are predominant. This indicates that links both to nearby local remnant residential areas and to the management and staff of commercial activities in the frame are also important. In terms of their function, such clusters correspond to what Garner (1966:8) has classified as 'community shopping centres'; these

> contain a group of retail and service premises for the community around . . . to allow for the purchase of necessities . . . and frequently demanded comparison goods. In addition they provide . . . groups of business and office services.

The northern cluster in Perth caters largely for immigrant community in the area around (see §2-3.3), and as a result has a distinct composition that includes continental groceries and delicatessens. The area has also formed the basis for the surrounding cluster of restaurants and night clubs, catering to both a local and a city-wide clientele. This cluster has grown rapidly with the continuing growth of the city, although the entertainment offered has not risen far above the 'striperama' level.

2-4 PLANNING PROBLEMS IN THE FRAME

2-4.1 BLIGHT

The preceding discussion has indicated that activity patterns within the frame display a marked degree of locational similarity from city to city. Although the comparisons have been somewhat limited, it is evident that constant forces are at work producing these patterns. The general composition of the area is explicable in terms of its location with respect both to the core and to the city as a whole. This is reflected in the prevailing land values in the area, which themselves exert an important influence on the patterns of space use and the evolution of the area.

The area is characterized by change in terms both of its composition and its structure. These characteristics give rise to many of the area's inherent problems, the causes and consequences of which will be discussed and clarified in Chapter 5. In the meantime, however, it has become clear even from a discussion of static structure of individual patterns that the frame is no longer the suitable location for a wide range of activities that it was; extensive activities in particular—such as large-scale industrial establishments or wholesaling premises—are declining in significance, and although other are moving in to take their place, vacant premises abound in the frame as a result of the constant process of adaptation and change. Preston (1966) regards vacant structures as 'non-transition uses' on the grounds that these areas tend to occur at the outer edge of the zone; in similar vein Outwater (1967) regards vacany as a non-frame use, owing to its not housing any activity. Such classifications, however, fail to recognize that vacancy is in fact a feature common to any segment of the city, but of the frame in particular because of its peculiar nature. Ironically, Preston (1966:258) recognizes this in his analysis, when he comments: 'Vacancies appear in older sections of the transition zone . . . it is also common in dilapidated residential areas.'

A similar pattern is repeated in Perth (as shown in Fig. 2-11). It is also true that vacant land (as opposed to buildings) often occurs at edge of the frame (cf. Davies 1965, Preston 1966), but to use this as evidence to imply that vacant premises or land are not a normal part of the central area is extremely unrealistic, for in all of the cities examined in terms of their frame content (Table 2-4) vacancy occupies an average of almost 7% of total activity space. The processes of land-use succession then appear to operate more slowly in the frame than in the core: in the same cities vacancy accounts for a much smaller proportion of core floorspace. This is probably due to a combination of factors, including a lack of demand for land and buildings in the locations where vacancy occurs, deliberate withholding of land from the market for speculative purposes, and fragmented patterns of property ownership. The already blighted nature of much of the frame, owing to the preponderance of old and functionally obsolescent structures, will further deter the development of prestige accommodation that is becoming the most common product of larger redevelopment projects.

It should also be mentioned that other factors besides the 'normal' operation of the land market, can contribute to the blighted nature of the frame in significant ways. Among these is the increasingly common feature of freeway construction.

2-4.2 FREEWAY IMPACT

Traffic congestion is a growing problem in city centres the world over. In recent years, traffic engineers have put increasing faith in the ring-road as a solution to this problem. The ring-road often takes the form of a freeway-grade loop around the most congested portions of the city so as to provide a by-pass route for through traffic, and superior access for traffic bound for the central area itself. Because of its peripheral location, such routes often pass through the frame of the central area; the so called 'inner city distributor loops' are a feature common to many traffic plans, particularly in the United States cities (Horwood & Boyce 1959:104-6). There is some proof that such networks do assist in lessening traffic congestion and also in improving access to the central area (see Smeed 1970). If this is so, the high cost of providing such facilities in terms of land acquisition (highest in inner city areas) and construction costs, may be offset by savings in motorists' time and frustration both on and off the network. However, recent studies suggest that such benefits are themselves often swallowed up through the increased traffic resulting from the improvements to the network (see Thompson 1969, Plowden 1972).

But even if it is possible to justify such traffic schemes in these terms, there are other costs that are rarely considered, and which no doubt are real to the people and activities affected. Amongst these, and particularly relevant to this context, is the impact of the network on the land-use pattern and linkages in the frame area. This has been little studied by urban analysts as Murphy (1966:314) points out; yet in view of the extraordinary space consumption of the networks and their associated interchanges (see Fig. 2-12c, Plate IX)—often 10 hectares per kilometre (Horwood & Boyce 1959) and nearly 16 in Perth—it would seem a crucial factor to consider in planning the traffic network and land-use pattern in the city centre.

The plan for a ring-road around the Perth central area was first mooted in the Stephenson Report (1955): it was to take the form of a dual-carriageway network closely circumscribing the inner central area, partially grade-separated, and partially connected to the existing traffic network *via* roundabouts (see Fig. 2-12a). The unprecedented increase in car ownership and the continued growth of traffic bound for and around the central area in ensuing years, coupled with the mania of engineers, led to proposals for upgrading this system into a complete motorway network around the centre (De Leuw Cather 1967; Fig. 2-12b). Such was the strength of opposition to these proposals, however, particularly from conservation groups concerned with the prospect of the city being alienated from the river, that the proposals were modified to a partial ring by 1968 (Fig. 2-12c). However, even this partial system is to occupy a total of 101 hectares if completed as planned (equivalent to 30% of the existing frame floorspace). Up to 1968 only the western leg of the network and part of the Narrows interchange had been completed; the

Fig. 2-11   *Vacancies in Perth frame 1968*

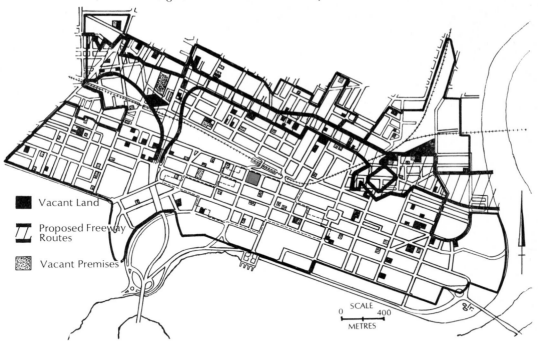

Vacant Land

Proposed Freeway
Routes

Vacant Premises

SCALE
0   400
METRES

Fig. 2-12   *Development of ring road concept*

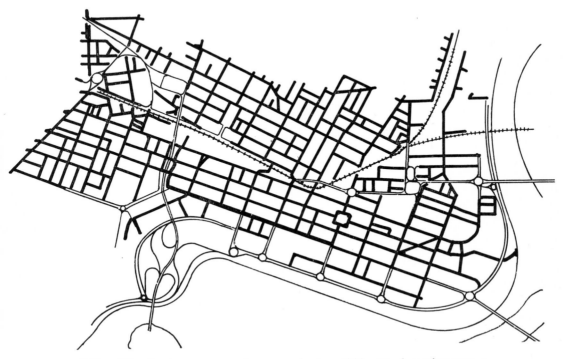

2-12a   The Stephenson central-area road plan 1955. (Dual carriageway=;
existing traffic network ——.)

Fig. 2-12 *Contd*

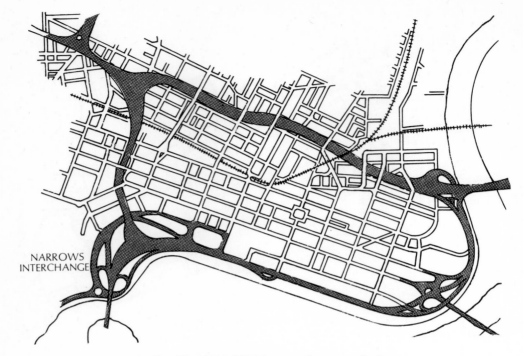

2-12b   The 1963 MRPA central-area road plan

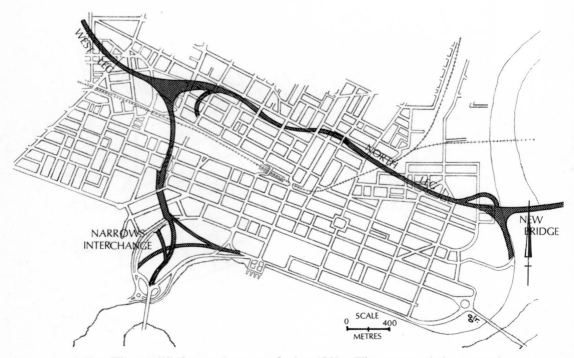

2-12c   The modified central-area road plan 1968. (The extent of the network
completed to 1968 is shown in Fig. 2-13.)

remaining portions were due to absorb a further 57 hectares of land devoted to frame uses (excluding existing roadspace; Perth City Council 1971*a*:53). By 1972 the network had extended slightly northwards, and the construction of the north-west interchange had begun, as illustrated in Fig. 2-14.

A glance at a map of vacant premises and land in the frame area at 1968 (Fig. 2-11) is sufficient to show that the freeway route is exerting an important influence on the pattern: there is a strong correlation between the distribution of vacancies and the freeway path. This is partly a result of the policies of the planning authorities to acquire land in advance of construction, but also seems to be caused by uncertainties over the final shape of the network and its effects on the land-use pattern. A recent survey has shown that there was a considerable increase in vacancy in areas in the freeway path and its immediate proximity between 1968 and 1972. Over the period, vacant land in the path of the freeway increased by 88%, from 71.8 thousand to 135.2 thousand m², as shown in Table 2-6 (refer also to Figs. 2-11 and 2-14); by 1972 vacant premises accounted for 30% of the total floorspace to be ultimately absorbed by the freeway, as compared to 16% in 1968. A closer examination of Table 2-6 shows that these increases were higher in the area of the frame that is scheduled for absorption by the freeway in the 1973-75 period (north-western sector of the frame) than in areas scheduled for later absorption (post-1975). Similarly the overall increase in vacancy in the freeway path area exceeds that in the immediate fringe area (Fig. 2-13a, 2-13b), although the increases in the latter case are well above those elsewhere in the frame.

Table 2-6

INCREASES IN VACANT SPACE: FREEWAY PATH AND ENVIRONS,
PERTH FRAME AREA 1968-72

		1968		*1972*		
	Zone	*Vacant space**	*% Total space*	*Vacant space*	*% Total space*	*% Increase*
A	Freeway path—					
	1973-75	44 332	25.76	91 377	48.92	+106.12
	1976-78	13 860	10.49	24 323	18.40	+ 75.49
	Post-1978	13 646	8.47	19 525	13.70	+ 43.08
	Total freeway path	71 838	15.90	135 225	29.32	+ 88.23
B	Freeway fringe†	21 265	4.69	41 657	9.04	+ 95.89
	Grand Total	93 103	10.26	176 882	19.91	+ 89.98

* In m².
† An area one block either side of the freeway route (see Fig. 2-14).

Source: 1968: Perth City Council and personal survey data; 1972: personal survey data.

Fig. 2-13 *Changes in vacancy in freeway area 1968-72*

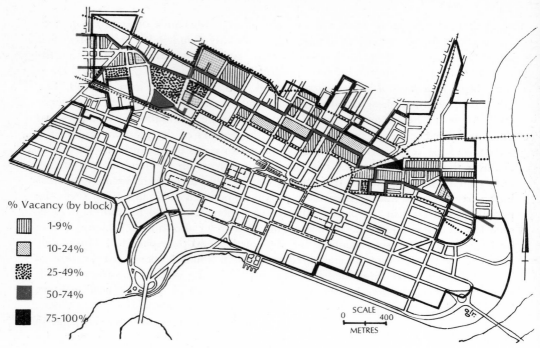

% Vacancy (by block)

▦	1-9%
▧	10-24%
▨	25-49%
▩	50-74%
■	75-100%

SCALE
0   400
METRES

2-13a   Pattern of vacancy 1968

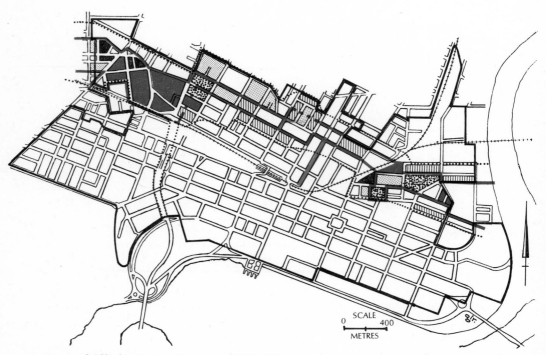

SCALE
0   400
METRES

2-13b   Pattern of vacancy 1972. (Key to vacancy as in Fig. 2-13a.)

Fig. 2-14 *Distribution of vacancy and resumed property in freeway path, Perth frame 1972.* (Solid [red] lines show boundaries of freeway path; dotted area marks boundaries of freeway fringe referred to in Table 2-6.)

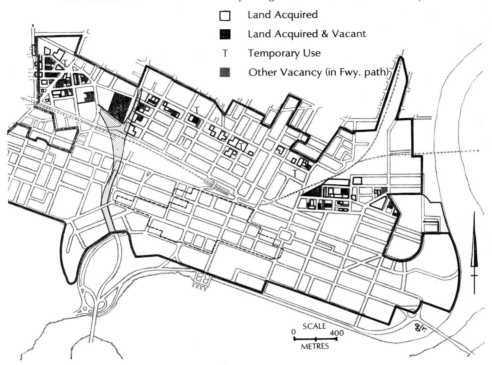

☐ Land Acquired

■ Land Acquired & Vacant

T Temporary Use

■ Other Vacancy (in Fwy. path)

These trends point to the 'creeping blight' that is preceding the construction of the freeway and interchanges. As mentioned, the spatial distribution of vacancies in the freeway path area (see Fig. 2-14) reflects in part the resumption policies of the construction authority (Main Roads Department). The authorities attempt to resume required land well in advance of the scheduled construction programme, but in so doing create a tract of advancing blight. Attempts are made to find short-term tenants for resumed properties, but there is a general lack of demand for such tenancies, except from low-investment activities such as car-parking, car-sales yards and contractor's depots. Thus many premises are left vacant, and this, in combination with sporadic low-investment activities creates a swathe of blighted property along the future freeway path. Even in cases where property has not yet been resumed, vacancies are high (see Fig. 2-14), and this indicates the uncertainty created by the freeway plans. Such situation is a direct consequence of the freeway plans, and undoubtedly represents an opportunity cost to the community. A more rapid construction programme would alleviate the problem somewhat; however, it must be pointed out that the increases in vacancies in the *fringe* area (see Table 2-6) also seem attributable to the uncertainty of the landowners as to the ultimate impact of the freeway on the northern frame area.

Fig. 2-15 *Frame floorspace to be absorbed by the proposed freeway, Perth central area*

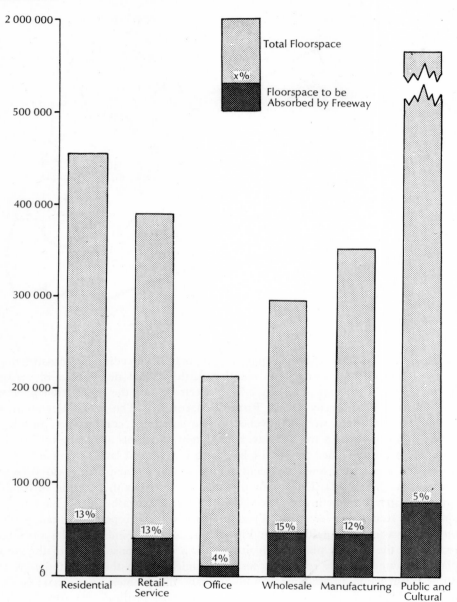

This impact is also felt by a wide range of activities that are to be compulsorily displaced by public authority resumption. Manufacturing is the hardest hit, owing to its concentration in the north-west and north-east sectors of the frame, where interchanges are sited (cf. Figs 2-8, 2-12c). Almost 60% of the space absorbed by the freeway is currently given over to industry and this represents some 12% of the total manufacturing space in the central area. Despite the current trend of decentralization of these activities from the frame, it is clear that the removal of such a large segment of land from the market will not only place increasing pressure on the remaining activities, but also seriously disrupt the existing land-use pattern. Other commercial activities are less affected, but nonetheless are to lose significant proportions of existing space, as illustrated in Fig. 2-15—a total of 147 business establishments alone are involved (Perth City Council 1971a:53). In view of the growing preponderance in the frame of activities exhibiting strong linkages to the core, and despite compensation to displaced businesses, the losses to the central area are incalculable.

In addition, some 344 dwellings and 49 flats with a residential population of nearly 1 400 are to be displaced. As the Perth City Council (1971a:53) has pointed out, 'approximately 14% [are] . . . of pensionable age many of whom are obliged to live as close as possible to the medical services and clinics in the central area.'

The impact on this sector of the population, many of whom are also central-area residents of long standing, has been completely overlooked by the planning authorities. Compensation will undoubtedly be insufficient to cover the real social costs involved in terms of loss of ties with nearby residents and institutions, grievance and hardship invoked by a forced move. That the city council has implicitly recognized such costs (in the quote above) renders their decision to zone single-family dwellings out of the central area (Fig. 2-7; see also Chapter 5) doubly ironic.

Not content with the extent of disruption to businesses and residences, the freeway proposals go further and threaten some 10 hectares of public open space with obliteration. Although this is only equivalent to 8% of the total open space in the central area, it will cause obvious loss of amenity and user value. The major areas to be affected are three large public parks and a sporting-oval complex in the northern segments of the frame. Indeed, the route of the freeway seems to have been carefully designed to pass through as many open spaces as possible (cf. Fig. 2-12c with Fig. 5-2a); of course there are no resumption costs involved here as the spaces are already under government ownership. When the social costs of the loss of amenity and use value are coupled with those arising from the displacement of privately-owned activities, the case for the completion of the network becomes much less convincing. But it seems unlikely that the bureaucracy will listen to such 'irrational' protests.

2-5 CONCLUSION

The foregoing discussion has referred to some problems that arise in planning the structure of the frame. It is evident that one of the major forces that planners have to contend with is the automobile. Its effects are widespread within the area, and range from pressure on properties in strategic locations for conversion into anonymous car-parks and car-sales yards, to the construction of freeways that can disrupt the land-use and linkage patterns. The automobile, therefore, is a significant contributor to the overall blighted nature of many segments of the frame. But the other factors contributing to this major planning problem cannot be seen in their proper perspective until a closer examination is made of the dynamic aspects of central-area structure.

This chapter has demonstrated that the frame area displays distinctive patterns that distinguish it from the core; yet it cannot be denied that strong linkages exist between the two segments of the central area, as Horwood and Boyce (1959) originally pointed out. On the other hand equally strong linkages have been identified between activities within the frame. Even so, it is not realistic to treat the frame and the core separately for planning purposes; for this reason attention is now turned to patterns within the core. Following this, the patterns are synthesised so that a picture of overall structure emerges. When combined with the analysis of the area's dynamic aspects, the stage is set for the construction of a model and proposals for solving the area's most acute land-use planning problems.

3

Central-area processes, activity patterns and problems

II: THE CORE

3-1 CHARACTER

The core of the city is undoubtedly the visual magnet of the central area: its tall buildings and intensive nature contrast sharply with those of the surrounding frame (see frontispiece). But this contrast (one dare not say beauty) goes further than skin-deep, for the core's distinctive character reflects its importance as a service and employment centre for the entire city and region. Although this importance tends to decrease over time and as cities grow, most core areas remain the focus of the greatest daytime population concentration. By contrast the resident population of the area is usually negligible, causing the area to be dubbed as the 'dead heart'.

The tidal waves of population movement to and from the area are at the root of many of the city's transport problems: they give rise to pressures for the construction of massive freeway networks (whose impact upon the frame has already received attention).

The core, then, is often marked by serious traffic congestion, arising not only from the large volume of vehicular movement, but also from pedestrian-vehicular conflict within its boundaries. The pedestrian traffic is generated by activities within the core; thus the area is further contrasted with the frame which, as we have seen, tends to be dominated by vehicle-generating activities. Other differences between core and frame—as seen by Horwood and Boyce (1959)—are evident from a comparison of Tables 2-1 and 3-1.

3-2 COMPOSITION AND CONTENTS

The intensive character of the core is reflected in its composition; the area is characterized by specialist retailing outlets (in the form of department stores, clothing and footwear retailers, jewellery shops and the like), personal-service activities (hairdressers, beauty salons, bootmakers and tailors being typical), and offices of many types (see Table 2-3). However, as stressed earlier, certain central civic and cultural facilities are also located within the area: these form just as important a segment of central activity as do the business concerns.

Nonetheless, it is clear that retailing and office-based activities are the main space users within the core which holds true in all cities regardless of size (see Table 3-2).*

Table 3-1

GENERAL PROPERTIES OF THE CBD CORE

Property	Definition	General characteristics
Intensive land use	Area of most intensive land use and highest concentration of social and economic activities within metropolitan complex	Multistoreyed buildings Highest retail productivity per unit ground area Land use characterized by offices, retail sales, consumer services, hotels, theatres, and banks
Extended vertical scale	Area of highest buildings within metropolitan complex	Easily distinguishable by aerial observation Elevator personnel linkages Grows vertically, rather than horizontally
Limited horizontal scale	Horizontal dimensions limited by walking distance scale	Greatest horizontal dimension rarely more than 1 mile Geared to walking scale
Limited horizontal change	Horizontal movement minor and not significantly affected by metropolitan population distribution	Very gradual horizontal change Zones of assimilation and discard limited to a few blocks over long periods of time
Concentrated daytime population	Area of greatest concentration of daytime population within metropolitan complex	Location of highest concentration of foot traffic Absence of permanent residential population
Focus of intracity mass transit	Single area of convergence of city mass transit system	Major mass transit interchange location for entire city
Centre of specialized functions	Focus of headquarters offices for business, government, and industrial activities	Extensive use of office space for executive and policy making functions Centre of specialized professional and business services
Internally conditioned boundaries	Excluding natural barriers, CBD boundaries confined only by pedestrian scale of distance	Pedestrian and personnel linkages between establishments govern horizontal expansion Dependency on mass transit inhibits lateral expansion

Source: Horwood and Boyce 1959:16. Reproduced with permission of Washington University Press.

---

* It is recognized in this connection that the content of the area will depend on the criteria used for delimitation; all cities listed in Table 3-2 have been defined by the Murphy/Vance technique with the exception of Perth, where the delimitation procedure explained in the previous chapter was used. Both these techniques (notwithstanding the weaknesses of Murphy/Vance) use a classification of activity to define the extent of the core; thus the content will clearly be a reflection of this classification. Nonetheless it is contended that the comparisons are worthwhile in pointing to similarities and differences between cities.

Table 3-2

COMPOSITION OF CORE AREAS OF SELECTED CITIES*

Land-use proportions

City	Survey date	Population (survey date)	Office	Retail	Public (incl. parking)	Residential	Service	Wholesale	Manufacture	Vacant	Total
Salt Lake City, U.S.A.	1954	182 000	22.0	30.0	20.0	13.0	4.0	3.0	4.0	4.0	100.0
Worcester, U.S.A.	1954	203 000	21.0	29.5	21.0	12.0	5.5	2.5	3.5	4.0	100.0
Phoenix, U.S.A.	1954	107 000	19.5	35.0	18.0	15.0	4.5	1.5	1.0	3.5	100.0
Derby, U.K.	1964	132 000	16.5	46.0	16.5	7.0	4.5	2.0	2.5	4.5	100.0
Southampton, U.K.	1964	204 700	23.0	39.5	12.5	12.0	5.0	1.0	2.0	4.5	100.0
Norwich, U.K.	1964	119 900	22.5	35.5	15.0	9.5	4.0	3.5	2.5	4.0	100.0
Capetown, S. Africa	1964	807 000	35.8	23.0	20.7	4.0	7.0	5.1	1.2	2.9	100.0
Perth, W. Australia	1968	600 000	37.7	22.0	11.5	6.3	7.0	3.5	3.4	2.6	100.0
Adelaide, S. Australia	1965	720 000	38.9	35.6	1.7	4.9	N.A.	5.6	2.4	N.A.	100.0
Dusseldorf, Germany	1966	702 600	42.0	11.0	6.0	30.0	—	11.0	—	—	100.0
Essen, Germany	1966	726 600	37.0	20.0	10.0	19.0	—	14.0	—	—	100.0
Stuttgart, Germany	1966	637 500	43.0	16.0	12.0	16.0	—	13.0	—	—	100.0
Mean			29.9	28.6	11.2	11.4	—	—	—	—	—

* Note: Core areas defined by Murphy/Vance (1954) technique for all cities, except Perth (see footnote p. 60).

Sources: U.S. cities: Murphy and Vance 1955:333; U.K. cities: Mika 1965:80; Capetown: Davies 1965:101; Perth: Perth City Council survey data 1968; Adelaide: City of Adelaide 1968:55; German cities: Hartenstein and Stack 1967:48.

N.A. = not available

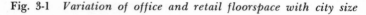
Fig. 3-1 *Variation of office and retail floorspace with city size*

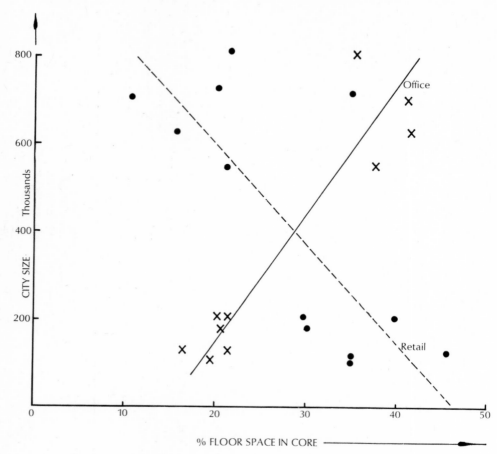

In Perth these two activity types in fact occupy over 70% of the total floorspace as against the mean of only 60%. In contrast, the same activities account for only 12% of the floorspace within Perth's frame.

But the folly of regarding public activities as non-central in character, as do Murphy and Vance and their followers (see Chapter 1), is proven by their accounting for an average 11% of core space. Similarly residential activities (including hotels) occupy significant amount of space in most core areas (averaging 11%). This tendency is particularly marked in the European cities, probably owing to their more concentrated nature in comparison to the 'New-World' cities of the United States, South Africa and Australia. Nonetheless, it is evident that in all cases examined here, the core is consistently dominated by intensive activities. Those that dominate in the frame (such as extensive sporting and public facilities, manu-facturing and warehousing) are all insignificant space occupiers in the core.

However, when we compare the content of core areas, the function and the size of the cities are also relevant. Thus the variable amount of office and retail space found in the various cities listed in Table 3-2 may be attributable to city size (see Fig. 3-1). The former has also been observed by Horwood and Boyce (1959:47) in the United States, where they found a high correlation between the amount of office space and the population of some eighty-one cities at 1956. The data in Table 3-2 do not permit the calculation of meaningful correlation coefficients, but it is nonetheless clear from Fig. 3-1 that similar relationship holds true for the sample of cities involved here; the smaller cities (ranging from 107 000-205 000 population) have around 20% of their core space devoted to offices, whilst the larger ones (637 000-807 000) 35%-40%.

There is an inverse relationship between amount of retail space and city size, but this is less definite; the scatter of points about the 'regression line' is far greater than in the case of offices (see Fig. 3-1). Nonetheless the trend is apparent; it would appear to arise from the decentralization and growth of suburban shopping facilities with increasing city size (see Smith 1961). On the other hand the office function's increasing importance with city size no doubt reflects the increasing emphasis upon administrative activities and financial dealings in large cities (cf. Hartenstein & Stack 1967:43).

But analysis of core floorspace at this level pays no attention to the horizontal and three-dimensional nature of the distribution patterns of space use within the area. In contrast to the situation in the frame, the floorspace of the core is distributed over several levels—seventeen in Perth (1968), giving the core a total height index of 3.1 as against 1.4 in the frame (Fig. 3-2).* Only one-third of all floorspace was located at ground level (compared with over 60% in the frame), 13% in basement premises, 21% at first-floor level, 11% at second and 6% at third; these percentages decrease with increasing height, giving the area an overall pyramidal appearance in profile, as initially noted by Murphy and Vance (1955:328).

The overall structure of the central area core is further differentiated by distinct vertical location patterns of the various activities characterizing the area. The subtleties of this structure will become clear from the detailed analysis of the distribution and association pattern of activities that follows. However, it can be noted here that certain activities show definite tendencies to favour particular floor levels within the core. Thus, as can be seen from Table 3-3, there is a very strong tendency for retail activities to reach their greatest importance at ground level; service and public facilities also tend to be most significant here. Other activities, conversely, are more important at upper levels. These tendencies reflect both the differing functional needs of the activities and their relative rent-paying ability.

---

* Height index (HI) is an expression that relates total floorspace (TFS) to ground floorspace (GFS), such that $HI = TFS/GFS$. By 1973, the index in Perth's core would undoubtedly have risen following the completion of several office towers of over twenty storeys in height.

Fig. 3-2 *Distribution of Perth core space by floor (1968 data)*

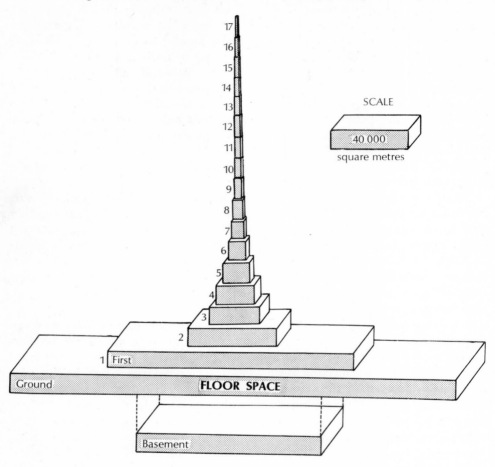

Thus retailing has a clear need for a street-level location and, as shall become evident, can generally afford high rents; wholesaling, on the other hand, tends to reach greatest significance at first-floor level, owing to its lesser need for a ground-level location and its generally more extensive nature. This differential arrangement of activity in the vertical plane has been overlooked or underplayed in many studies.

Differentiation of activity types is also evident in the horizontal plane; as in the case of frame, definite clusters are evident. This point has been established by a number of studies that followed the comparative work of Murphy and Vance (1955). The analyses of Diamond (1962), Mika (1965), Carter and Rowley (1966), Goddard (1967) and Hartenstein and Stack (1967) provide European

Table 3-3

RELATIVE RANK ORDER OF CORE USES ACCORDING TO AMOUNT OF
SPACE OCCUPIED ON SEPARATE FLOOR LEVELS

Activity	Ground				First				Upper floors			
	Perth	Kuala Lumpur	U.S.* cities	U.K.† cities	Perth	Kuala Lumpur	U.S. cities	U.K. cities	Perth	Kuala Lumpur	U.S. cities	U.K. cities
Retail	1	1	1	1	2	2	2	2	3	3	3	3
Office	3	3	3	3	2	2	2	2	1	1	1	1
Service	1		1	2	2		2	1	3		3	3
Public & organizational	1	—	1	3	2	1	2	2	3	—	3	1
Residential (perm.)	1	3	3	3	2	1	1	2	3	2	2	1
Hotels	3	—	3	3	1	1	2	1	1	—	1	2
Wholesale	3	3	1	2	1	1	2	1	2	2	3	3
Industry	2	NR‡	2	3	3	NR	1	2	1	NR	3	1
Vacancy	1	NR	3	1	2	NR	1	2	3	NR	2	3

* U.S. cities: Roanoke, Tulsa, Phoenix, Worcester, Grand Rapids, Tacoma, Salt Lake City, Sacramento, Mobile
† U.K. cities: Derby, Southampton, Norwich
‡ NR = not recorded

Source: Perth: Perth City Council survey data 1968; Kuala Lumpur: Sendut 1965:130; U.S. & U.K. cities: Mika 1965:115.

examples; those of Scott (1959), Robinson (1965), Davies (1965) and Pain (1967) some antipodean equivalents. Such work provides a sound basis for comparison, but many of these studies have concentrated on questions of composite core structure at the expense of considering individual activity patterns, whilst others have dealt only with ground-floor patterns.

Studies of particular sectors of core activity have been undertaken by such workers as Morgan (1961) and Goddard (1968, 1970, 1971) in the field of office location, Getis and Getis (1968) on shop groupings, and Simons (1966) on wholesaling. Their research has thrown light upon these particular aspects of core organization and structure. However, in the present chapter an attempt will be made to deal with the patterns of all major activity groupings within the core, both in a horizontal and a vertical context. Perth will be used as a base, and such data as are available for other cities (and for Perth itself from Scott 1959) will be used for comparative purposes. In the next chapter attention will be turned to the total structure of the core.

3-3   OFFICE LOCATION*

3-3.1   THE GENERAL PATTERN

The significance of offices within the core is readily apparent: it is the multi-storey offices that dominate the skyline of most city centres and account for its most marked vertical extension (see frontispiece, Plate X).

Offices tend to concentrate within particular segments of the core, giving rise to distinctly recognizable 'office zones', of which the best example is the City of London (see Morgan 1961). In Perth there is a strong linear concentration of office structures along the St George Terrace axis (hereinafter referred to as the 'Terrace'). All frontages along this axis within the core have over 30% of their floorspace devoted to offices (see Fig. 3-3). This concentration housed almost two-thirds of the core's office space (at 1968), of which one-half has been found within the central hub area between William and Barrack Streets, regarded as the prestige location for offices. This is reflected in high land values that average 60% of the peak (the highest of any office area; see Fig. 3-4); in office rentals, up to 50% above those elsewhere;† and also in the concentration of recent redevelopment in the area (see Chapter 5). The façade of offices fronting this hub area is broken only by two street-level arcades that connect northwards to the core's retail heart, a church and a hotel. A few frontages to the north of the Terrace house significant amounts of office space, but there is a sharp fall in building height away from the Terrace (Plate VIIb) and a general lack of office space within the core's central blocks, where land values are at a peak (Fig. 3-4), and where retailing predominates. This spatial segregation is now reinforced by zoning ordinances (Fig. 2-7), but developed naturally as a result of the normal operation of the land market.

But it is misleading to discuss offices as if they contained a homogeneous group of activities: whilst office buildings do provide a specific type of accommodation, they house a multitude of different activity types. These tend to have differing locational requirements and linkages to other activities and hence behave in spatially distinct patterns. The degree of resulting spatial differentiation appears to become stronger as a city grows and takes on more sophisticated functions; thus Robinson (1965:44) found that in Hamilton, a city of only 60 000 population, office districts (such as financial and professional) were in an 'embryonic' stage of development, whilst other studies in larger cities have shown a higher degree of spatial segregation of office types (e.g. Capetown, population c. 800 000 [Davies 1965]; Auckland,

---

* The following sections all refer to patterns within Perth's core at 1968; changes between 1968 and 1973 are discussed in Chapter 5.
† Data based on Perth City Council survey of offices 1968-69. Information supplied by the Planning Department.

Fig. 3-3 *Distribution of office space, Perth core 1968*

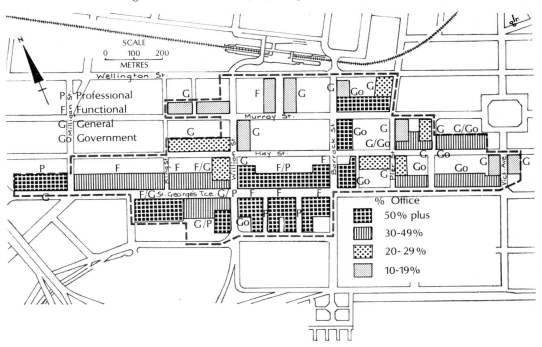

Fig. 3-4 *Market land values, Perth core 1968*. Source: a Perth real-estate agent. (Since some following core maps do not show street names, reader may have to refer back to these figures [3-3, 3-4] when checking on textual references to core streets.)

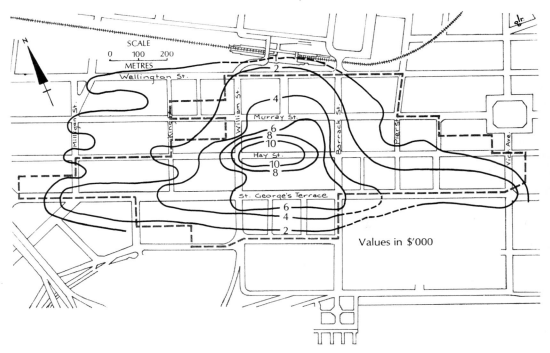

population *c*. 500 000 [Pain 1967]).* The ultimate situation appears in the 'world cities' such as London and New York, where office-type districts become a distinctly recognizable feature of overall central area structure.

In Perth, a medium-sized city (*c*. 600 000 in 1968; closer to 800 000 by 1972), a certain degree of such spatial segregation is observable in broad terms within the areas, where office space is prevalent (see Fig. 3-3). Offices dealing with finance in some way or another are the most concentrated, and are confined mainly to that section of the Terrace west of Barrack and east of William Streets. In sections of this area financial and general offices are intermixed. (Question of locational association of office types is pursued further in Chapter 4.) In general, however, the latter groups are widely scattered over the core, thus contrasting with government offices which tend to concentrate in the eastern sections of the core, and with professional offices which concentrate both in the hub area and in the western segments of the Terrace.

It is at this general level of description and analysis that most studies of core areas have stopped; either all offices are considered as one activity type (as in many planning reports—see City of Adelaide 1968, City of Hobart 1968, Perth City Council 1971), or at best they are divided into the broad categories discussed above. The pattern was set by Murphy and Vance (1955) and has been followed in many studies since (e.g. Davies 1965, Mika 1965, and Pain 1967). Such an approach can give a broad picture of city-centre office structure and can lead to certain inferences concerning the rationale of the patterns observed. However, in order to gain a clearer insight into the detailed structure of the core a finer level of analysis is necessary, for within the broad categories such as 'financial' and 'general' offices, a myriad of different categories of activity are found (see Appendix II). It would be tedious to analyse each pattern in detail, but some recognition of the wide spectrum of the activity-mix is essential. Similarly, reference to the actual functional linkages between offices—an important locational influence as noted in Chapter 1 —is necessary in order that the patterns observed may be validly explained. Such objectives are attempted in the following pages, with reference to the patterns of office location within Perth's core.

3-3.2 FINANCIAL OFFICES

Offices housing concerns connected with the city's financial functions—and these include stockbrokers, bank (head) offices, insurance and finance companies and real-estate agencies—show a high degree of concentration within Perth's core (see Figs 3-5a - 3-5d). The actual degree of concentration can be expressed by reference to a 'standard-distance' measure that relates the degree of scatter of a distribution to the number of points in the distribution, such that:†

---

* Population figures relate to survey year.
† *Source:* Bachi 1963:87. This measure is equivalent to the 'dynamical radius' employed by Stewart and Warntz (1958) to measure population dispersion. It has been used recently by other workers for examining activity concentrations (see Varley 1968, Goddard 1973).

$$D = \sqrt{\frac{\sum\limits_{i=1}^{n} d^2_{(ic)}}{n}},$$

where D = standard distance;
$d_{(ic)}$ = distance from c (centre of gravity of distribution) to i (each point in the distribution);
n = number of points in the distribution.

On this basis, financial offices show a mean concentration value of $D = 12.5$, as against 18.8 for general offices, and 12.1 for professional chambers (see Table 3-4). This strong clustering tendency has been noted in other cities, such as Capetown, where Davies (1965:124) found a 'nodal cluster' of financial offices adjacent to the retailing district, Auckland (Pain 1967:81), Manchester (Varley 1968:221) and London (Goddard 1968:125). The latter grouping in London forms a part of the City office area already referred to, and whilst it would be facetious to compare the grouping in Perth with this world-famous area, it would appear that the same processes are at work producing the concentrations, albeit at vastly different scales.

Table 3-4

CONCENTRATION INDICES AND NUMBERS OF OFFICE ACTIVITIES
IN PERTH'S CORE AT 1968*

Activity	Designation	Index	Number of offices
Stockbrokers	Financial	8.2	18
Doctors	Professional	8.9	40
Lawyers	Professional	9.2	64
Transport Co. Travel agents	General	12.4	37
Estate agents	Financial	13.3	92
Insurance	Financial	13.9	76
Architects Engineers Surveyors	Professional	14.7	33
Bank (head office)	Financial	15.0	42
General business	General	15.1	52
Dentists	Professional	15.4	47
Accountants	Professional	15.5	66
Clubs & associations	General	18.1	71
Government		18.1	48
Production-distribution	General	22.1	171
Mean values and total numbers:	Financial	12.5	228
	General	18.8	231
	Professional	12.1	250

* Calculated from distribution maps of activities concerned

Note: Index explained in text. The general order of concentration of these activities shows some marked similarities with that discovered in Manchester by Varley (1968) and London by Goddard (1973): financial and professional offices are most concentrated, and general offices least.

Fig. 3-5 *Distribution of financial offices, Perth core 1968.*

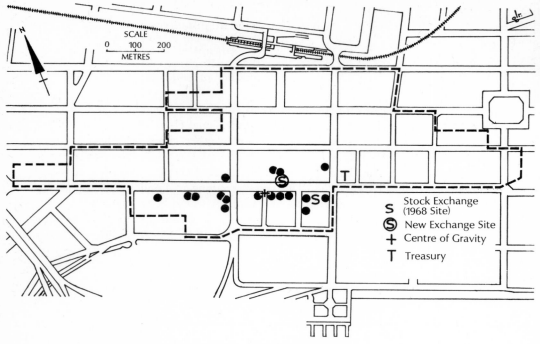

3-5a Stockbrokers

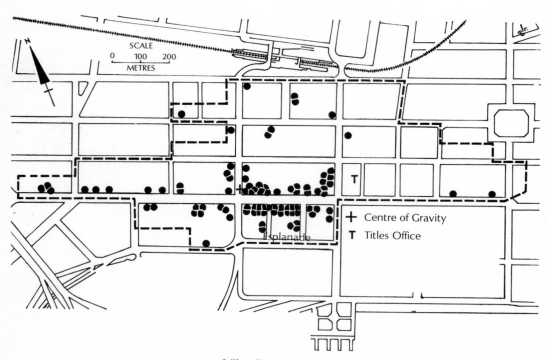

3-5b Estate agents

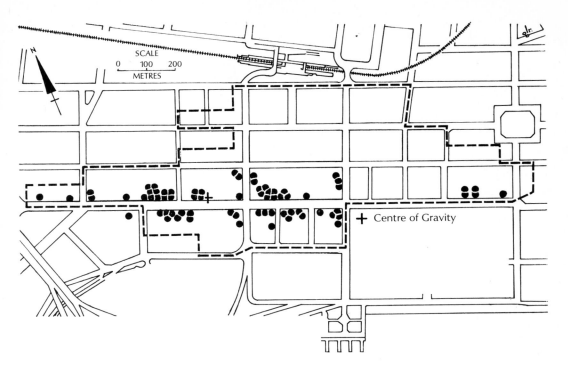

3-5c   Insurance offices

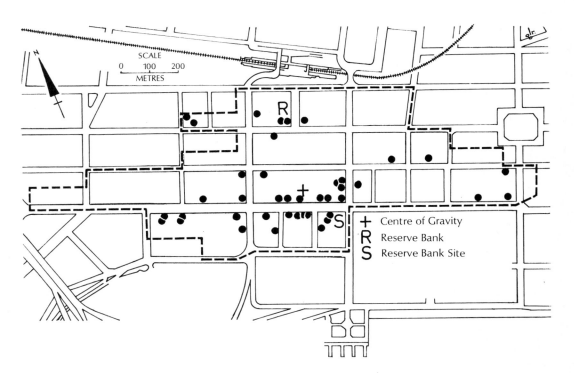

3-5d   Banks and finance companies

It is of course hazardous to attempt an explanation of a clustered pattern simply from a spatial analysis; yet recent work by Goddard (1971) in London has confirmed that offices that cluster strongly together in space tend to have strong functional interlinkages (contacts) with one another and with nearby institutions. Thus the extremely strong concentration of stockbrokers' offices in Perth ($D = 8.2$, the lowest of any office-type [cf. Manchester, Varley 1968], and second lowest of any element in the core) would appear to result from the obvious link to the stock exchange. None was found further than 500 metres from the exchange in 1968 and the new exchange (operating from 1969) located even closer to the distribution's centre of gravity (Fig. 3-5a).* It appears, in fact, that the stock exchange acts as a 'magnet' for the entire financial office sector as has been observed elsewhere, for example Johannesburg (1967:22), or Manchester (Varley 1968).

Other locational 'anchors' also exercise influence upon the spatial behaviour of financial offices. Thus real-estate agents are more widely distributed ($D = 13.1$; cf. Manchester, Varley 1968), but are nonetheless predominantly concentrated close to the State Land Titles Office; 85% are located within the central hub office area (Fig. 3-5b). The attraction to this hub area is probably also influenced by a need for location close to similar activities as well as by prestige. The need for real-estate agencies to be accessible to the public also motivates their location, at least in the vertical plane. More premises are located at ground level than any other, and 80% are located on or below the second-floor level, including basement locations (see Table 3-5), which offer cheaper rents while providing street-level advertising.

The accessibility factor can also be seen at work influencing the vertical location of insurance offices. Although these occupy space at all levels up to the tenth floor, 70% of all their floorspace is located at or below second-floor level (54% of all premises), with 26% at ground level. The prestige factor is again significant here, however, for along with banks, insurance companies are investing considerable sums on construction of office towers in prestigious locations and occupy the prominent ground-level suites (see Plate X).†

Insurance companies' investments in office redevelopment has been one of the main factors behind the recent office-building boom in Perth and other Australian capital cities (see Chapter 5). This has caused one observer (Archer 1967) to suggest that the planning of the future structure of the city centre should be left to the property investors, a rather bizarre suggestion given the havoc these companies have already wrought upon the structure and appearance of the city core (Plates X, XIII).

The importance of the prestige factor in the location of insurance offices also helps explain the fact that these offices are overwhelmingly concentrated within the Terrace (69 of the 76 are found here; see Fig. 3-5c). Their spatial concentration ($D = 13.9$) is not so great as that of real-estate chambers or stockbrokers, but

---

* The State Treasury building is also located close to this area (see Fig. 3-5a).
† Bank and finance company offices also have over two-thirds of their floorspace at lower-floor levels (see Table 3-5).

Table 3-5

PERCENTAGE (BY NUMBER AND FLOOR AREA) OF VARIOUS OFFICE TYPES
AT ALL FLOOR LEVELS: PERTH CORE

Floor	Manufac.		Wholesale Distr.		Associations Clubs		Transport Travel		Business service		Business advisory		Insurance		Banks		Stock-broker		Real estate		Accountant		Lawyer		Doctor		Dentist		Engineer Architect Surveyor		Health service		Government		Travel agent	
	FA*	No†	FA	No	FA	No	FA	No	FA	No	FA	No	FA	No	FA	No	FA	No	FA	No	FA	No	FA	No	FA	No	FA	No	FA	No	FA	No	FA	No	FA	No
Basement	10‡	9	—	—	15	12	8	24	4	13	21	—	15	3	20	—	6	7	21	16	2	2	2	5	8	10	—	—	2	—	5	3	—	6	23	8
Ground	10	9	32	24	31	17	29	33	19	21	26	14	26	16	25	19	17	26	28	26	7	5	6	7	49	40	27	13	41	15	22	34	11	16	55	62
1	27	32	24	15	32	23	8	12	35	19	31	28	16	18	21	21	11	21	18	21	23	26	20	26	21	30	27	26	9	12	29	28	10	13	22	—
2	18	24	15	13	15	13	13	15	29	24	8	14	13	18	6	5	6	11	13	13	18	24	20	20	11	8	21	23	16	21	24	25	8	10	—	—
3	12	8	8	5	13	2	5	5	6	11	4	14	8	8	7	7	11	8	7	5	25	15	17	12	4	5	18	21	11	9	11	6	4	7	—	—
4	6	3	4	—	5	10	—	—	—	9	7	14	3	3	5	—	16	11	10	7	16	14	9	10	5	5	7	11	4	12	9	—	6	7	—	—
5	6	4	2	—	1	2	7	2	2	4	—	—	1	1	5	—	6	4	—	—	2	1	8	12	—	—	1	—	10	6	—	—	4	6	—	—
6	4	2	—	—	—	—	4	4	—	—	—	—	3	1	4	—	6	7	2	2	—	—	—	—	—	—	3	3	5	6	—	—	6	6	—	—
7	3	3	—	—	—	—	—	—	—	—	—	—	2	—	2	5	—	—	1	1	1	1	6	6	—	—	4	4	—	—	—	—	5	5	—	—
8	1	1	—	—	—	—	—	—	—	—	—	—	5	3	2	—	6	4	—	—	—	—	1	1	—	—	—	—	—	—	—	—	7	7	—	—
9	1	1	—	—	—	—	—	—	2	4	—	—	5	2	2	—	—	—	—	—	3	—	—	—	—	—	—	—	—	—	—	—	2	2	—	—
10	—	—	—	—	—	—	—	—	—	—	—	—	5	5	2	—	—	—	—	—	—	2	—	—	—	—	—	—	1	6	—	—	1	1	—	—
11	—	—	—	—	—	—	—	—	—	—	—	—	—	5	1	—	—	—	—	—	3	—	—	—	—	—	—	—	—	—	—	—	2	2	—	—
12	—	—	—	—	—	—	—	—	—	—	—	—	—	5	—	—	—	—	—	—	—	—	—	—	—	—	—	—	—	—	—	—	4	4	—	—
12+	1	2	—	—	—	—	—	—	—	—	—	—	—	—	—	—	—	—	—	—	—	—	—	—	—	—	—	—	—	—	—	—	9	9	—	—

* FA = floor area (%)
† No. = number (% of total establishments; totals are less than 100 as multi-floor establishments are excluded).
‡ Rounded to nearest whole number

Note: Only single-floor establishments noted here

Source: Data from land-use survey, Perth City Council.

they are nonetheless located in close proximity to these and other financial offices and close to the legal cluster (Fig. 3-6b), to which according to Morgan (1961:209) they have something of a functional link.

Bank and finance offices are more widely distributed than any other element in the financial office set ($D = 15.0$), and yet tend to cluster both in the Terrace hub area and also close to the Reserve Bank in Murray Street (see Fig. 3-5d), to which there is an obvious functional link. The latter institution was due to shift into new premises in the Terrace hub area (at the time of writing), thus reinforcing the concentration of financial offices and institutions in this vicinity. In time, depending on the strength of the functional link between the bank offices and the Reserve Bank, and on the need for close physical proximity, the cluster in the Terrace areas may become even more pronounced.

In general, therefore, financial offices are concentrated in the prestige office locations within Perth city core, and form the backbone of the 'hub' area. They appear to be drawn to one another and to state and other financial institutions, such as the Stock Exchange, State Treasury, Reserve Bank, Titles Office and the courts. Recent research in London has shown that interlinkages between different types of financial offices in the form of inter-office contacts are rich (Baker & Goddard 1972). The spatial distribution of office types in terms of their clustering tendencies appears to reflect their need for connection with one another. However, many of the 'contacts' were found to be transacted by telephone rather than by personal meeting; personal contact proved numerous within the financial sector in absolute terms, but less significant in relative terms (Baker & Goddard 1972). Nevertheless, as the authors admit, such data do not give any guide either to the 'importance' of these contacts or to the significance of the linkage pattern in general; thus the cost of severing this pattern cannot be calculated. Further research, currently in progress (outlined in Goddard 1973), may throw more light upon this question. In the meantime, the danger of attributing spurious significance to linkages and contacts as a location factor must be borne in mind; particularly since telephone communications are already playing a significant rôle in contact patterns.

The growing importance of such telephone and other non-direct methods of communication between offices (telex, TV-type phones, etc.) as substitutes for personal contact implies that the linkages may be 'stretchable' over distances; indeed certain critics (e.g. Cowan 1971) predict that the already noticeable trend towards the suburbanization and scatter of central offices will accelerate rapidly in the near future. On the other hand, it appears that at least the decision-making sectors of these offices will remain in the city centre. It is the routine and clerical sections of firms that tend to decentralize first, owing apparently to low intra-firm contact at this level in comparison to the executive level (Goddard 1971). But again a measure of the importance of the contacts is lacking, and it should be noted that another recent survey has shown that personal contact patterns of completely decentralized offices can adjust to location without difficulty (see Location of Offices Bureau 1969). Thus further research into the significance of contact patterns between offices may be misdirected; it would appear more fruitful to attempt an assessment of the true significance of the central institutions that apparently act as locational anchors for the financial office sector. It seems that these anchors, rather than intra-group linkages, are continuing to maintain the strong financial office cluster as a typical feature of many city centres.

3-3.3 PROFESSIONAL OFFICES

The development of a node of professional chambers in the frame of Perth's central area was outlined in the last chapter. It was seen to be a trend typical of many central areas and to result largely from relocations of professional chambers from the city's core (see Chapter 5 for analysis of locational rationale). Nonetheless, a good proportion of these chambers in Perth have not as yet chosen to relocate, thus leaving important clusters within the core.

Among these are the offices of accountants of which 60% remained in the core at 1968. Clearly accountants are closely associated with the financial activities carried on within the core, and an examination of their location pattern in Perth shows that they do tend to concentrate ($D = 15.5$; Table 3-4) within the already delineated financial zone; almost 60% are located within the office hub area or its immediate vicinity as shown in Fig. 3-6a, which suggests that functional links with other financial offices and institutions are an important location factor. However, as noted above, it is dangerous to attach too much significance to spatial concentrations and associations. Moreover, the fact that a large number of accountants have recently moved out of this area to the frame insinuates that the linkage factor is not so strong as might be supposed, and that pressures within the core may become so great as to outweigh the need for close spatial proximity to the financial zone (see Chapter 5).

A contrast to this trend is noticeable in the case of legal offices which display a very marked clustering tendency within Perth's core (as they do elsewhere: Varley 1968, Goddard 1973); 85% are found within the hub area and in the narrow streets running south from this area (Fig. 3-6b). Their dispersal index of 9.2 renders them the third most concentrated element within the core, and it seems significant that no legal offices have been involved on the core-frame migration of professional chambers. A similar trend in Christchurch (Merriman 1967) was found to be attributable to the importance lawyers attached to a core location and to linkages to other offices and institutions within the core. Therefore, the strong concentration does reflect an important linkage pattern, for the cluster is in close proximity to the Supreme Court (Fig. 3-6b), an institution noted by Morgan (1961:209) as an important localizing influence for legal offices. The Titles Office is no doubt another significant localizing factor, and it is also probable that there are important linkages to the rest of the hub activity set. Such a grouping has long been a tendency within Australian capital cities, for Scott (1959:309) noted that lawyers' offices cluster near the courts in all core areas; a similar tendency has been noted in many cities (see Murphy 1972:62).

In contrast to certain financial offices, lawyers and accountants are found predominantly above ground level in Perth's core (also noted by Scott 1959:309).

Fig. 3-6 *Distribution of professional offices, Perth core 1968.*

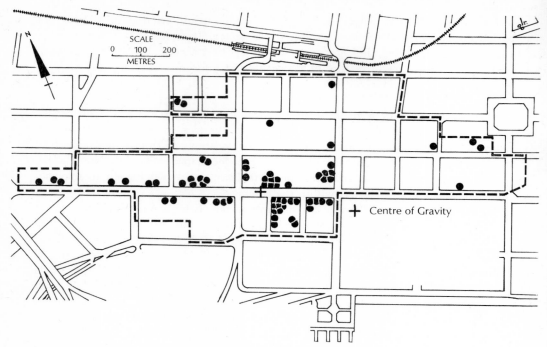

3-6a   Accountants

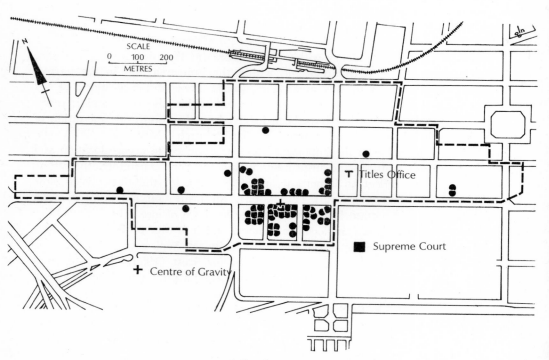

3-6b   Lawyers

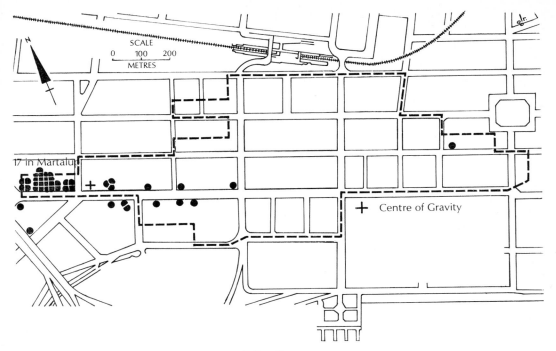

SCALE
0   100   200
METRES

17 in Martalu

N

+ Centre of Gravity

3-6c   Doctors

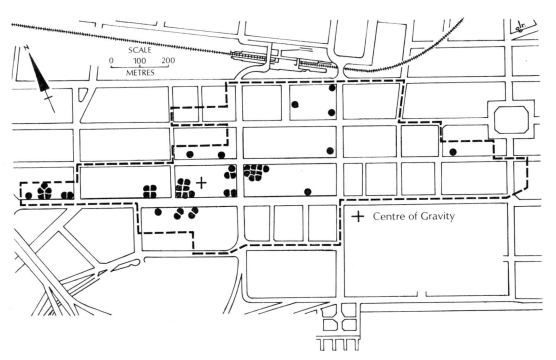

SCALE
0   100   200
METRES

N

+ Centre of Gravity

3-6d   Dentists

Thus 92% of legal and 93% of accountants' offices were located at first-floor level or above (predominantly first to third) in 1968 (Table 3-5). This is a reflection of their *modus operandi* in that they do not depend on public advertising or locational prestige to gain custom.

Offices occupied by doctors (almost entirely specialist practitioners) are, as shown in Fig. 3-6c, concentrated in a tight cluster in the western segments of the core ($D = 8.9$). These are the remains of a once much larger concentration in this area (Scott 1959:309), that has been weakened by the continuing drift to the frame (cf. Chapter 2). At the time of the survey (1968) over half of this remainder were located in a purpose-built medical centre. Reasons for the tendency of medicos to concentrate in few buildings have already been advanced.

A similar tendency is noticeable in the case of dentists' premises, since, although their overall scatter within the core is relatively high ($D = 15.4$, i.e. almost twice that of doctors; see Table 3-4), over 60% are located in two buildings (Fig. 3-6d). Specialized building requirements, not readily found in general office blocks (Robinson 1965: 48), and desire for locational proximity help explain this. Their need to be relatively accessible to the public is reflected in their marked propensity to locate on lower-floor levels (83% below fourth-floor level; Table 3-5).

3-3.4 GOVERNMENT OFFICES

As indicated above, the offices housing governmental functions are scattered throughout Perth's core, which coincides with the situation observed in Auckland by Pain (1967). However, as Fig. 3-7 shows, Perth's offices show a marked tendency to avoid peak-value areas, with commonwealth offices gravitating to the west and state government to the east. This inclination has been altered since the survey, following the completion of a new commonwealth office tower just *to the south-east* of the core (see Fig. 3-7); this has caused a general shift of the locus of commonwealth offices to the east.

Similarly, the concentration of state offices in the Terrace and in western Hay Street has been weakened by the construction of a government block close to Parliament House in the western frame area (see Chapter 2). The remaining concentration is found close to the original centres of government power, the courts and Government House.

The trend of the government to occupy purpose-built premises is on the increase in the central area, although as Whipple (1967) has noted in Sydney, the government nonetheless remains an important tenant in many privately-constructed office towers. Given the large amount of space occupied by government offices (28% of office space in Perth's core), the rent bill must be a considerable expense.

With regard to location, it can be seen from Fig. 3-7 that despite a fairly high degree of dispersal (index of 18.1), the seventy-one different state and governmental departments present within the core in 1968 exhibit definite sub-clustering tendencies within buildings; some of these are based on functional links between departments. In general they show a preference for ground- and first-floor locations (30% area

Fig. 3-7 *Distribution of governmental offices, Perth core 1968*

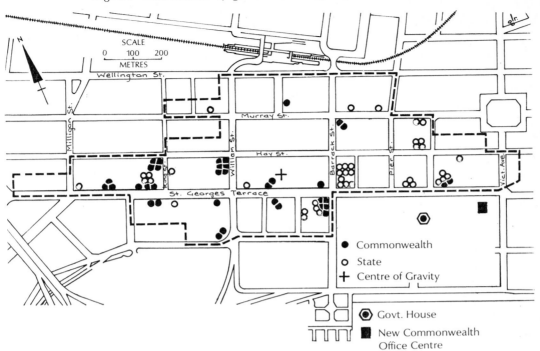

Fig. 3-8 *Distribution of general offices, Perth core 1968*

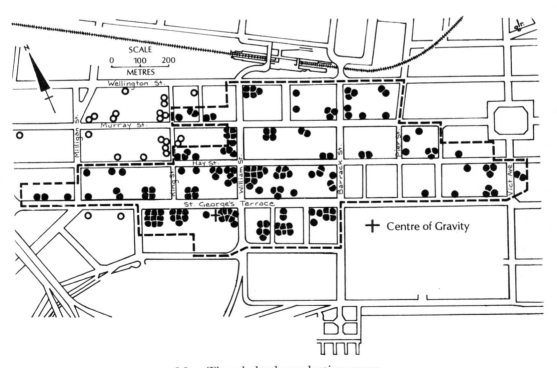

3-8a The wholesale-production group

Fig. 3-8 *Contd*

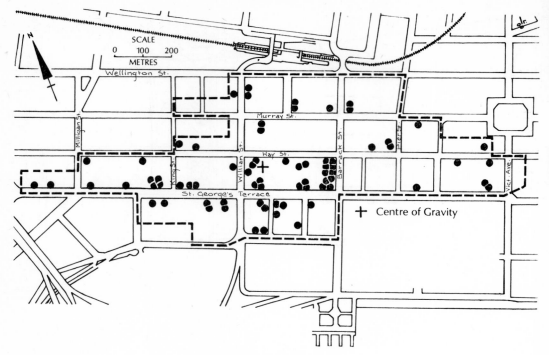

3-8b   Business services

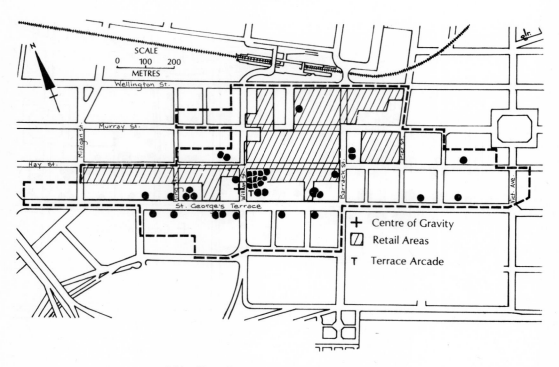

3-8c   Travel agents and travel companies

and 20% numbers), although they are found at all floor levels, which makes them one of the most widely distributed office elements in the vertical plane (Table 3-5). Those locating at lower levels require most direct contact with the public (e.g. electricity accounts, immigration, labour exchange).

3-3.5 GENERAL OFFICES

This category is composed, as its name suggests, of a wide variety of elements including the offices of manufacturers, wholesalers and distributors, customs agents, importers and exporters, clubs and associations, business services, and travel agencies. As noted earlier they have a high mean dispersal index (18.8) and in fact all have values above 18 with the exception of travel agencies ($D = 12.4$; see Table 3-4). Apart from the latter group, which are sandwiched between the retail and office segments of the core, the 'general' category are all widely spread throughout the core with little tendency to concentrate in particular areas, apart from slight gravitation towards the Terrace office zone (see e.g. Figs 3-8a, 3-8b). Many are located in upper-floor premises of buildings given over to retailing at lower levels; here rents are cheaper than in the prestige office areas and yet the location is fairly readily accessible. The overall picture, therefore, is of a fairly footloose locational procedure. Their tendency to scatter within the core has been noted in other studies. Davies (1965:55) notes that in Capetown 'the distribution of general offices correlates rather closely with the position and size of the CBD.' Similar comments are made by Murphy (1955:38) and Mika (1965:102) in their respective studies of the United States and British city centres.

Nonetheless, *some* locational tendencies are noticeable in Perth. Thus the wholesale-production group (Fig. 3-8a), although having the highest dispersal index of any core element (22.1), does gravitate towards the western areas of the core and spill over into the adjacent frame, where wholesaling assumes significance (see Chapter 2). They also favour upper-floor locations, reflecting their lack of public contact.

Clubs and associations tend to locate in older premises offering cheaper rents, and several have migrated to the frame in recent years. In contrast, business services locate broadly in response to the overall distribution of offices (Fig. 3-8b), which is a logical outcome of their function. Their vertical location depends on the need for public contact with such concerns as typing pools and plan printers in accessible ground-floor premises, whilst management consultants (with more specific contacts) gravitate to upper levels. Travel agencies, on the other hand, not only concentrate in the horizontal plane close to the retail heart of the core, to benefit from 'comparison shopping' (Fig. 3-8c), but also vertically, owing again to their need for public accessibility.

3-3.6 OFFICES—SUMMARY

It has been demonstrated that the different activities performed within offices display distinctive locational tendencies both in a horizontal and vertical plane.

Nonetheless, common tendencies have been noted and can be generalized. The question of spatial groupings is taken further in the next chapter, when more objective methods of analysis are explored. Here, however, it can be said that three distinctive office groupings are noticeable in Perth's core:

1. *The financial-legal grouping:* this is centred in the high-value Terrace hub area, and contains several tightly clustered groupings with a mean dispersal index of 12.8 (range 8.2-15.5). The clusters are explicable in terms of intra and inter-group linkages and ties to nearby locational anchors such as the courts, Stock Exchange, Titles Office and State Treasury. Such clusters have been well documented elsewhere and seem a relatively stable element of core structure, although the extent and significance of the linkages is imperfectly understood at the present time. Many offices in the group show a preference for ground-floor location, the strength of this tendency depending on the need for display and ready public accessibility.

2. *The medical grouping:* covering only a handful of doctors' offices remaining from the drift to the frame, this grouping is nonetheless tightly clusterd in the western Terrace area, which has relatively low land values.

3. *The government group:* polarized into eastern (state) and western (commonwealth) sectors, this grouping is conspicuous by its absence from areas of high land values and yet accounts for over 25% of the core's office space. Public contact and accessibility requirements appear to influence both horizontal and vertical location.

The general office sector cannot be regarded as a spatial grouping as it includes a wide variety of activities which all tend to locate throughout the core, with the single exception of travel agencies. The wholesaling area to the north-west of the core exerts a weak pull on the location of offices connected with the production-distribution process, and requirements of accessibility and rent-paying ability determine the differential vertical location of different members of this set.

These groupings form the basis of the functional zoning of office areas not only in Perth, but in many cities (see Murphy 1972:62). Before such spatial patterns can be seen in perspective, however, an examination of the patterns of other core activities is required.

3-4 LOCATION OF RETAIL AND SERVICE ACTIVITIES

3-4.1 INTRODUCTORY REMARKS

It was pointed out in Chapter 1 that retailing is a central activity which tends to become less significant in metropolitan-wide terms, both over time within a city and with increasing city size. Nonetheless, the city core continues to house a significant variety and concentration of retailing activity, and these display a wide variation in location. In addition, a large number of service activities such as hairdressing, tailoring and bootmaking are also found in the area and add a significant component to its three-dimensional structure.

Retailing itself is a predominantly ground-floor activity, as was demonstrated in Table 3-3. Reasons of accessibility to pedestrian flows and hence custom are clearly the dominating influence here, and thus in Perth 70% of the area devoted to retailing (and a higher proportion of establishments) occur at street level. The remainder is almost exclusively located at basement and first floors; of the twenty-four retailing categories within the core only seven are areally represented above ground-floor level, and these are either the upper floors of multi-floor establishments, or of department or variety stores (see Appendix IIIA).

Personal-service activities, on the other hand, display a vertical location pattern that varies with both the type of activity and position within the core. Thus, whilst certain establishments are found predominantly at first-floor level in overall terms, and others at street level, both elements tend to be forced to upper levels in the most intensive areas, whilst gravitating to street level towards the peripheries of the core. Reasons for this pattern are advanced later.

The location pattern of retail-service activities within the Australian core has been dealt with in some detail by Scott (1959). As has already been noted, the fact that his study dealt only with ground-floor patterns is a limitation on its completeness. Even so, the data will be useful for comparisons of locational patterns at ground level and in gauging changes between the two survey dates (1957, 1968).

According to Scott (1959:292), the retail dominated segments of the Australian CBD (at ground-floor level) are divisible into an inner- and outer-retail zone, distinguishable from one another in terms of their composition and locational attributes. As will become evident, this structure still seems broadly valid in Perth, even when upper-floor patterns are taken into account. Yet the functional zoning of the area is most logically seen as an outcome of an analysis of individual-activity patterns, rather than a precursor.

In the meantime, however, Scott's classification of retail elements into groups is of interest. On the basis of their differential location he derived groups of 'inner', 'outer' and 'dispersed' retail elements. Broadly speaking, the inner group was dominated by speciality stores, selling 'personal requisites and demanding a central location', whilst the outer group was dominated by household-goods stores (Scott 1959:292; see Table 3-6). Within the former group primary and secondary classes were identified on the basis of centrality of location.

An examination of the location pattern of retail and service elements in Perth at 1968 shows that such groupings are still identifiable, although many of the details of the classification have altered and a new 'miscellaneous' category has been created (see Table 3-6). In deriving the classification, attention has been paid to the location patterns of each main retail-service element, with respect to land-value levels and the degree of concentration as measured by the dispersal indices (listed in Table 3-7) as follows:

(*a*) *Primary inner elements:* those showing a high degree of concentration, located predominantly within areas, where land values average over 40% of the peak value.

Table 3-6

LOCATIONAL CLASSIFICATION OF RETAIL-SERVICE ELEMENTS,
PERTH CORE 1957 AND 1968*

Establishment type	Classification 1968	Classification 1959	Establishment type	Classification 1968	Classification 1959
Department—variety	IP	IP	Hotel	M	D
Women's clothing	IP	IP	Branch bank	M	D
Men's clothing	IP	IS	Food	M	IS
Drapery	IP	—	Restaurant-cafe	M	D
Footwear	IP	IP	Hardware	O	OP
Clothing accessories	IP	IP	Furniture	O	OP
Jewellery—gifts	IP	IS	Disposals/auction		
Cinema	IP	IP	room	O	OS
Coffee lounge	IP	IS	Electrical goods	D	D
Dressmaker	IS	—	Dry-cleaning agency	D	D
Beauty salon	IS	—	Newsagent/books	D	D
Optician	IS	—	Tobacconist	D	D
Jewellery repairs	IS	—	Sports goods/toys	D	OS
Bootmaker	IS	OS	Men's hairdresser	D	D
Chemist	IS	IS	Florist	D	OS
Photographer	IS	—	Photographic		
Business college	IS	—	equipment	D	—
Women's clothing			Automobiles	—	OP
mnfctr	IS	—			
Tailor	IS	D			
Clothing softgoods					
w/sale	IS	—			

Key: IP = inner element (primary)   OP = outer element (primary)
      IS = inner element (secondary)   O = outer element
      M = miscellaneous   OS = outer element (secondary)
      D = dispersed

* *Sources:* 1957: Scott 1959; 1968: based on location patterns plotted from land-use survey data: see text for explanation.

(*b*) *Secondary inner elements:* located *either* at ground level in areas with land values averaging between 20% and 60% of the peak value, *or* at first-floor level in peak-value areas.

(*c*) *Outer elements:* concentrated on the margins of the core in areas of between 10% and 40% of peak value.

(*d*) *Dispersed elements:* scattered throughout the retail segments of the core, with dispersal indices of 15.0 or over.

(*e*) *Miscellaneous elements:* elements regarded by Scott (1959) as dispersed, but showing a definite propensity to concentrate between the inner and outer elements in areas of 20% to 40% of peak land value.

Table 3-7

DISPERSAL INDICES AND NUMBERS OF RETAIL-SERVICES ACTIVITIES,
PERTH CORE 1968

Element	Index	Number
Inner primary		
Department stores	5.3	7
Drapery	6.1	9
Men's clothing	9.1	24
Women's clothing	11.0	60
Jewellery	11.9	49
Inner secondary		
Dressmaker	7.1	25
Optician	10.5	16
Boot repair/jewellery repair	11.2	31
Beauty salon	11.8	48
Tailor	12.0	24
Florist/chemist/photographic equipment	14.3	45
Outer		
Hardware	13.1	6
Furniture	14.0	10
Disposals	12.0	9
Miscellaneous		
Hotels	14.4	15
Branch banks	15.8	28
Food	9.0	31
Dispersed		
Electrical goods	17.3	26
Barber	18.5	22
Dry cleaner	18.5	16
Newsagent/books	16.5	40

Source: Calculated from distribution maps, using index of Bachi (1963—see § 3-4.1).

In toto, the differential location pattern of all retail-service establishments within the core forms the basis of the functional zoning of the area discussed in the next chapter. First, however, the location patterns themselves will be analysed in detail.

3-4.2 INNER ELEMENTS: SPECIALIST RETAILING

The most prominent mixture of retail elements found within the core is composed of a grouping of establishments catering to a wide market and to specialist needs. Most significant are department and variety stores and specialist retailing premises, dealing in goods such as clothing, footwear, jewellery, gifts and fabrics. It is these outlets, and the department stores in particular, that provide the main

Fig. 3-9 *Distribution of inner retail elements, Perth core 1968*

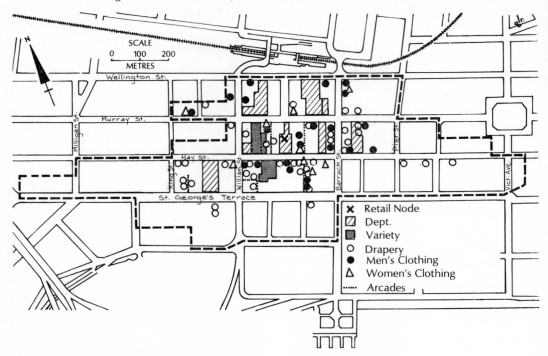

3-9a   Department, variety and clothing stores

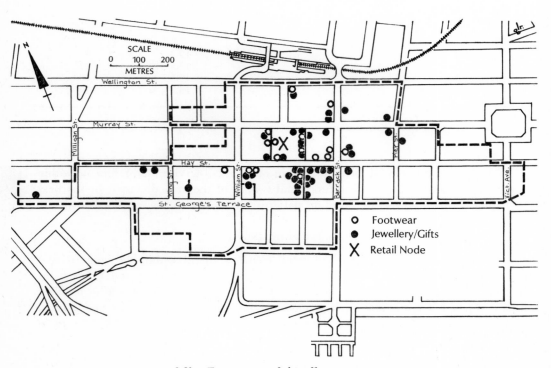

3-9b   Footwear and jewellery stores

draw of custom (and particularly female custom) to the core, and on which many other elements within the area depend for trade. According to Nelson (1958:70-6) this grouping of establishments are highly compatible to one another in terms of their interdependence; this applies particularly to the department-apparel group.

They thus provide something of a focus within the retail sections of the core, generating high levels of pedestrian flows. This renders the areas within which they locate of high value, and land values often reach their intra-metropolitan peak here. Conversely, the stores can well afford the high rents in these areas; less intensive and profitable activities are forced to upper floor or peripheral premises where rents are lower.

According to Ratcliff (1949:398) a concentration of specialist retail establishments in the inner peak-value segments of the core is a feature typical of all central areas. This hypothesis is confirmed by common observation and by subsequent studies of Australian (Scott 1959:295-301), of United States and British cities (Murphy & Vance 1955:33, Mika 1965:109, Getis & Getis 1968:320), and of South African and New Zealand cities (Davies 1965:49, Pain 1967:51, Robinson 1965:42).

In Perth, the vast majority of specialist stores are found within the areas bounded by the 40% isoval, where pedestrian flows are at a peak (see Figs 3-9a, 3-9b, 3-10), and many are clustered in the central Hay Street area, where land values consistently average over 80% of the peak (Fig. 3-4). This concentration is reflected by their low-dispersal indices, ranging from 5.3 for department and variety stores, to 11.9 for jewellery stores (Table 3-7); hence their designation as 'primary' inner elements.

The high volume of pedestrian flows in this area, which in combination with heavy vehicular traffic and narrow carriageways led to considerable congestion, was the main cause of the development of plans for the partial closure of central Hay Street to vehicular traffic in 1970 (see Plate XI). Eventual plans call for the complete closure of this section as part of a pedestrian network which is to thread through the entire core area (see Fig. 3-16).

The department stores form a framework for the core's specialist retailing elements; most are found within the area bounded by the department stores. Scott (1959:295) regards the centre of gravity of the latter stores as the 'retail node' of the core since it coincides fairly well with the point of maximum retail intensity and pedestrian flow (see Figs 3-9a, 3-10). In this respect, as Scott notes, the node is a more satisfactory reference point for the core's retail areas than is the peak land-value intersection, since the latter lies on the periphery rather than in the centre of the retail areas.

The dominant rôle of the department stores within the retail sector of the core has already been noted; in Perth all are multi-storey structures that front onto two streets, thus acting as important linkages for pedestrians in conjunction with the many arcades that lace through the area. There is some specialization of function within the department group: whilst all carry a wide range of merchandise, the most central ones concentrate on soft-goods and apparel. According to Pasdermadjan (1954:84) such stores cater mainly to middle- and upper-class clientele—this profitable trade enables the maintenance of a highly-accessible location. Upper

Fig. 3-10 *Pedestrian flows within Perth's core 1968.* Based on Geography Dept student survey, Sept. 1968.

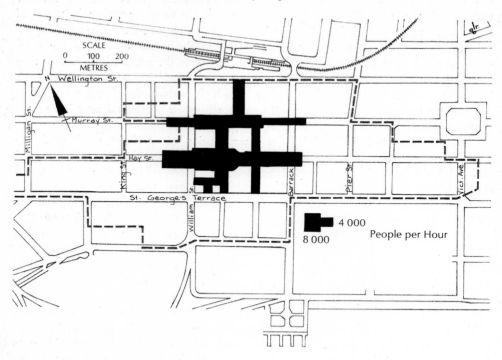

floors in all department stores show a tendency to be given over to the sale of bulky items of low value, such as furniture and household goods; this is a reflection both of the slow turnover of such items and the difficulty of drawing customers to upper floors (Pasdermadjan 1954:43). The vertical differentiation within the department stores is, as will be seen, reminiscent of the horizontal differentiations of retail elements within the core.

The specialist retail group centred in the peak-value areas of the core is dominated by stores catering to women's needs; they draw their custom both from the resident non-working population in the surrounding and suburban residential areas, and from the female workforce in the nearby office areas—lunch-hour trading is a major boost to an otherwise declining trade in the core. As Scott (1959) has shown, each store type has distinctive location patterns, depending on their particular need for contact with high pedestrian volumes, their rent-paying ability and their accommodation needs. In Perth, they all cluster towards the retail node (Figs 3-9a, 3-9b), while footwear and jewellery stores tend to occupy prime locations within arcades and on corner sites. In contrast to many other retail types within Perth's core, the department-apparel-jewellery group showed an increase in numbers between 1957 and 1968 (as detailed in Appendix IIIB).

I *Residential premises in the frame: traditional style.* Such dwellings are typical of many sections of the frame; processes of land-use succession are gradually obliterating them, however (see **Plate VIII**).

II *Residential premises in the frame: modern style.* Such flats, constructed in the late 1950s and early 1960s, are found in isolated nodes close to the core. They cater largely to lower-income and office workers—clearly the utilitarian function has influenced their aesthetics. Whether they are really any improvement on housing of the type shown in Plate I seems doubtful. But note the contrast with higher-income housing in Plate XV.

III *Transitory residential premises in the frame*. Another important component of the frame's residential function. Many are formerly high-income housing. They now provide a welcome home for many single people working in the central area, and for disadvantaged members of society. But their future is threatened by rising land values and freeway construction. Such is the fate of those who cannot avail themselves the prosperity evident elsewhere within the city centre (see Plate X).

IV *The significance of parking areas and automobiles in the frame*. The amount of space devoted to cars in the inner segments of the frame is dramatically illustrated by this aerial shot. This is always on the increase as the demand for parking space, car yards and automotive-service establishments increases; despite their necessary function such areas undoubtedly loosen the fabric of the frame. The diversity of activity within the frame is also well illustrated. (Photo by R. Webber)

'Automobile row' in the frame. These areas commonly locate along the approach roads to the core, where they are both prominent and accessible. Unfortunately, aesthetics are often sacrificed to commercialism.

Blight in the frame. Dilapidated structures, lack of maintenance and ugliness are characteristic of many segments within the frame. Economists explain them away as 'imperfections of the land market', and undoubtedly externalities are often significant barriers to redevelopment. Impending freeway construction, however, can perpetuate and worsen these conditions (see § 2-4.2).

VII *Wholesaling premises in the frame*
(*a*) Time has passed such structures by
their outdated nature is indicated by the
gantries and the multi-storey character of
the buildings. These conditions have en
couraged the decentralization and reloca
tion of much central-area wholesaling in
recent years. But while these premises may
be unsuitable for the original users the
often 'filter-down' to more viable activities
Nonetheless these areas are now seen by
developers as being 'ripe for redevelop
ment'.

(*b*) An aerial view of the 'zone of discard
in Perth's core, which contains man
structures of the sort shown in Plate VIIa
The difference in scale between the olde
structures and the redeveloped offic
areas is dramatic.

A considerable number of men's clothing stores are also found in the peak-value areas of the core. In Perth they are concentrated in inner areas ($D = 9.1$), although in other Australian capitals they are apparently less clustered and thus regarded by Scott (1959:302) as a secondary rather than a primary element (see Table 3-6). Apart from such retail elements, cinemas are an important primary inner element. In Perth six of the eight are located in central Hay Street. Most, whilst occupying frontages at street level, house the actual cinema at first floor or basement level, which is an indication of their high mean space occupancy (1 720m² as opposed to 190m² for clothing stores) that renders them an uneconomic proposition at ground level.

3-4.3 INNER ELEMENTS: PERSONAL SERVICES

Personal-service activities within Perth's core tend to exhibit a dual location pattern. Some, such as men's hairdressers, bootmakers and dry cleaners clearly depend very much on accessibility to passing pedestrian traffic. Hence they behave in a similar fashion to the inner retail elements, and locate predominantly at ground level (see Appendix IIIA). Others, like opticians, beauty salons, photographers, dressmakers, tailors and jewellery repairers have a lesser need for direct contact to passing trade and yet still desire a central location. This causes them to locate in first- or second-floor level premises above the primary inner elements that generate the pedestrian traffic, or at ground level in more peripheral locations (western and eastern Hay, and Barrack and William Streets). Since rents in these segments of the core vary according to land-value level in the horizontal plane and floor level in the vertical plane (reductions of up to 50%), the rent levels in these alternate locations are approximately equivalent. The choice of location represents a trade-off between display and direct accessibility afforded by a peripheral street-level location, and the lesser direct accessibility but larger potential market afforded by central upper-floor location. In general terms, it is clear that these secondary inner elements have a lower rent-paying ability than the primary elements and that this influences their overall locational pattern as shown in Fig. 3-11. Furthermore, their relatively dispersed location pattern (dispersal indices range from 11.2-14.0; see Table 3-7) suggests that their degree of interdependence is lesser than that of the primary inner elements as Nelson (1958:76) has hypothesized—this is to be expected in view of the specific nature of the services they offer.

In addition to such personal-service activities, space at upper-floor levels in the peak-value areas is shared by a wide range of activities, including general offices (as discussed in the previous section), and activities that are functionally linked to the primary elements of this area. Most conspicuous among them are clothing and soft-goods wholesalers and manufacturers, and jewellery manufacturers, which have clear links to the speciality shops below and to the wholesaling district to the west. However, many of these premises at upper-floor levels in the main retail areas are left vacant. Such trend is common to many cities (see e.g. Murphy & Vance 1954b:317, Davies 1965:67, Mika 1965:117) and reflects the somewhat obsolescent

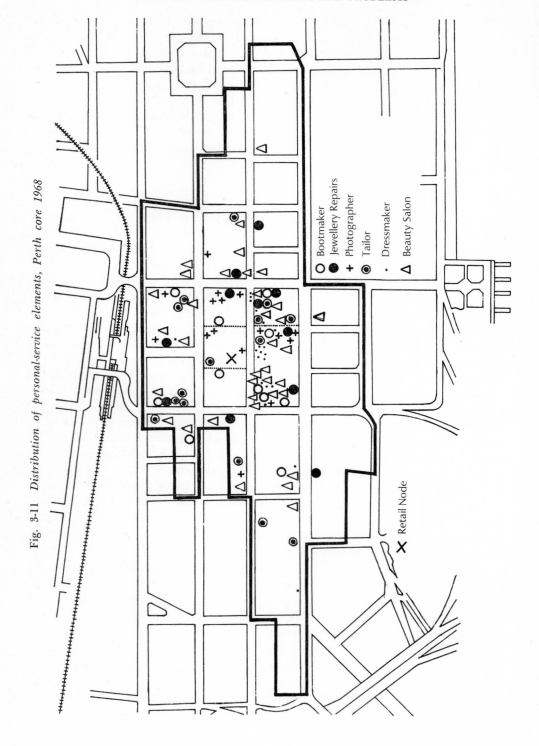

Fig. 3-11 Distribution of personal-service elements, Perth core 1968

Bootmaker
Jewellery Repairs
Photographer
Tailor
Dressmaker
Beauty Salon

Retail Node

nature and difficulty of access to the upper-floor levels of older structures (see Plate XI). As Andrews (1962:68) has pointed out, these premises find themselves in a 'cut-throat market' in that they are having to compete with the more modern office structures to a certain extent. Although the older premises undoubtedly offer cheaper rents, they cannot offer the air-conditioning, views, lifts or the prestige of the modern office blocks.

3-4.4 OUTER ELEMENTS: HOUSEHOLD-GOODS RETAILING

The retailing of household goods is an activity that is commonly found on the peripheries of shopping areas. Murphy and Vance (1955:38) note in their United States city study that household-goods outlets become increasingly significant towards the outer areas of the core, and Mika (1965:107) found a similar tendency in three British cities. Getis and Getis (1968:329) state from a series of comparative observations of the United States and British city core areas that the same stores are found 'on the fringes rather than in the very heart'. The designation of the household group as outer retail elements in all Australian capitals (Scott 1959; see Table 3-6) shows the pattern is similar here. In Perth, this location pattern had not altered by 1968, when household-goods stores were found grouped in two distinct clusters, one to the west and one to the north-east of the peak-value areas, as shown in Fig. 3-12. Despite the similarity of pattern, however, there has been a sharp decline in numbers of furniture and hardware stores in the core since 1957, as illustrated in Appendix IIIB. This would appear to reflect the increasing suburbanization of this type of store over time,* which is probably at least partly explicable in terms of the relative lack of rent-paying ability these stores possess (see Scott 1970:23). This arises from their typically bulky and slow turnover stock that requires large display-floor areas (Ratcliff 1949:383). As a result, they are confined to somewhat peripheral and hence relatively quiet locations within the core. As noted above, the same activities are located on upper floors of department stores for similar reasons.

Within the household group, furniture stores are, despite a relatively high dispersal index ($D = 14.0$), strongly clustered in the western portions of the retail area (Fig. 3-12); seven of the core's ten furniture stores are located here, a relatively more potent concentration than at 1957, when only nine of eighteen were present. However, Scott (1959:304) did note that 'since furniture is normally bought on special shopping expeditions, furniture stores benefit from clustering.' Those stores not located within the cluster have almost entirely disappeared, suggesting that in this instance clustering is a significant benefit to trade.

Hardware and disposal stores are found both in the west and north-east cluster, although as Appendix IIIB indicates, the former are no longer a significant element

---

* Between 1957 and 1969, the value of hardware and furniture sales within the core fell from an average of 63% of metropolitan sales to 34%. Meanwhile, the value of all sales within the area, although remaining constant in absolute terms, fell from 38% to 21% of the metropolitan total (see Appendix IV). Clearly, the major growth of retail sales in recent years has occurred outside the central core area.

Fig. 3-12   *Distribution of household-goods stores, Perth core 1968*

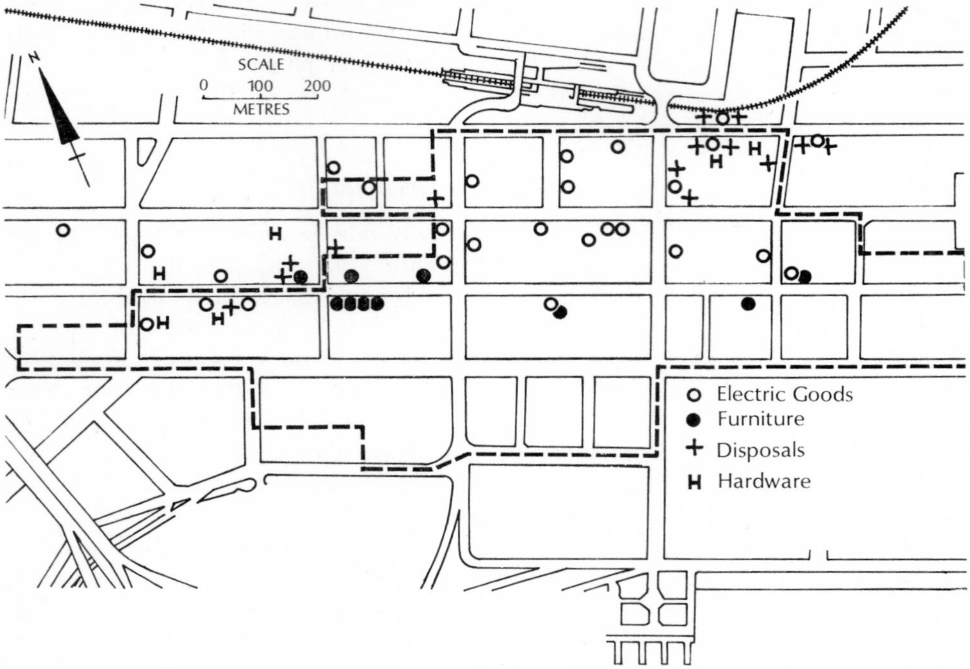

within the structure of the core. The disposal stores are generally of a low-grade nature, and those in the north-east are located within buildings of somewhat dilapidated nature, which is indicative of the low land values prevailing in this area (Fig. 3-4). This concentration of low grade and low value suggests that this area forms the core's 'zone of discard', which, according to Murphy and Vance (1955:42), lies in the wake of core expansion and is characterized by an accumulation of low-grade establishments. However, the identification of these dynamic aspects of structure will be easier and more certain following an analysis, undertaken in Chapter 5, of the processes of change within the central area as a whole.

3-4.5   MISCELLANEOUS AND DISPERSED ELEMENTS

Elements that are classified as 'miscellaneous' (in Table 3-6) are found clustered at street level in certain areas of Perth's core, where land values are between 10%-40% of the peak. These clusters consist of hotels, branch banks, food stores and restaurant-cafés, and provide something of a transition buffer between the inner cluster of clothing and department stores and the outer clusters of household-goods stores. They are most noticeable in northern areas of the core (Fig. 3-13a), although they are also located in other areas throughout the retail-dominated sections of the

Fig. 3-13 *Distribution of miscellaneous retail elements, Perth core 1968*

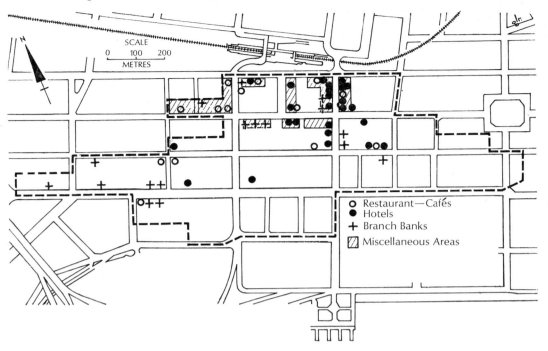

3-13a Banks, hotels, restaurants

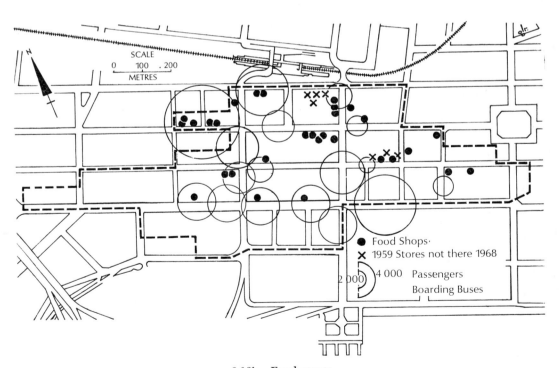

3-13b Food stores

core, as their dispersal indices (ranging from 9.0-15.8—see Table 3.7) indicate. Similar location patterns were observable in all Australian capitals at 1957, when despite their differential classification by Scott (1959:303, 307), it was admitted that restaurants and food stores were localized in marginal areas.

Food stores have shown a sharp decline in representation within Perth's core since 1957, reflecting continuing decline in the food trade within the central area.* Their current location pattern (Fig. 3-13b), shows that they are strongly influenced by transportation termini: both clusters are in close proximity to important bus pick-up and set-down points. A cluster located opposite the railway station in 1957 has since dwindled, no doubt partly revealing the declining patronage received by the railway system in recent years.

Other retail-service elements within the core are all dispersed throughout the area, reflecting in some cases their 'parasitic nature'. Such establishments as snack-bars, coffee shops, tobacconists, newsagents and florists depend to a large extent on passing trade and thus scatter widely over the areas of maximum pedestrian flow. Their linkages, therefore, are to other retail outlets rather than to each other.

3-4.6 SUMMARY

In general terms, it is clear that the location of retailing and service activities within the core is influenced by a large number of variables. In summarizing the patterns several points seem worth noting:

1. A strong cluster of clothing and speciality stores occurs within the peak-value areas of many city centres. The department stores form a framework for this cluster, which generates high pedestrian flows and has an extremely high collective rent-paying ability.

The cluster is complemented by a number of personal-service elements, at upper-floor levels in central sections and ground level towards the peripheries. Some manufacturing and wholesaling establishments occupy similar locations.

Despite the apparent prosperity of the cluster, however, a number of vacant premises occur on upper-floor levels, betraying a degree of obsolescence in the structures. Congestion is also rife in these areas, owing to conflict between the high volumes of pedestrian and vehicular traffic.

2. The central cluster of speciality stores gives way to clusters of household and miscellaneous stores towards the margins of the core, where land values decline sharply. These latter elements often have greater space requirements and slower turnover of goods, and hence a relatively low order rent-paying ability. Many of the members of these activity-groups have shown a sharp decline in numbers in recent years, indicating the increasing specialization of the core's retailing function.

* Between 1957 and 1968, there was a decrease of 5% in the numbers of food stores within the core (see Appendix IIIB). Over the same period, the proportion of the metropolitan food sales transacted within the core fell from an average of 11% to 5%, and fell in absolute annual value by $6 000 (see Appendix IV).

3. Within the inner and outer retail elements groups, certain spatial associations of activities have been noted by visual analysis, as in the case of offices. Whether such groupings are statistically valid, as suggested by Getis and Getis (1968), can only be determined through a more objective analysis. This is undertaken in the next chapter.

4. The overall structure of the core will also receive further attention in the next chapter. However, it is clear that the retail-service group is arranged in a logical and consistent manner within the core in response to a number of factors.

The concentration of specialist and apparel stores in peak-value areas of the core (60%-100%) is surrounded and overlain by a three-dimensional arcuate distribution of department stores and personal-service elements (20%-60% peak-value areas). Groupings of food stores, restaurants, banks and hotels are found sandwiched between this group and the belt of household-goods stores which are located in lower value (20%-60% peak) peripheral areas.

As land economists (e.g. Ratcliff 1949, Alonso 1960, Goodall 1972; see also Scott 1970) have suggested, there appears to be strong competition for sites amongst these activities. The arrangement of elements suggests that the prime sites are occupied by those activities with the highest rent-paying ability (i.e. those yielding the highest economic rent—*à la* von Thünen),* with others occupying either peripheral or upper-floor sites. This pattern, however, is clearly modified by varying accessibility requirements between activities and the differential need for clustering.

It has been suggested by Garner (1966) that the structure of retail nucleations is explicable in terms of a relationship between threshold population for different activities and their rent-paying ability. Thus high threshold functions (with extensive hinterland) will occupy prime sites, whilst low threshold (small hinterland) functions are relegated to the peripheries. This model is derived from a study of non-central-area retail nucleations within Chicago and is based largely on an analysis of ground-floor patterns. To some extent its derivation seems dubious since the relationship hypothesized above between threshold and location failed to yield a significant correlation in the largest centres (Garner 1966:156). Even so, the general arrangement of functions within the core may, to some extent, be related to threshold since the speciality functions in the inner areas cater to a wider market than the food and household functions on the peripheries; and the latter elements are decreasing most in significance as suburbanization continues apace.

The inclusion of personal-service elements confuses this pattern somewhat, since they occupy both central and peripheral locations within the core; Garner (1966) found a similar pattern in the nucleations he studied, although he did not incorporate explicitly this into his model. Personal-service establishments are generally dependant upon trade initially generated by the nearby speciality stores, and in this sense are low threshold activities. But their dual location pattern could be seen as

* Whether economic rent is suitable as a measure of the value of all activity, as the economists suggest, is seriously questioned in Chapter 5.

3-14 *Diagrammatic representation of core structure*

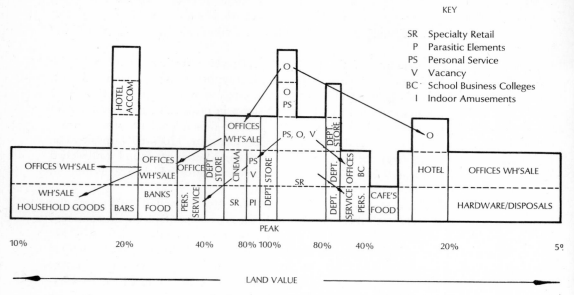

3-14a   Activity arrangement

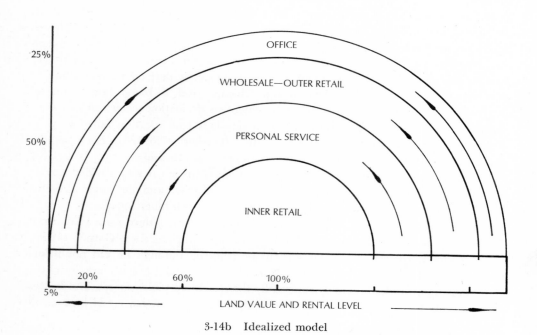

3-14b   Idealized model

a reflection of threshold since the central locations they occupy are mostly on upper floors, and hence 'peripheral' to the main retailing areas. However, it is clear from the preceding discussion that many factors other than threshold are at work in determining the location of retail-service activities within the core. Even so, and regardless of threshold considerations, the overall arrangement of these elements within the core bears strong resemblances to that observable in non-central-area nucleations. This points to the operation of consistent forces and influences. A diagrammatic representation of the patterns within the core is contained in Fig. 3-14 (a, b). This illustrates the tiered, dual-location pattern of various activities in relation to variable rent and value levels in the horizontal and vertical planes; it bears some resemblance to Carter's (1972) depiction of the three-dimensional structure of the entire city.

3-5 WHOLESALING AND OTHER ACTIVITIES

It was seen in the previous chapter that wholesaling is an activity located predominantly in the frame of the central area. However, a certain number of establishments are located within the core: in Perth these are confined almost exclusively to upper-floor levels (93% of their area is found above street level). As we have seen, a certain number are located on upper floors within the speciality retail areas; but the bulk are clustered in upper-floor premises in northern William and western Hay Streets (see Fig. 3-15), and are the spatially dominant activity. These areas represent a 'spill-over' fringe of the wholesale-zone proper (to the west), which has already been shown to have a three-dimensional boundary (§ 2-3.6). Most of the core wholesalers occupy smaller premises than their frame counterparts, and deal in high-value low-bulk goods, such as clothing and soft-goods (55%) and electrical appliances (25%). This links them both to the wholesaling area of the frame, and the retail and office segments of the core.

The location of the major churches and cathedrals within the core is worthy of comment. According to several authors, such structures are 'anachronistic' in central areas and should, therefore, be encouraged to vacate their sites (see e.g. Murphy & Vance 1955, Horwood & Boyce 1959). The unjustifiable narrowness of such an attitude has already been exposed (Chapter 1); apart from their regional religious function, such structures within the core provide a welcome relief from the developing canyons of faceless commercial offices within the centre. However, it cannot be denied that rising land values within the core place increasing pressure on such facilities, as they become hemmed in by office and/or retail development. In terms of the theory of the land market, their lack of rent-paying ability in the face of such competition would indicate the advisability of relocation. But clearly the value of such premises cannot be measured in terms of land values; it is essential, therefore, that such sites should be afforded planning protection from economic forces.

The effects of rising land values are also seen in the location patterns of such facilities as private hotels and clubs. In Perth both have shown a tendency to

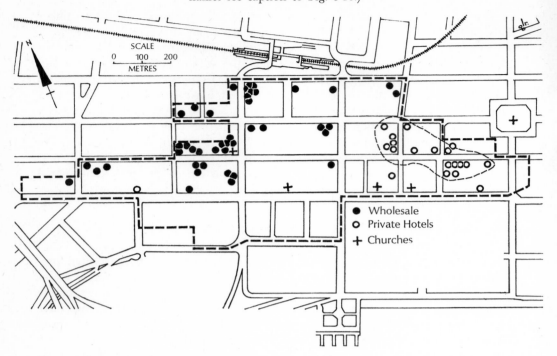

Fig. 3-15 *Distribution of wholesaling outlets, Perth core 1968.* (For street names see caption to Fig. 3-10.)

SCALE
0   100   200
METRES

N

● Wholesale
○ Private Hotels
+ Churches

Fig. 3-16 *Plans for central Hay Street mall*—artist's impression of future development proposed by Perth City Council. (Courtesy of W.A.N. Ltd.)

decrease in significance within the core, whilst becoming more important within the frame in recent years. As will be seen in Chapter 5, continuing redevelopment in the areas where these facilities are concentrated (private hotels to the east of the peak-value areas and clubs within the Terrace office zone) only serves to accelerate this trend.

3-6 CONCLUSION

The examination of the location patterns of activities within the city's core has pointed to the operation of a host of influential factors and in particular to the significance of land value and rental levels in shaping the pattern of land utilization. It has also emphasized that the area is typified by a number of important clusters of activities that form the basis of the marked functional zoning of the core. The full implication of this is examined in the next chapter, when attention is turned to the overall structure of the central area, both core and frame.

It is clear that the core in general is an area of intense activity and flows (pedestrian and information) between its components, and in this sense it can be regarded as a system. However, it is also clear that there are significant links between the activities of the core and those of the surrounding frame, and thus it would be more accurate to describe the area as a sub-system within the central area and city system. The core is subject to different pressures than the frame area, and this generates different planning problems. The blight that was seen to be a typical feature of the frame, is only present in small pockets of the core; on the other hand, redevelopment pressures are stronger in the core and hence the activity groupings are subject to greater pressures. The importance of the structure of land values in determining space-use patterns should not be overlooked in planning the future content and structure of the area.

A planning problem that has attracted much special attention is that of pedestrian-vehicular conflict arising from the high intensity of activity within the area. In combination with high volumes of traffic, this leads to considerable congestion and danger to pedestrian and motorist alike. In many cities, certain of the busier shopping streets have been closed to traffic, and as in Perth, plans for converting them into permanent pedestrian ways have been implemented (Fig. 3-16). This has generally helped in improving the environment considerably, and has often bolstered a declining central-area shopping trade. If alternative access and servicing arrangements can be made, such approach is clearly an important and relatively easily-implemented method of reducing the pedestrian-vehicular conflict in the core.

A more radical solution has come from the traffic engineers, which involves a complete vertical segregation of pedestrian and vehicular traffic via comprehensive redevelopment of the entire fabric of the city centre. Superficially this approach has much to recommend it since it offers an improved environment to both modes of traffic; however, as will be argued in Chapter 5, it can also have a disastrous impact on the existing fabric and activity groupings within the core. At the very least, this impact must be weighed against the benefits which the improved environment offers.

But the activity patterns that have been examined in both the core and the frame are clearly far from static; thus before a full understanding of the implications of redevelopment and change within the area can be gained, it is necessary to study these processes in some depth. It is simply not sufficient to be content with a static analysis, and attempt to diagnose problems and forecast trends from this basis; too many mistakes in the past have hinged on such incomplete analysis.

4

Synthesis of activity patterns: perspectives
on regionalization

4-1 OVERALL STRUCTURE: A CONVENTIONAL
APPROACH

4-1.1 FUNCTIONAL ZONES

The identifications and definition of meaningful regions is a question that has
long attracted the attention of geographers and one that has raised considerable
controversy and confusion over the years. This situation has become more acute as
the techniques of regionalization have multiplied (see Taylor & Spence 1970).

As far as the central area is concerned, it is a matter of common observation that
distinctive zones are present there, the most obvious of these being the core and the
frame. It has been suggested that both of these areas are subdivisable into further
zones that reflect the tendency of activities to cluster together (see e.g. Fig. 1-1).
Such tendencies have been confirmed by the analyses of preceding chapters, but
the extent to which these clusters form distinctive zones or sectors of differential
character and properties is thus far indeterminate. This brings us back to the thorny
question of defining regions within the area.

One attempt in this direction has been made by Davies (1965) in his study of
central Capetown. Having defined clusters of various activity types within the
central area, he then combined these together into 'functional areas' which 'represent the basic divisions of the central area' (Davies 1965:68). This process, however, seems somewhat dubious since the clusters that are used as a basis for the
exercise are themselves of doubtful validity since they include a wide mixture of
uses within their bounds.*

A more fruitful approach stems from the work of Goddard (1967). It involves
an analysis of the activity composition of sub-areas within the centre, a classification
according to major use, and the grouping of similar areas.† Following this procedure
in Perth (using the block as a basic analytical unit in the frame and the street

* In this connection see Chapter 2, § 2-1.
† Goddard utilized the 'least squares' technique to classify by major use squares of a grid laid
over central London. This technique was first used by Weaver (1954) in an agricultural context
and involves the summing up deviations from an ideal split of activity in each area, i.e. if two

frontage in the core), the central area can be resolved into sixteen zones: eleven in the frame and four in the core, with one overlapping the core-frame boundary (Fig. 4-1).* The latter area is spatially dominated by wholesaling activities and its overlapping character casts some doubt on the validity of the core-frame boundary in this region. As will be seen, this validity is further questioned by the application of a statistical division technique and it appears to be explicable in terms of the zone's dynamics.

The composition of other zones (as illustrated in Fig. 4-2) makes clear the overall pattern of land-use arrangement within the central area; this consists of a spatially restricted centre zone of offices and retail-service activities which are surrounded by more extensive zones of public, residential, office, automotive-retailing, retail-service, manufacturing and wholesaling activities and transportation termini. However, it is also clear that each zone, whilst dominated spatially by a particular activity, also contains a considerable quantity of other uses. In most cases it is possible to identify at least two and often three 'major uses' (as defined in the footnote on p. 101) within a zone; only in the case of zones eight and eleven does one use predominate to the exclusion of other major uses (see Fig. 4-2).

The most significant areal combinations of activities within the frame (on the basis of spatial coherence and extent) are: (a) residential premises and professional offices to the west of the core (zone 3); (b) manufacturing and wholesaling activities with residential remnants to the north-west (zone 6); and (c) manufacturing and wholesaling activities in combination with storage and transport termini to the north-east (zone 9). Apart from these, zones of automotive outlets are found in combination with residences on all flanks, with zones of high-density residential activity to the east and west. Areas dominated by public and cultural facilities form a definite ring around the core. The zonation of the frame is more complex to the east of the core than in other directions, possibly reflecting the active transition forces at work within this segment (see Chapter 5).

In the core, the zones as defined are more segregated, with the major uses occupying an average of almost 50% of each zone's floorspace as against 40% in the frame. The implication is that rather than forming discrete nodes of single activity type, those uses that typify the frame tend to cluster with one another, with the possible exception of public services (zone 5) and high-density housing (zone 11). In the core, on the other hand, the segregation of activities is greater, possibly reflecting the increased competition for sites within the area and the larger differential land values there.

* In Fig. 4-1, the core's four zones are shown as 1-1 to 1-4, those in the frame are numbered 2 to 13.

activities are present within an area, an 'ideal' split would be 50/50; for three 33.3/33.3/33.3, etc. Those activities yielding the least square of deviations are mapped as the significant ones for that area. In our study, this technique was simplified to the extent that the summing and squaring procedure was eliminated. Blocks were classified according to major uses: a major use is one that occupies more floorspace within a block than an even split of all uses within the block would predict. For these purposes the broad categories of activities such as 'retailing', 'office', etc. were utilized, unless one particular category of activity within these sectors was predominant.

Fig. 4-1 *Functional zones within Perth's central area 1968*

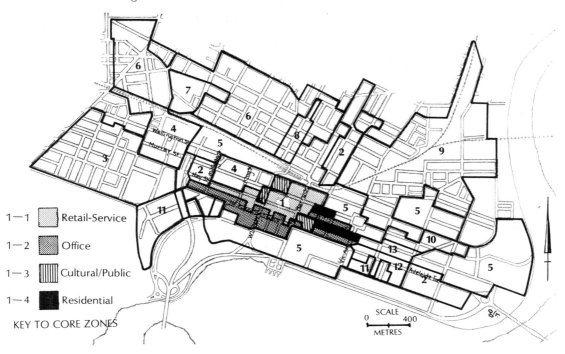

KEY TO CORE ZONES

1—1 Retail-Service
1—2 Office
1—3 Cultural/Public
1—4 Residential

SCALE
0   400
METRES

Fig. 4-2 *Space use within functional zones, Perth frame 1968.*
(M.F.R. = manufacturing.)

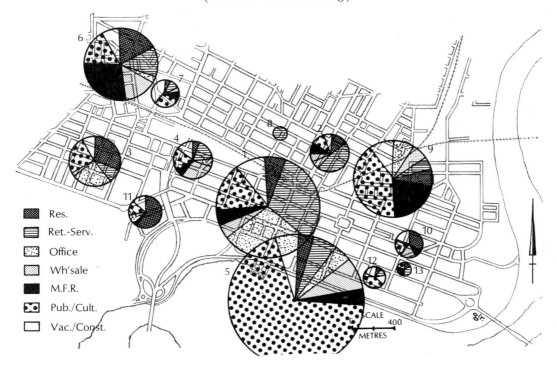

Res.
Ret.-Serv.
Office
Wh'sale
M.F.R.
Pub./Cult.
Vac./Const.

SCALE
400
METRES

The pattern in Perth is similar to that apparent in other cities, as examination of Fig. 4-3 shows. In all of these cities certain activities show a propensity to concentrate together rather than to separate; most significant in this regard are: (*a*) residential premises in combination with offices—these are clearly a product of the invasion of former purely residential areas by offices; (*b*) manufacturing and wholesaling activities in combination with storage and transport termini; and (*c*) retail and service activity combinations within the core. The general validity of the core-frame concept (with a core of intensive uses surrounded by a frame of extensive activities) is confirmed by these comparisons; however, it is clear that there is more combination of activities within the frame, and indeed more activity types present than suggested by the original schematic model of Horwood and Boyce (1959).

In this respect, the 'poly-nuclear' structure of the frame area proposed by Preston and Griffin (1966) has more validity (Fig. 4-3g), in that it explicitly contains reference to combinations and clusters of various activity types. As we have seen in Chapter 1, Preston and Griffin (1966) also suggested that the clusters could then be further classified into areas of 'passive assimilation', 'active assimilation' and 'general inactivity' (Fig. 1-4). Although an analysis of static patterns of activity within the frame (such as undertaken in Chapter 2) can point to processes of change, to use this as a basis for a classification is clearly dubious. A classification must be based on detailed analysis of the processes; this is attempted in the next chapter.

But despite the superficial treatment of the processes of change in the static models of central-area structure, the general similarity of the arrangement of activities within the central areas in itself points to the operation of universal factors shaping the internal differentiation of the urban heart. As seen in previous chapters, the functional linkages between activities, the structure of the land market, the relative rent-paying ability and the differing locational requirements of activities with respect to one another and to pedestrian and vehicular traffic are amongst these factors. The core-frame model does point to the operation of some of these factors, but it overlooks others and does not explicitly incorporate any processes into the conceptual structure. An attempt is made to remedy this in the final chapter.

Issue can also be taken at this stage with another hypothesis put forward both by Preston and Griffin (1966) and by Horwood and Boyce (1959). They propose that the various zones of activity found within the frame are discrete or unlinked in nature and possess ties to areas outside the frame rather than to each other. It has been discerned from this study that clear functional relationships do exist between frame and core, and to this extent the hypotheses are verified. However, it is also equally clear that significant linkages exist between activities within the zones (such as between manufacturing and wholesaling, and the latter and transportation termini) and between zones themselves (such as from residential areas to retail-service nodes in the frame, or from office areas to manufacturers and wholesalers). On the other hand it must be noted that many apparently unlinked activities occur in proximity to one another: for example manufacturing or offices, and

II *Land-use succession in the frame*. Sandwiched between two new office blocks (whose scale is typical of the frame), the fate of these houses is clearly sealed. Conversion of houses to temporary offices is often a precursor to redevelopment.

X *Freeway interchange*. This complex lies on reclaimed land to the south-west of Perth's central area, and occupies an area of 36 hectares (Main Roads Dept information). This illustrates the huge area the car requires when given free reign. The space occupied by the interchange is the equivalent of approximately the total ground-floor area of the entire core. It effectively alienates a large segment of the city from the river. It is ironic that the reclamation was recommended in the 1955 Stephenson report which stated: 'through thoughtful action in the past, the setting of Perth has been enhanced rather than destroyed.' The interchange has been variously described as an engineering marvel, a 'heap of spaghetti' and a tribute to political megalomania, but it undoubtedly serves an important distributory function (although its connecting roads are sadly below its own capacity).

X *Offices in the core hub area*. T[?] development is typical of the structu[?] that are increasingly dominant in t[?] core's office segments; these concrete a[?] glass towers are rapidly replacing t[?] older buildings still evident within t[?] area. At present the latter buildings p[?] vide at least some contrast to the mus[?] rooming monuments to finance, [?] progress will soon take its toll.

XI *Retail-services premises in Pert[?] core*. The contrast of building age a[?] scale with the office areas is clear fr[?] a comparison with Plate X. Buildi[?] owners in the retail hub area are findi[?] it increasingly difficult to rent upp[?] floor space, although ground-floor usa[?] remains intense in response to the hi[?] land values. Heavy pedestrian flows [?] this area of Perth's core are grea[?] facilitated by the mall developme[?] which, although only partially comple[?] creates an attractive and informal sh[?] ping atmosphere.

Perth's skyline 1955. The low profile of development and the relatively peaceful
...osphere of the city is evident from this shot. (Photo courtesy Govt. Printer)

Perth's skyline 1973. The dramatic contrast with the earlier skyline (Plate XII)
...ds no emphasis; it is a stark reflection of the strength of the office boom that has
...ected the area in the intervening years; it has been a typical feature of all Australian
...es since World War II.

XIV *High-status housing*. The spacio
and luxurious air of this block of hom
units to the west of Perth's core contras
sharply with the functional high-densi
housing shown in Plate II. The uni
here command superior views an
naturally, prices: they are definitely r
served for high-income sectors of th
community.

XV *Foreshore activities, Perth centr
area*. This again demonstrates the dom
nance of the car within the city cent
Such car parks serve an important fur
tion for daily commuters; unfortunate
in Perth they help to alienate the ci
from the river.

Fig. 4-3 *Comparison of functional zoning in central areas of eight cities*

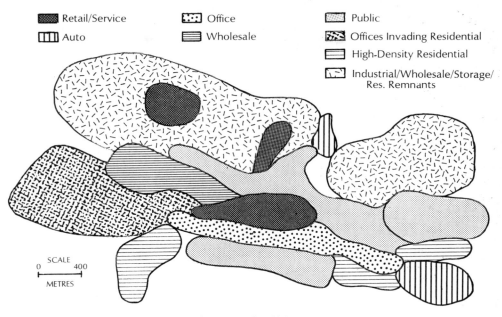

4-3a   Perth 1973

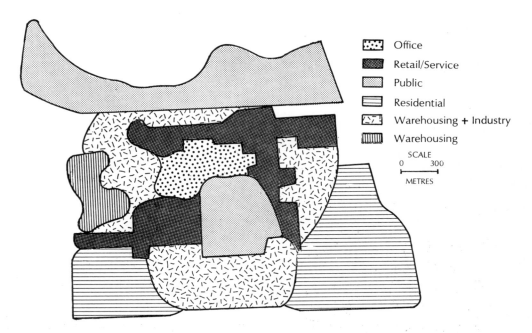

4-3b   Adelaide 1973. After City of Adelaide 1973.

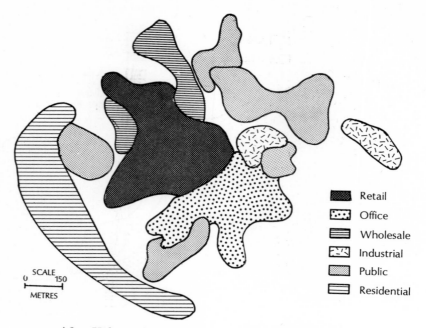

4-3c   Hobart 1968. Source: City of Hobart 1968: Fig. 14.

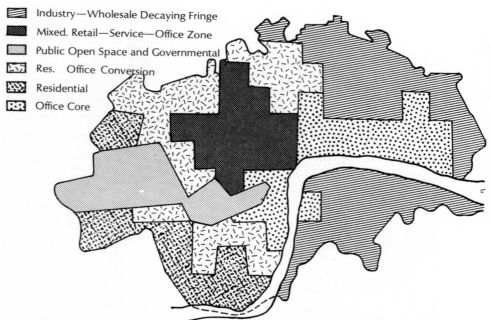

4-3d   London 1966. After Goddard 1967: Fig. 12. Reproduced with permission of the publisher.

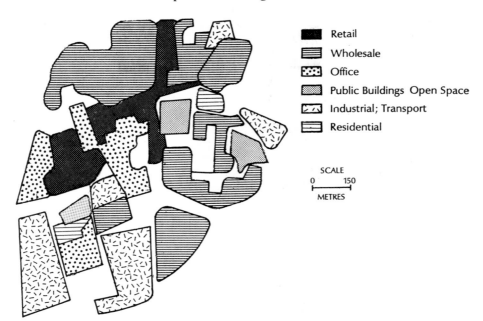

Retail
Wholesale
Office
Public Buildings Open Space
Industrial; Transport
Residential

SCALE
0   150
METRES

4-3e   Manchester 1966. After Varley 1968.

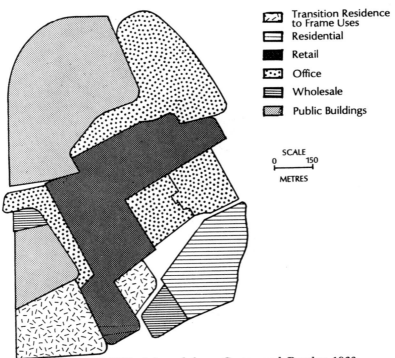

Transition Residence to Frame Uses
Residential
Retail
Office
Wholesale
Public Buildings

SCALE
0   150
METRES

4-3f   Cardiff 1966. Adapted from Carter and Rowley 1966.

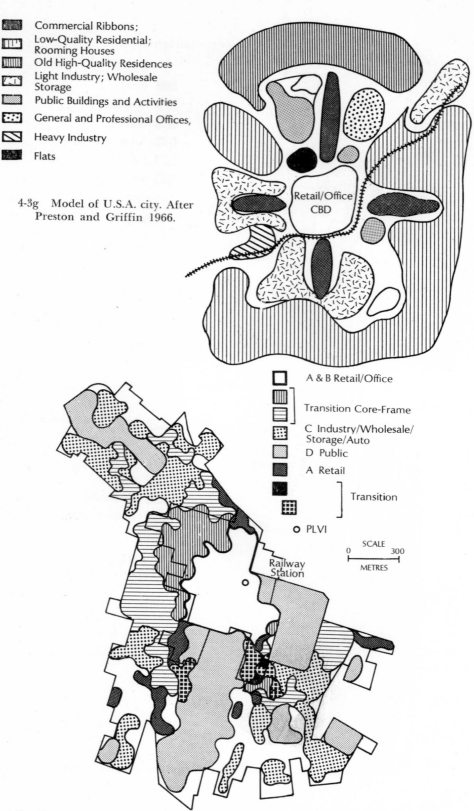

Commercial Ribbons;

Low-Quality Residential;
Rooming Houses

Old High-Quality Residences

Light Industry; Wholesale
Storage

Public Buildings and Activities

General and Professional Offices,

Heavy Industry

Flats

Retail/Office
CBD

4-3g   Model of U.S.A. city. After
Preston and Griffin 1966.

A & B Retail/Office

Transition Core-Frame

C Industry/Wholesale/
Storage/Auto

D Public

A Retail

Transition

O PLVI

SCALE
0   300
METRES

Railway
Station

4-3h   Capetown 1965. After Davies 1965. (PLVI = peak land value intersection.)

housing. But such juxtaposition results from an invasion of former housing areas by central activities. In other cases the locational proximity may result not so much from functional linkages between activities as from similar locational requirements (e.g. government depots and transportation termini).

Within Perth's core, four major zones have been identified: retail-service, office, public-cultural, residential (hotels) with, as we have seen, a wholesaling zone over-lapping the core-frame boundary (Fig. 4-1). Within the retail and office areas, however, a subdivision can be made into sub-zones on the basis of the predominance of a particular activity type. Thus the retail-service area is resolved into an inner, outer and miscellaneous zone (Fig. 4-4a) in accordance with the classification adopted in the previous chapter (Table 3-6). As noted, these activities show distinctive clustering tendencies in conformity with their rent-paying ability and locational requirements. Apart from the inclusion of a 'miscellaneous' zone within the retail-service segments, the functional zones correspond relatively closely with those defined by Scott (1959).* The miscellaneous zone in Perth has been identified on the basis of a clustering of banks, hotels, restaurant-cafés and food stores. As noted in the previous chapter, these agglomerate in several pockets on the outskirts of the inner specialist stores towards the main public transport termini.

A further contrast to Scott's classification is that the retail-service zones identified in Fig. 4-2 also take account of upper-floor activities. This means that personal-service elements and offices become significant components in inner areas, whilst wholesaling and other activities are supplementary components of outer areas. Thus, analysis of the contents of the inner-retail service zone reveals that the specialist-department retailing group is dominant in terms of space occupancy, yet also shows that personal-service elements are a significant component (see Table 4-1). To-gether, this combination of retail-service elements occupy some 69% of the zone's floorspace, and department stores alone occupy some 40%. The balance of the space is occupied by cinemas and a small quantity of office activities. The latter become more significant in the outer retail and miscellaneous areas, where retailing as such is less dominant (Table 4-1). The supplementary activities tend to occupy upper-floor locations.

The office areas (already discussed at the commencement of the preceding chap-ter [Fig. 3-3]), are divisible into three distinct zones: a financial-professional area within the hub, a professional office (largely medical) area to the far west, and a government area to the east. To a large extent these areas reflect the clustering tendencies discussed in the last chapter. The most viable area is undoubtedly the highly intra-linked financial zone in the vicinity of the hub area, and indeed this

---

* Dynamic aspects of these zones over the 1957-68 period are discussed further in Chapter 5. With regard to the definition of these areas, Scott (1959) used predominance of frontage as a major criterion: if 50% (or more) of a frontage was devoted to inner retail elements (as de-fined in Table 3-6), that frontage was classified as part of the inner retail zone; if 50% (or more) was devoted to outer elements, the frontage became part of the outer retail zone. A similar technique was used in this study, although total floorspace was used as the classification base in preference to ground-floor frontage. This reflects the three-dimensional structure of the core to a greater degree.

Table 4-1

PERCENTAGES OF FLOOR AREA OCCUPIED BY MAJOR USES WITHIN
FUNCTIONAL ZONES, PERTH CORE

Zone	Description	Major uses		Secondary uses	
1-1 (a)	*Inner retail service*	Department stores	48.9%	Cinemas	14.2%
		Clothing stores	7.8%	Offices	5.8%
		Variety stores	7.6%	W/sale	1.1%
		Personal service	4.5%	Household retail	3.3%
				Vacancy	3.9%
		Total	68.9%		19.3%
(b)	*Outer retail*	Household retail	27.0%	W/sale	13.7%
		Miscellaneous retail	11.5%	Office	13.0%
				Personal service	5.3%
		Total	38.3%		32.0%
(c)	*Miscellaneous retail*	Hotels	26.0%	Office	10.6%
		Banks	17.2%	Household retail	5.3%
		Restaurants	4.0%	Vacancy	4.8%
		Food shops	2.7%		
		Total	50.9%		20.7%
1-2 (a)	*Financial office*	Financial office	25.5%	Gen. office	11.3%
				Prof. office	8.9%
				Govt. office	6.8%
				Under construct.	9.9%
				Parking	14.3%
				Newspaper	7.0%
					58.2%
(b)	*Professional office*	Prof. office	33.5%	Fin./Gen. office	27.1%
				Parking	13.2%
					40.3%
(c)	*Government office*	Govt. office	50.0%	Gen. office	13.0%
				W/sale	11.0%
				Under construct.	4.2%
				Parking	4.6%
					32.8%
(d)	*Office construction*	Offices under construction	48.3%	Gen. office	12.8%
				Prof. office	6.3%
				Govt. office	9.3%
				Parking	10.0%
					38.4%

Zone	Description	Major uses		Secondary uses	
1-3	*Residential*	Hotels	32.7%	Parking	21.0%
		Flats	4.2%	Office	11.0%
		Other res.	0.4%	Vacancy	5.5%
		Total	37.3%		37.5%
1-4 (a)	*Public facilities*	Post Office	78.1%	Theatre	6.6%
		Parking	5.4%	Parking	5.4%
		Education	2.8%		
		Total	83.3%		12.0%
(b)	*Cultural facilities*	Churches	31.8%	Clubs	5.1%
		Entertainment	19.8%	Service	5.8%
				Parking	11.4%
				Retail	5.1%
		Total	51.6%		27.4%

zone has been referred to in numerous studies of city centres; next to the retail areas it appears to be the most distinctive component of core structure. Even so, despite its significance in Perth, there are a number of other office activities intermixed with the financial set within the financial office zone (Table 4-1). The importance of these mixtures is more fully investigated in § 4-1.3.

4-1.2 VERTICAL DIFFERENTIATION

The preceding analysis of the internal differentiation of the city's central area has demonstrated the existence of viable 'zones' of activities which tend to show a high degree of interdependence. However, this tends to mask the pattern of vertical differentiation; as we have seen, certain core activities are confined to particular floor levels, giving the area a distinct three-dimensional structure. The composite result of these patterns is illustrated for Perth's core in Fig. 4-4 (a-h). Viewed in conjunction with the composition of each level's structure (Fig. 4-5) an image of the total structure begins to emerge.

It is immediately apparent from these maps and diagrams that the retail-service area, which predominates in a spatial sense at ground level (except in the Terrace office zone), becomes increasingly less significant at each succeeding level; conversely offices become more widespread and dominant in spatial extent until they are virtually the only activity present at fifth-floor level and above.

Little *retail-service* space occurs above ground-floor level except within the inner segments of the inner retail-service zone (IRZ). This comprises personal-service activities, the upper floors of department stores and isolated specialist-retail outlets. The high amount of vacant space found at upper levels in these areas is also evident from Fig. 4-4 (b-g).

Floorspace above second-floor level accounts for a mere 22% of the total, which reflects the lack of vertical development within Perth's core in comparison with

Fig. 4-4 *Functional zones, by floor, Perth core 1968*

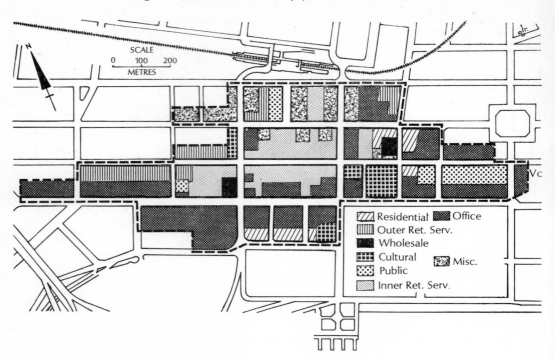

4-4a Ground floor

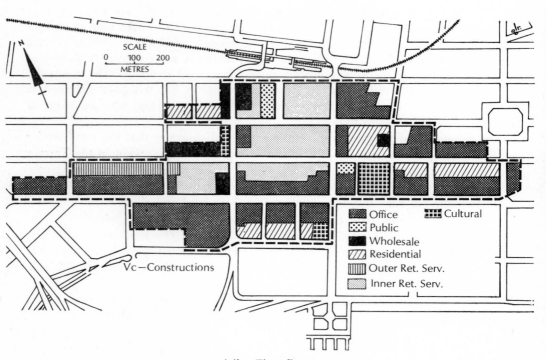

4-4b First floor

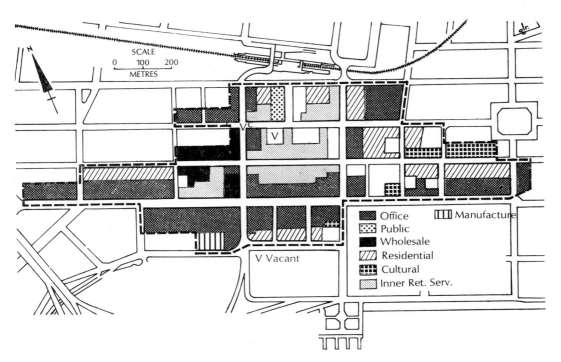

SCALE
0   100   200
METRES

Office   Manufacture
Public
Wholesale   Residential
Cultural
V Vacant   Inner Ret. Serv.

4-4c   Second floor

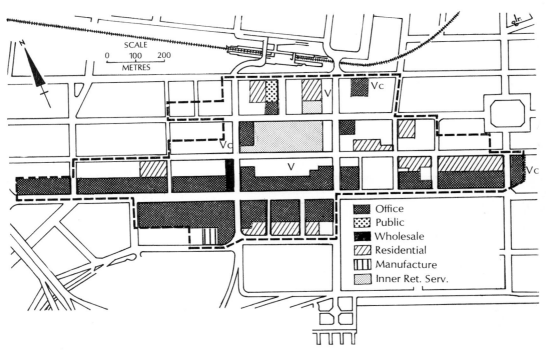

SCALE
0   100   200
METRES

Office
Public
Wholesale
Residential
Manufacture
Inner Ret. Serv.

4-4d   Third floor

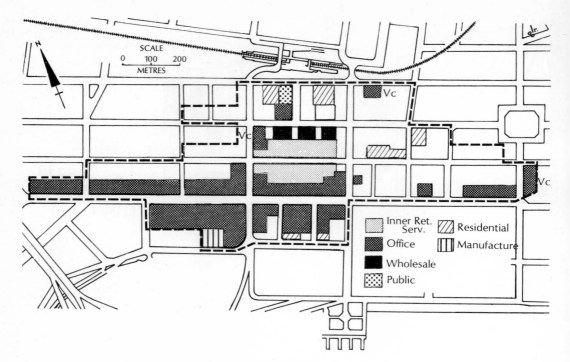

4-4e   Fourth floor

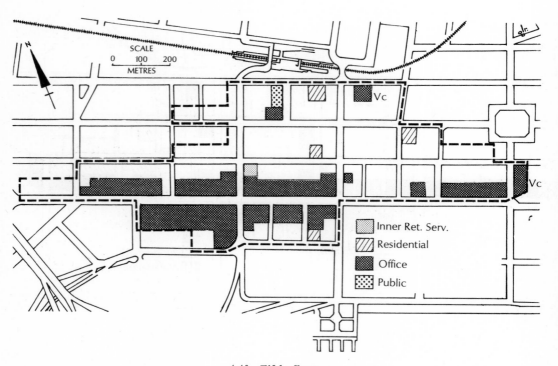

4-4f   Fifth floor

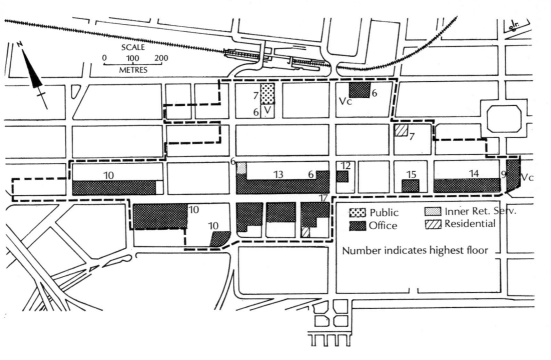

SCALE
0   100   200
METRES

7
6 V
Vc   6

7

6
10
13   6
12
15   14
9 Vc

10
10
17

Public   Inner Ret. Serv.
Office   Residential

Number indicates highest floor

4-4g   Sixth floor

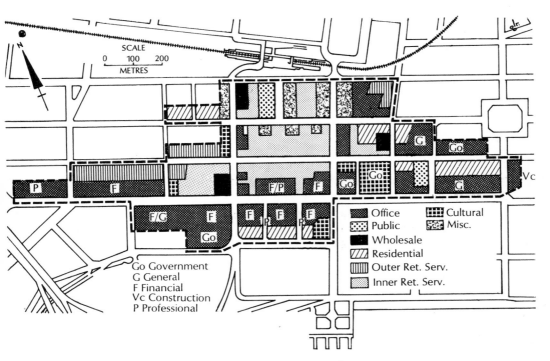

SCALE
0   100   200
METRES

G
Go

Go   Go
Vc

P
F
F/P   F
G

F/G   F
F   F   F
Go

Office   Cultural
Public   Misc.
Wholesale
Residential
Outer Ret. Serv.
Inner Ret. Serv.

Go Government
G General
F Financial
Vc Construction
P Professional

4-4h   All floors combined

larger cities. As the next chapter shows, however, this situation is rapidly changing with the office-building boom of recent years; indeed, offices under construction account for up to 40% of the floorspace at upper levels (Fig. 4-5).

It is generally clear from Fig 4-4 (d-g) that the only activities of any spatial significance above second-floor level are the remnants of the IRZ, isolated residential accommodation in the form of hotels, and office structures. Other activities are totally insignificant at these levels, generally being found at lower floors towards the peripheries of the core. In this sense, the remaining area (at all floor levels) can be seen as a 'hard core', an area which Davies (1965:21) suggests is distinguished from the balance of the core by 'more intensive space use, higher land values, heavier pedestrian traffic and generally taller buildings'. The latter characteristic is obvious from an examination of Fig. 4-4 (a-h); the area of taller buildings encompasses the IRZ and the Terrace office zone. Space use here is clearly most intensive and it is of interest to note that the land values are generally above 20% of the peak, which corresponds fairly closely with the situation in Capetown, where the hard core was found to be within the 30% isoval. It is doubtful whether such an area should be regarded as the 'quintessence' of the core as Davies (1965:21) insists, since its major components are offices and retail premises. To suggest that such development represents 'the purest form' of core development implies that other activities are in some sense undesirable. To adopt this standpoint is to revert to the narrow philosophy of the 'CBD for business only' that must be rejected if the core is to retain anything of its diminishing life and character.

4-1.3   THE NEED FOR ALTERNATIVE STRATEGIES*

The preceding section has illustrated the zonal structure of the central-area core and frame and has pointed to the existence of several clusters of different activities. The zones have been defined on the basis of floorspace-use distribution: such a method has proved possible, owing to the comprehensive data base at our disposal. Needless to say surveys that afford such data are costly to mount and hence are only enacted infrequently. In addition, once such data are available, problems arise as to its organization and analysis, to the effect that much collected data go unused. Electronic data processing has helped remedy this situation, yet the need remains for techniques that are capable of identifying the salient characteristics of the central area with a minimum of data input.

There is also a need for the development of more 'objective' methods of classifying data; the clusters of activities referred to in the preceding sections have been only determined on the basis of subjective visual impression, whilst there is some room for doubting the validity of certain boundaries drawn between zones. The development of numerical methods of classifying data (numerical taxonomy for those *au fait* with the terminology!) offers a possible answer to both the data and

* Some of the material in the following sections has been previously discussed in Alexander (1972a); here however, the discussion is elaborated in more detail by reference to other techniques, recent similar studies, and possible explanations for patterns.

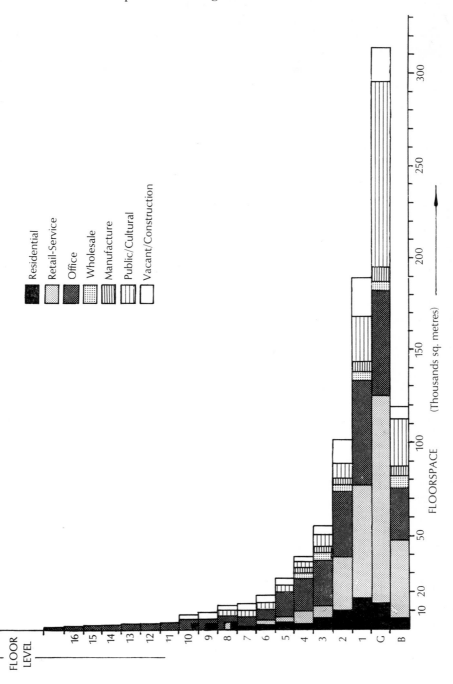

Fig. 4-5 *Space use by floor, Perth core 1968*

objectivity dilemma. Such techniques have predominantly originated from the field of plant taxonomy, where botanists have long sought for more objective and reliable methods of identifying meaningful groups of phenomena (see e.g. Grieg-Smith 1964).

Many numerical techniques that set out to produce such a classification of data have been developed in recent years: indeed the whole field of taxonomy has undergone a virtual information explosion since 1960. This explosion has been ignited largely by the availability of increasingly sophisticated computing machinery that enables the rapid handling of large data sets and the implementation of complex classification strategies. Scientists in many fields have realized the potential of such techniques and are becoming increasingly enamoured with them (see e.g. Cole 1969). Urban analysis is no exception in this regard, and the ordination technique of factor analysis in particular has been increasingly applied as a means of identifying groups of 'key variables' that better explain the composition of the urban fabric (see e.g. Berry & Horton 1970; *Econ. Geogr.* 1971). Similarly, techniques that seek to identify significant clusters of phenomena by progressive fusions or subdivisions of a population (cluster analytical techniques) have been used to classify urban areas according to various criteria (see e.g. Caroe 1968, Stimson 1970).

As yet, however, few studies that recognize the relevance of such techniques to the question of land use and activity analysis have appeared. An exception in this regard is provided by the discussion of Johnston (1968), who uses land-use data from Melbourne's central area as a basis for testing the viability of various techniques. He shows that such methods can be used for identifying 'regions' within the area. Similarly, the work of Goddard (1968) illustrates the potential of taxonomic techniques in identifying significant spatial groupings of activities: they certainly seem superior to the arbitrary and subjective methods utilized in the previous section. However, a few warning notes should be sounded.

First, the tendency to invest the results of a classification with spurious significance must be avoided. The previous chapter illustrated the danger of inferring functional linkages from spatial groupings of activities. Certainly classification techniques enable the identification of significant spatial clusters of activities within an area; however to imply then that such groups have a *prima facie* functional rationale, as does Goddard (1968), is not only dangerous, but can be positively misleading. Goddard's later studies (1970, 1971) recognize this point as they concentrate on identifying contact patterns between and within clusters of activities. Unfortunately, others have inferred a great deal more from Goddard's original analysis than is reasonable. Thus Spence and Taylor (1970:9) state:

> Theoretically one would expect certain groups of city centre activities to be linked in *both business and spatial* terms. This is exactly what the principal components solution [i.e. Goddard's (1968) study] produced.*

* My italics.

The spatial links cannot be denied, but to suggest that a mathematical classificatory technique can also define business linkages is patently false. As we have seen, spatial groupings are often linked in business terms, but this can only be established by independent survey.

Secondly, the adoption of numerical taxonomic techniques often leads to claims of an indisputable objectivity in the results. The review carried out by Johnston (1968) has clearly put the lie to this argument, since he demonstrated that the results of a classification are to some extent dependent on the strategy adopted. Clearly, the internal operation of a technique will affect its output. However, to intimate that such techniques are completely subjective is 'to argue the concept of objectivity out of existence' (Spence & Taylor 1970:6). On the other hand, it is equally absurd to suggest that the results of a classificatory technique are in some way infallible.

Given this tendency for results to be affected by the choice of technique, it is clear that a careful choice of method must be made. As Williams (1971:304) points out, this choice will be conditioned by the nature of the problem. Yet there still remains a bewildering array of techniques—each claiming to be the answer to the taxonomist's prayer—from which to choose. To accompany this, there is an equally bewildering array of opinions on the comparative merits of the techniques. Thus, several reviews of available techniques have appeared recently, but in the main they are rather inconclusive (see e.g. Johnston 1968, Spence & Taylor 1970, Abler *et al.* 1972). This is partly attributable to the lack of comparative studies, but it is also due to uncertainty over the full implications of the relatively sophisticated mathematical machinery that the techniques employ. The only way to resolve such a situation lies not in the abandonment of the field, in the pious hope that a perfect technique will suddenly materialize, but in the continued application of the techniques to a wide range of data and frequent reviews of their comparative merits. The following sections outline the application of one such technique—Information Analysis (as developed from Lambert & Williams 1966)—to the problems of regionalization and identification of meaningful clusters of activities within the central area. Before embarking on this discussion, however, it is necessary to see where it stands within the fertile field of taxonomy.

4-2 CLASSIFICATORY TECHNIQUES: THE TAXONOMIST'S DILEMMA

4-2.1 CHOICE OF STRATEGY

The apparent success with which the relatively conventional factor analysis has been applied to the study of urban structure in recent years and its application to activity-association and regionalization in central London by Goddard (1968, 1970) suggest that the technique has considerable potential for application to the problem in hand. This technique is basically concerned with identifying the 'unknown interdependencies in a particular set of data' (Spence & Taylor 1970:9), by collapsing a series of variables onto several key factors that, ideally, explain most of the variance within the data set. In this way the redundant variables are eliminated from consideration as significant explanatory factors within the total pattern (Abler et al. 1972:166).

The factor analytical model measures the degree of similarity between individuals (each possessing certain attributes) by way of the correlation coefficient. Although this measure is widely used in taxonomic exercises (see Spence & Taylor 1970, Sokal & Sneath 1963), it is argued by some critics that it is not necessarily a suitable measure. Thus Eades (1965) notes that spurious taxonomic similarity can be inferred from correlation coefficients in certain circumstances owing to the measure's emphasis on statistical likeness rather than on similarity of content between individuals. Similar objections are raised by Harvey (1969:344). More significantly and despite its widespread use, it is but rarely mentioned that the model assumes that the correlated variables are all relatively normally distributed. It also assumes that each observation of a variable is independent. Such conditions may be easy to fulfill in certain circumstances, but with discontinuous data such as land use and activity distribution it seems unlikely. In order to offset the problem of data skewness Goddard (1968) subjected his data to a log 10 transformation; while this is normal practice, Goddard does not state how successful his transformation was in overcoming skewness. Furthermore, it seems significant that the first six factors that emerge from his analysis, and on which the bulk of the interpretation is based, account for a mere *one-third* of the total variance in the data. Similarly a factor analysis of several United States city centres carried out by Morris (1966), as a means of identifying important activity groupings and districts, took twelve factors to account for 70% of the variance. Goddard's results have been validated to some extent, both by subsequent survey (1971) and by comparison of activity groupings with those yielded from a cluster analysis. However, while the results may have some value for comparative purposes, the factor analytic model would seem to be based on assumptions that simply cannot be fulfilled by land-use data.

A trial application of the factor analytic method to Perth's central area confirmed these suspicions.* It was not possible to achieve a meaningful transformation of the data, owing to the concentration of individual activities in particular areas to the exclusion of others; most variables were irredeemably skewed. In these circumstances the fact that the first six factors accounted for only 20% of the variance was not surprising. And since the subsequent factors each contributed little to the pattern, it was felt that such results could not be meaningfully or validly interpreted. As Poole and O'Farrell (1971) note, analysts should pay more attention to the mathematical bases of techniques before applying them with such fervour. To violate the assumptions of mathematical models because of ignorance is perhaps excusable; to do this knowingly and then gloss them over in interpreting the results is sheer chicanery.

* The analysis was carried out in late 1972.

Clearly, therefore, other techniques have to be found. In this context those techniques that seek to cluster data into hierarchical groups undoubtedly have more potential. Such methods are not so much concerned with identifying the significant underlying dimensions within a data set, but more with isolating groups of linked phenomena. This may be achieved either through progressive subdivision of the total population (divisive methods) or through progressive grouping of individuals (agglomerative methods; Fig. 4-6). In either case the objective is to choose an optimal route between 'the entire population and the set of individuals of which it is composed' (Williams 1971:308); and furthermore to produce groups with minimum within-group variance and maximum between-group variance. Both strategies have been widely employed in many fields, and again opinion on their relative merits is far from unanimous. This question is complicated by a further choice that has to be made between monothetic and polythetic sorting strategies. The former method seeks to define groups on the basis of a single 'indicator' attribute, whilst polythetic systems make reference to overall group structure. It would be tedious to rehearse the many arguments concerning the divisive-agglomerative choice and those for and against these strategies; these have in any case been well covered elsewhere (see McNaughton-Smith 1965, Williams *et al.* 1966, Spence & Taylor 1970, Stimson 1970, Williams 1971, Alexander 1972*a*). Suffice it to say that each has its disadvantages and yet each has been applied successfully to a wide range of problems; true, results may be affected by the strategy employed, but this is a matter for another study.

4-2.2   INFORMATION ANALYSIS

The statistical information analysis utilized in this study was developed, as are many clustering strategies, within the field of plant ecology (as outlined by Williams *et al.* 1966). Since that time various versions have been developed and applied with success to many classification problems (see Lambert & Williams 1966, Stimson 1970, Daly 1970, Dale *et al.* 1971). The model was originally developed as an agglomerative polythetic system and derives its name from its use of the 'information statistic' measure of group similarity. According to its authors this statistic is superior to conventional measures of group similarity (such as the correlation coefficient or euclidean distance) since it is based on probabilistic procedures; they also claim that it produced a 'more satisfactory' grouping of an ecological community on a spatial and a species level than did the conventional measures (see Williams *et al.* 1966). The statistic can be expressed in the following form:*

$$I = pn \log n - \sum_{i=1}^{p} [a_j \log a_j + (n - a_j) \log (n - a_j)],†$$

where I = amount of information,

     p = number of attributes in the population,

     n = number of individuals, there are a_j individuals possessing the jth attribute.

* *Source:* Williams *et al.* 1966:431.

† As it stands this statistic is not capable of handling truly quantitative data: it relies on a presence-or-absence matrix. While later versions of the analysis have corrected this (see Lance & Williams 1968) this weakness is more apparent than real (see § 4-3).

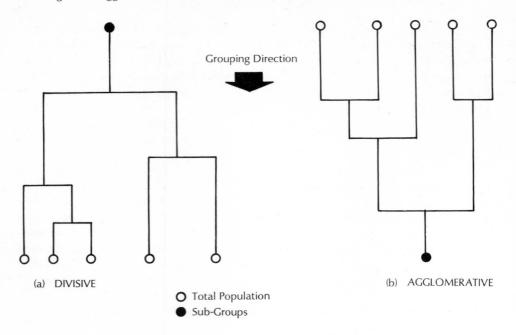

Fig. 4-6 *Agglomerative* vs *divisive strategies for classification: linkage trees*

Grouping Direction

(a) DIVISIVE

○ Total Population
● Sub-Groups

(b) AGGLOMERATIVE

Fig. 4-7 *Regionalization of Perth central area by information analysis at the general level (1968 data)*

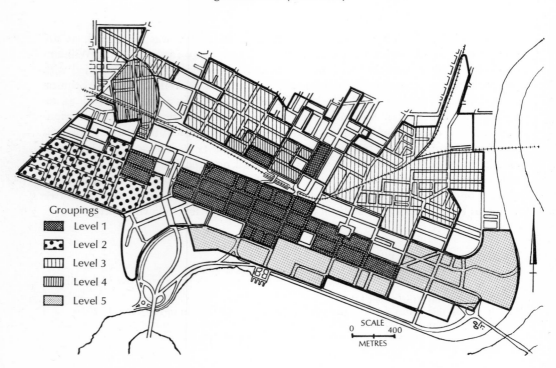

Groupings

▨	Level 1
⬡	Level 2
▥	Level 3
▦	Level 4
▨	Level 5

SCALE
0   400
METRES

The statistic thus measures the similarity between individuals (or attributes) in terms of the difference in information carried by the total population ($pn \log n$) and that carried by each of its members. In this context, information can be regarded as providing a measure of the amount of disorder (entropy) within the system; it becomes zero in the event of a completely uniform population.

The monothetic-divisive version of the analysis utilized in this study operates by dividing the population into groups on the basis of their internal similarity and external differences from the total pattern as measured by the information analysis statistic. The groups are specified by an 'indicator-attribute' which is present in all of the members; it is the attribute that carries the greatest amount of information at each level of the hierarchy. Division proceeds until the number of groups specified by the user is identified. Alternatively, it is possible to invoke a 'stopping-rule' at each stage, so that division of the population proceeds only when the information gap between the total and the sub-population is significant in terms of an equivalent X^2 measure (see Lance & Williams 1967:195). In either case, the result of the analysis is a hierarchy of groups with the information content indicating the group's relative significance within the population. Groups will be composed of either individuals (in this case areal groupings) or attributes (in this case activity types), depending on whether a normal or an inverse analysis, respectively, is enacted.

4-3 OVERALL STRUCTURE: NEW PERSPECTIVES

4-3.1 ANALYSIS AT THE GENERAL LEVEL

A test of the suitability of the information analysis strategy at the broad level is provided by its application to a total central-area data set, using a sixty-four-category classification with input by street block. Despite the relatively coarse nature of such a classification, the analysis resolved the central area into five distinct spatial regions (as shown in Fig. 4-7) which show a high degree of correspondence with the division resulting from conventional procedures (Fig. 4-1).

Perhaps the most striking feature of the division is the emergence of a central segment that corresponds to a fair extent with the boundary of the core, as originally defined in Chapter 2. The discrepancies lie first in the inclusion of peripheral areas to the north and east: these display the characteristics of the core in terms of their activity mix, although the height indices precluded them from the original definition. As we shall see in the next chapter, the zone to the east of the core was in fact one of expansion and assimilation in 1968. By 1972 it qualified as part of the core in terms of the definition criteria previously established. The other zone included as part of the 'core' in Fig. 4-7 is that area to the north-west identified in the preceding section as one overlapping the core-frame boundary. Its corroboration by the information analysis confirms that the core boundary *is* more indefinite in this area than it is elsewhere; again this appears to result from the processes of transition at work within the area (see Chapter 5). Thus the analysis clearly has potential as a tool for pointing to zones of transition and change. Furthermore, the fact that the analysis identifies a 'core' area at all, points both to its ability to identify meaningful 'regions' within the central area and to the strength of the core as a distinctive component of central-area structure.

The most coherent area to emerge from the analysis, apart from the core, is a zone to the west that corresponds closely with the previously defined professional office zone (see Figs 4-1, 4-7). Reference to the results of the inverse analysis of this data set shows that the area is identified as a zone of residential activity in combination with professional and general offices—this reflects the transition that is currently affecting the area.

The frame is further resolved into three main site groupings, which is not as detailed a 'regionalization' as achieved in the previous section in which land-use data were used (see Fig. 4-1). Nonetheless, the zone of public and cultural facilities around the core emerges clearly as a grouping (see Fig. 4-7), as do the industrial-wholesale areas to the north-west and to the north-east of the frame. Finally, the retail-service ribbon to the north of the core is also identified.

It is clear from the preceding discussion that the application of information analysis is of immense assistance in gaining a ready division of a land-use mosaic into its major components. This being the case, it is worthwhile to discuss the results of its application to the more complex data matrix within the core of the city.

4-3.2 DETAILED ANALYSES: THE CORE AREA

It has already been established beyond doubt that the core is by far the most complex segment of the central area. The intensity of land use and activity association within this core has rendered its analysis more difficult than that of the frame; the need for more objective techniques of analysis is greatest here. Hence the detailed applications of the information analysis procedure were restricted to the inner segments of Perth's centre.*

In order to shed light upon questions of vertical structure, analyses were carried out on a floor-by-floor basis in the first instance at ground, first- and second-floor levels. Analysis of the composite patterns, using data from all floor levels (including those above second) was then undertaken. Both normal and inverse analyses were carried out in all cases so that a grouping of sites within the area† and a grouping of activity types emerged from each analysis. The results of these analyses are summarized in Fig. 4-8 (a-d) and Table 4-2.

It is clear from an examination of the site groupings that the areas defined as significant areal clusters show a relatively close correspondence with the sub-regions

* Based on the individual activity categories (331) shown in Appendix II.
† As seen in Fig 4-8 (a-d), the sites were units of a grid placed over the area for purposes of analysis. The size of grid unit was chosen in the light of the capacity of the programme, and the increasing effects of 'noise' in the analysis with decreasing attribute/site content (see Alexander 1972a:96). Other orientations of the grid were tested, but that shown in Fig. 4-8 (a-d) proved the most viable.

identified (on the basis of floor area by frontage) in Fig. 4-4 (a-c, h). This correspondence is greatest in the case of ground- and all-floor analyses, although in all cases there are some significant discrepancies between the two patterns.

Table 4-2

ACTIVITY GROUPINGS RESULTING FROM INVERSE ANALYSIS OF
GROUND-FLOOR GRID (BLOCK-ORIENTED)

Group		Activity-mix
A	*Retail:*	food, furniture, newsagent, chemist
	Service:	milk bar, barber, dry cleaner
B	*Retail:*	grocery, meat, confectionery, men's clothing, women's clothing, general footwear, department store (4),* sporting goods, toys, tobacconists, photographic equipment, musical instruments, liquor bar
	Service:	beauty salon, photographer, bootmaker, optician
	Other:	sporting goods, instruments wholesale, hotel, cinema, crockery/glass wholesale
C	*Retail:*	service station
	Service:	jewellery repair, bank, hire service
	Office:	vacant, construction, manufacturing-wholesale, general business, associations (2), insurance, accountant, builder, legal, state govt.
	Other:	hall, printer, private hotel
D	*Retail:*	food (NEC),† clothing (NEC), hardware, furniture, miscellaneous, automotive sales & accessories, vacant
	Office:	travel agent, credit bureau, government (2)
	Service:	auction, hire cars, bank
	Wholesale:	textiles, clothing, leather, machinery, electr. instr., food, hardware, general
	Other:	private parking, night club, snacks
E	*Retail:*	motor cycles, machinery, bread
	Office:	estate agent, importer, engineer, medical, health service, local government
	Other:	flats, caretaker, pharmaceutical, chemicals wholesale, clothing manufacturer, clubs
F	*Retail:*	auto., marine, industrial equipment
	Other:	auto repair, panel beating, vacancy, electrical repair (2), wholesale appliances, electroplating, drama school, theatre

* Number of different departments shown in brackets
† (NEC) Not elsewhere classified

At ground level it is significant that the grouping of sites contributing most information to the overall pattern (level 1, Fig. 4-8a) delineates an area that coincides closely with the extent of the previously defined IRZ (shown in Fig. 4-4a). It was suggested that this zone is distinctive in terms of its activity content of specialist

Fig. 4-8 *Regionalization of Perth core by information analysis at the micro level (1968 data)*

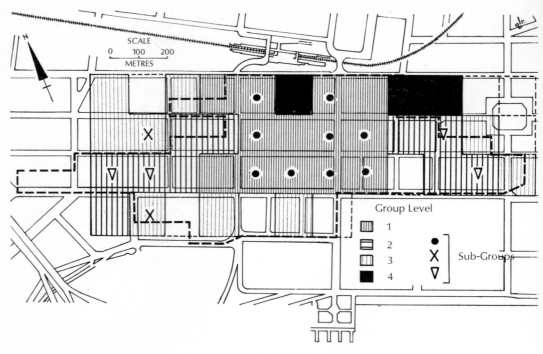

4-8a Ground floor

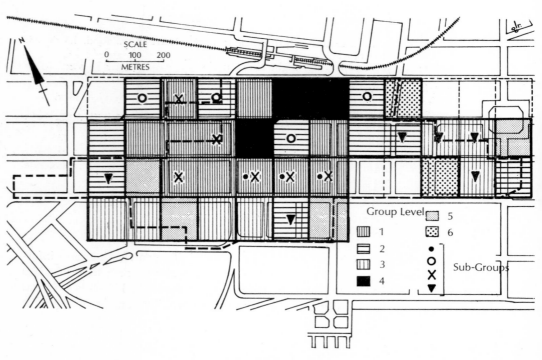

4-8b First floor

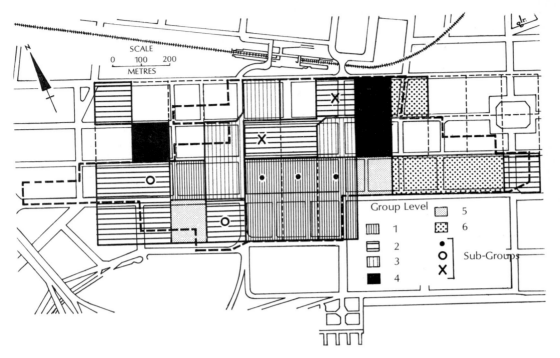

4-8c Second floor

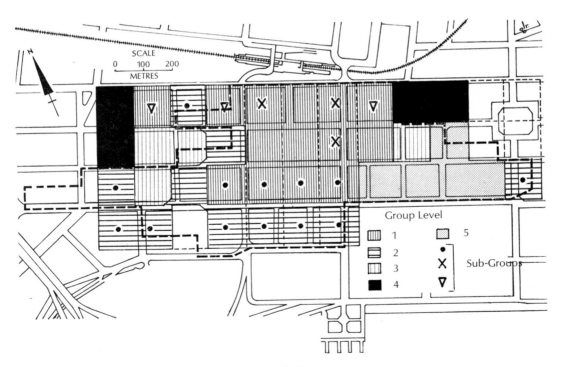

4-8d All floors

and department stores at ground level. Such a mixture of elements is shown to be a statistically significant group in the inverse analysis of the ground-floor level data set; groups A and B (Table 4-2) are representative of this area. Group B contains a strong mixture of specialist stores and dispersed elements together with certain personal-service elements. The latter two sets tend to be located towards the periphery of the area, and this is reflected by their being split from the specialist stores when the probabilistic stopping rule is invoked. Group A is also typical of peripheral retail areas. As has been pointed out (Alexander 1972a), these groupings of retail-service elements have been found to be statistically significant in other cities, thus reflecting their basic compatibility and viability as a core mix.

The other groupings of sites to emerge at ground level are slightly less coherent in terms of their correspondence with functional zones (cf. Fig. 4-8a, 4-4a), although the level 2 site-grouping approximately defines the major office areas. Group C from this area (Table 4-2) reflects this in that its main components are general and financial offices; however, the overlapping nature of the level 2 area is shown by the contents of group D, which contains a variety of peripheral retail-service elements. In this case, therefore, the coarseness of the grid structure is a limitation on the usefulness of the analysis as a key to the micro-structure of the central area.

The lower-level groupings (3 and 4, Fig. 4-8a) are sited in peripheral areas, largely outside the core boundary. As shown in Table 4-2, the representative activity groupings (E and F) contain a mixture of heavy retailing and wholesaling activities that are typical of the frame rather than the core.

However, the core-frame dichotomy is less apparent in other analyses (Fig. 4-8b-d); thus the groupings of sites correspond much less closely with boundaries drawn earlier.* Nonetheless, the level 1 site grouping at first-floor level (Fig. 4-8b) shows some correspondence with the limits of the IRZ (Fig. 4-4b), although it also extends into the wholesaling zone. But this latter phenomenon does not necessarily point to a weakness of the analysis itself, since it has already been pointed out that the presence of wholesaling and other frame-type elements increases at upper levels within the core, thus rendering the core-frame boundary less definite in this plane. Reference to the activity groupings resulting from the inverse analysis confirms this point: the groups representative of the level 1 area contain a wide mixture of wholesaling and office elements in addition to specialist retailing and personal-service elements. The question is not applicable at second-floor level, since the majority of the sites in the fringe areas are not classified as belonging to any group as they contain very few activities at this level.

Only a very small fragment of the IRZ remains at second-floor level in parts of the level 2 area; as Fig. 4-8c shows, the IRZ is grouped with an area in the eastern Terrace zone. According to the inverse analysis, it is dominated by a mixture of general offices. Indeed, in general terms, the upper-floor analyses reflect the

---

* This probably reflects the more fragmented nature of the activity pattern at upper levels. There are fewer activities present at this level, which restricts the validity of the analysis (see Alexander 1972a:96).

increasing significance of offices at these levels in comparison to retail-service activities. Thus the level 3 grouping in the first-floor analysis (Fig. 4-8b) defines segments of the Terrace general office zone, whilst the most significant (level 1) grouping at second-floor level corresponds to the 'hub'. Its contents includes a good number of the financial-legal set identified in the previous chapter. This firmly establishes the spatial significance of this set.

The composite analysis of all-floors' contents (Fig. 4-8d) provides the closest correspondence with the previously defined functional zones of all the analyses. The IRZ and the office areas in particular, are especially well defined.* However, the wholesaling/outer retailing zones are again not particularly well defined. As noted above, this is undoubtedly partly the result of the three-dimensional nature of the boundary in this zone; an analysis in one plane only cannot take account of this phenomenon. But it also points to the mixture of uses in the area. As will be seen in the next chapter there are grounds for regarding this area as the core's 'zone of discard': a zone of transition and change resulting from expansion of the core on an opposite flank (Murphy & Vance 1955).

4-3.3 CONCLUDING COMMENTS

The information analysis procedure clearly has a considerable potential as a tool for the analyses of land-use patterns. Further testing of the technique against similar strategies is obviously needed before it could in any way be claimed as 'best'. However, it can be stated with certainty that the procedure is superior to the factor analytic method both technically and practically in context of analysing land-use patterns. The data assumptions for the factor analysis model are very difficult (if not impossible) to meet where a discontinuous phenomenon such as land-use is involved. The classificatory models of the information analysis type are much more suitable for handling such data. Analysts should be wary, however, of applying such models without full knowledge of their operational characteristics and limiting assumptions. Mathematical elegance is not the only criterion by which to measure the worth of a technique.

It should also be recognized that whatever the utility of the mathematical models and the seeming viability of their results, the analysis of land-use patterns such as discussed in this chapter, should be regarded only as one aspect of the total comprehension of the nature of the city centre. It has enabled the confirmation of hypotheses concerning the polynuclear structure of the central area and has pointed to the existence of linkages within. This has clear implications for the future planning of the area, for if the structure as it currently exists is a rational one, planners should direct their efforts towards strengthening this structure and controlling processes of change in such a way as to minimize undesirable disruption. However, such processes of change cannot be effectively controlled until they are more fully comprehended; it is towards this goal that the next chapter is directed.

---

* The activity groupings from the office-dominated areas show marked similarities with those resulting from cluster analysis of the City of London (Goddard 1968).

5

Central-area dynamics

5-1 CHANGE: THE DYNAMIC ELEMENT

The city undergoes a constant change. Alterations in the composition, form and structure of the urban fabric are nowhere more evident than in the city centre, owing to its multiplicity of activities and buildings; this is borne out by the constantly fluctuating skyline of the area. In recent years one of the major concerns of planners has been the control of these processes of mutation in the name of that elusive phenomenon, the public interest. Unfortunately, this awareness of and desire to control change has not been matched by a sound understanding of the processes producing the changes:

> land use change and succession of uses which occupy units of urban space are nominees for the most cited but least understood aspects of the dynamics of urban spatial structure. [Bourne 1971:1]

Such a situation can all too easily lead to the adoption of planning policies that are to the detriment rather than the benefit of the city.

A central concern of this study has been the analysis of the patterns of land use and activity arrangement within the city centre. Previous chapters have utilized various techniques to discern major characteristics and spatial associations of these activities; explanations have been attempted in the light of functional associations and the economic competition between activities, and relationships to other variables such as pedestrian flows and traffic patterns. But this analysis presents a static view of the city centre: clearly this is incomplete in view of the dynamic nature of the area. In any case a complete understanding of structure cannot be achieved without a parallel analysis of changing patterns and of the processes inducing these changes.

The study of change, however, requires comprehensive data from successive dates if it is to proceed with accuracy; the inadequacies of subjective studies of city-centre change such as that of Preston and Griffin (1966) have already received attention (Chapter 1). Unfortunately, the complexity of the central area means that the requisite data are rarely recorded. In Perth's case, for example, there has been only one previous survey comparable to the 1968 data base used in this study.

This was carried out in preparation for the metropolitan region plan (Stephenson & Hepburn 1955). Tragically the detailed statistics have been destroyed; the only legacies remaining are a somewhat generalized land-use map (Fig. 5-1) and some broad land-use statistics for the central area. These will permit some superficial analysis of changing patterns of land use and altering composition of the area; but alone, they are clearly inadequate.

Faced with similar data problems other workers have resorted to alternative approaches. One of the most common of these is the 'directory method', whereby the changing composition of the area in question is established using data from past business directories. Such an approach was adopted originally by Ratcliff (1953) in studying the changing functional composition of central Madison, and has subsequently been used in a central-area context by several workers including Rannells (1957) in analysing Philadelphia, Pain (1967) in Auckland, Johnston (1967), and Bonhert and Mattingley (1964) in Melbourne and New York respectively. This method is useful for providing a record of the changing numbers and distribution of business establishments of differing types; but apart from its narrowness, a serious limitation (noted by Johnston 1967:183) is that it gives no indication of the changing intensity of land use. Also, the accuracy of business directory information and classifications is often open to question (Weiss 1957:17). In general it would seem that *floorspace* data provide a sounder analytical base; however, it must be remembered that even so, an analysis of functional change *per se* tells us little of the causes and mechanics of the processes involved.

Some studies have come closer to an examination of the actual process of physical change through a study of building and redevelopment activity over time. In analysing the recent office-building boom in central Sydney, Whipple (1967, 1970) approached the builders to gain data concerning value and area of buildings involved. This, however, is a tedious task and in certain cases municipal authorities collect the relevant data; thus Bourne (1967) had access to such records in Toronto, on which he was able to base a comprehensive study of private redevelopment over the period 1952-62. This underlines the fact that the quality of results depends to some extent on the quality of the data base. Some Australian capital cities are fortunate in having available similar comprehensive records of building activity— e.g. Johnston (1967) made reference to building surveyor's records in determining the location and number of buildings erected in central Melbourne since 1920. In Perth *areal* statistics are also recorded, and whilst these refer to gross rather than usable floorspace constructed, they provide a sound data base from which analysis of the patterns and type of building activity can proceed.*

* The records, kept by the Perth City Council Building Surveyor's Department, contain details of all permits issued for council and private rebuilding activity within the council's area of jurisdiction; all such building projects must have a permit before proceeding. There are also details of the location, type of building and gross floor area involved. Open car-sales yards, depots, service stations and car parks are, therefore, not included in the figures. Details of government-building projects were obtained from the Commonwealth Department of Works (Perth office) and relevant state departments.

Fig. 5-1 *Land use, Perth central area 1953.* Source: Stephenson and Hepburn 1955. (Interrupted line - - - between Pier St. and Vict. Ave indicates estimated core boundary.)

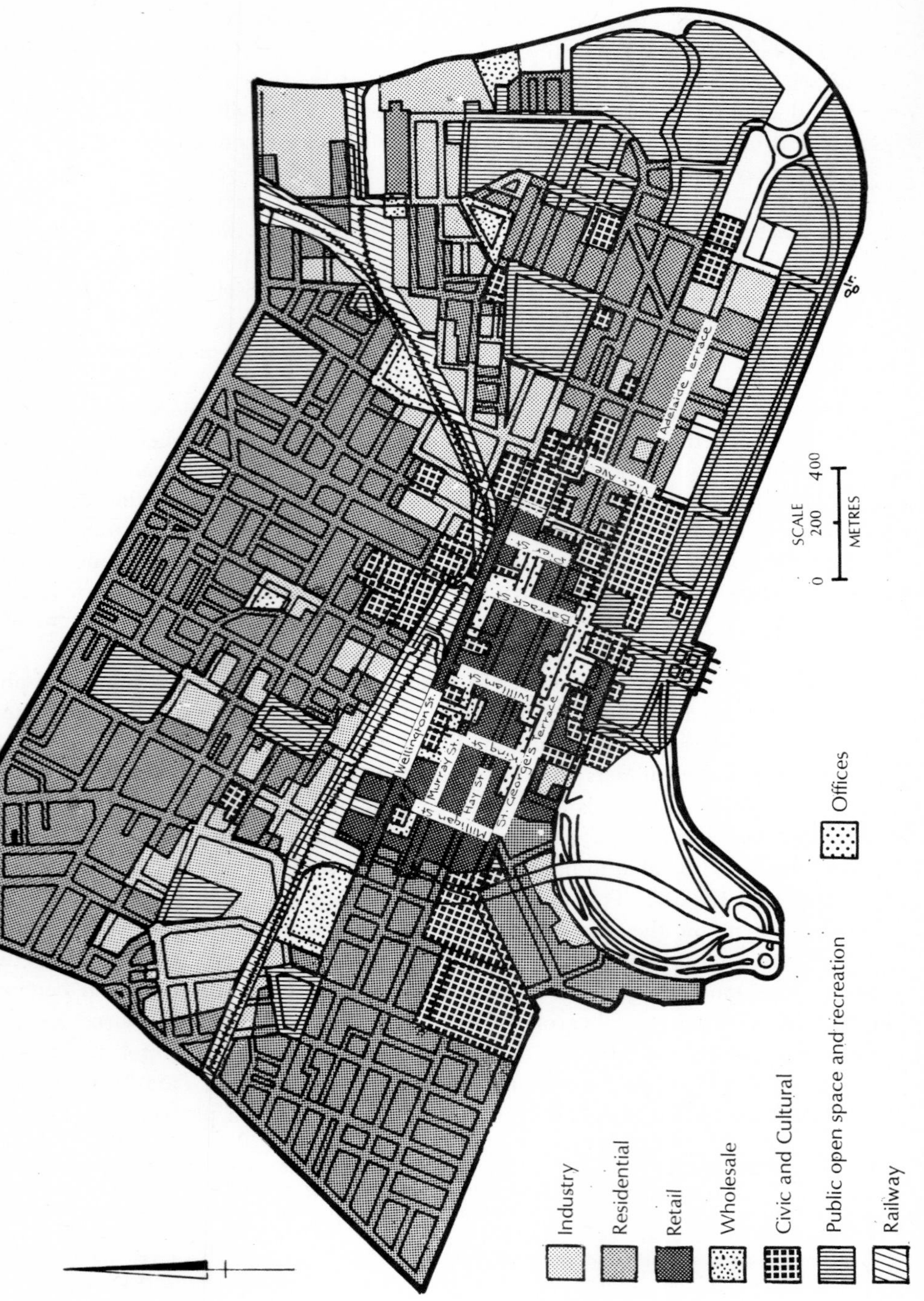

5-2 BOUNDARY MOVEMENT

Recent studies have demonstrated that central area boundaries move over time in response to changing land-use and activity patterns within the area (Bonhert & Mattingley 1964, Bowden 1971).

The studies have also shown that the concept of a 'zone of assimilation' and a 'zone of discard', occurring on opposite flanks of the core (as originally proposed by Murphy & Vance 1955; see Fig. 1-2) is valid. The concept appears to have greatest relevance in the core, and previous chapters have suggested that such zones may be identifiable in Perth. Comparison of 1953 and 1968 land-use maps (see Figs 5-1, 5-2a) confirms that the core shifted in an easterly direction over the time period, by expansion of its south-easterly office axis, and by contraction along the wholesale-heavy retail north-west periphery. A further comparison of the boundaries of Scott's retail zones (1959) with those defined on the basis of the 1968 survey throws additional light on these trends (see Figs 5-2b). Contraction of the outer retail zone is evident along the north-western flank of the core, whilst the IRZ showed some marginal expansion to the south and south-west. Developments since the 1968 survey suggest that this latter trend will continue over the next few years, as there has been a concentration of interest in retailing expansion in this area. Meanwhile, the core is continuing to shift in an easterly direction; a supplementary survey showed that there was a marked shift of the boundary between 1968 and 1973 as a result of the continued development of office towers along the Terrace axis (Fig. 5-2c).*

These trends emphasize the zonal nature of any boundaries within the centre; any linear boundary must be an approximation. However, they also point to processes of invasion and succession of land use within the area. Such processes are also evident along the outer boundary of the central area, although to a lesser extent, possibly due to the relatively stagnant nature of the frame. Over the period 1953-68 the Perth frame area expanded laterally to the west, due to the invasion of this once purely residential sector by professional offices. Some marginal expansion to the north is also evident, although the 1953 boundary seems to have been poorly placed, with little differentiation evident on either side. Minor expansion occurred over the 1968-72 period along the north-western flank due to the increase of frame-type wholesale and commercial establishments to the west of Loftus Street (see Fig. 5-2c). Development has been channelled in this direction both by permissive zoning in the vicinity, and the residential zoning to the north of the current frame boundary (Fig. 5-3). This illustrates the importance of exogenous barriers as an influence on change within the central area.

5-3 BUILDING ACTIVITY AND CHANGING LAND USE

5-3.1 OVERALL CHANGE

Comparison of the space occupied by various functions within the central area over time reveals certain trends in its evolution. London and Perth are vastly

---

* Office expansion is discussed in greater detail in § 5-3.2.

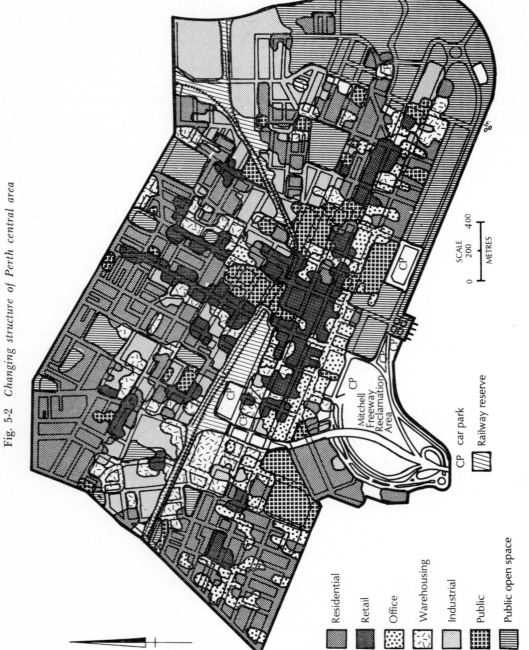

Fig. 5-2   *Changing structure of Perth central area*

Residential

Retail

Office

Warehousing

Industrial

Public

Public open space

CP   car park

Mitchell
Freeway
Reclamation
Area

CP

Railway reserve

SCALE

0   200   400

METRES

5-2a   Land use, Perth central area 1968. After Perth City Council.

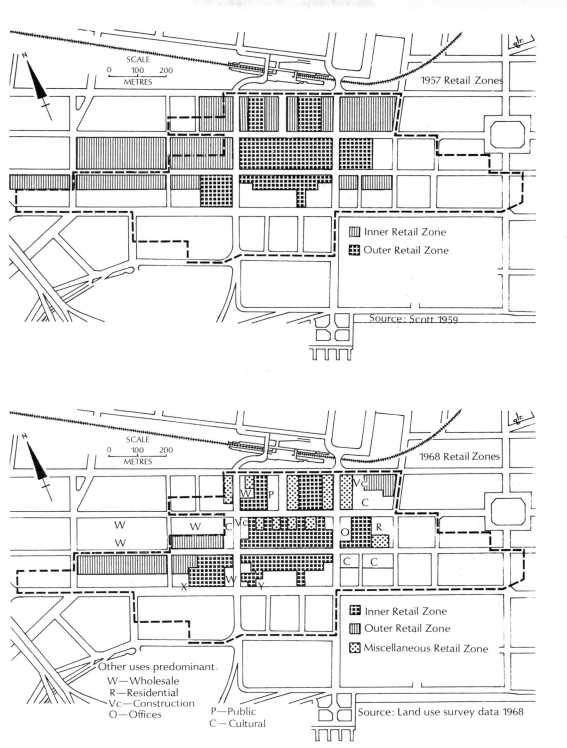

SCALE
0   100   200
METRES

1957 Retail Zones

Inner Retail Zone
Outer Retail Zone

Source: Scott 1959

SCALE
0   100   200
METRES

1968 Retail Zones

W   P
Vc
C

W   W   C   Vc
W   W
O   R
X   W   Y
C   C

Inner Retail Zone
Outer Retail Zone
Miscellaneous Retail Zone

Other uses predominant.
W—Wholesale
R—Residential
Vc—Construction   P—Public
O—Offices   C—Cultural

Source: Land use survey data 1968

5-2b   Internal boundary changes in Perth core 1959-72

Fig. 5-2 *Contd*

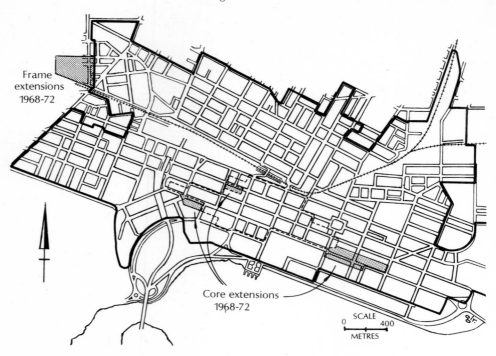

Frame extensions 1968-72

Core extensions 1968-72

SCALE
0   400
METRES

5-2c   Boundary changes, Perth central area 1968-72

different cities in terms of size, character and even function. Yet the trends in changing relative significance of various activities over time are similar—this points to the operation of similar processes of change, and underlines points made earlier concerning the possibility of generalizing about the area. The relevant figures of changing functional composition over the periods 1957-66 (for London) and 1953-68 (for Perth) are set out in Table 5-1. There has been a considerable increase in total floorspace in both cases. This is an indication of the process of intensification of land use through redevelopment, for while there has been lateral expansion of the boundaries of the central area in Perth, there was a floorspace gain of 0.5 million m² within the 1953 boundary.* Similar intensification process has also been discerned in Toronto, where Bourne (1967) found that space-intensive activities were constantly replacing space-extensive activities, since it is 'generally uneconomic' to replace an existing structure 'with anything but a more intensive use' (Bourne 1967:44). The phenomenon can be attributed to the high prices that most central-area sites command: non-intensive uses become an increasingly poor investment.

* In London the central area boundary is fixed for purposes of data collection.

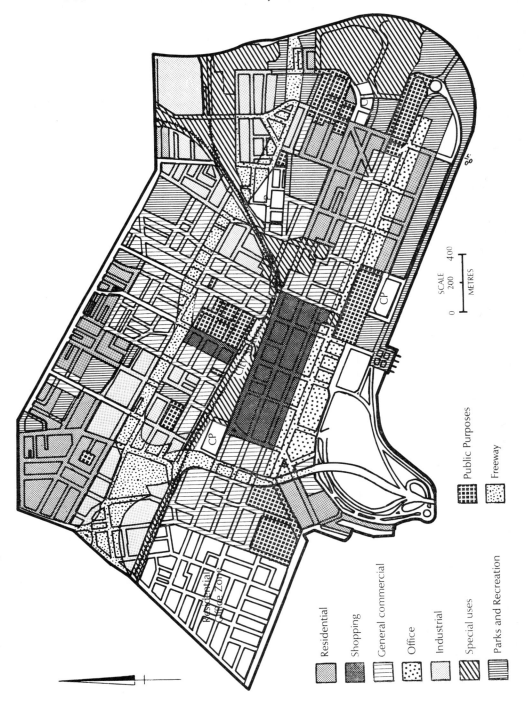

Fig. 5-3 *Proposed zoning ordinances for Perth central area 1971.* (CP = car park.)

SCALE

0   200   400

METRES

Residential

Shopping

General commercial

Office

Industrial

Special uses

Parks and Recreation

Public Purposes

Freeway

Residential Future Zone

Table 5-1

FLOORSPACE CHANGES: PERTH AND LONDON CENTRAL AREAS 1953-68, 1957-66, RESPECTIVELY

Activity	London 1957 area*	%	1966 area*	%	% trend	Perth 1953 area*	%	1968 area*	%	% trend
Office	13.61	31.64	16.68	37.03	+	0.44	20.09	0.73	24.66	+
Retail	3.30	7.67	3.20	7.10	−	0.33	15.07	0.45	15.20	++
Wholesale	3.76	8.74	3.57	7.92	−	0.18	8.22	0.32	10.81	++
Manufacture	3.19	7.42	2.47	5.48	−	0.49	22.37	0.56	18.92	−
Residential	12.74	29.62	11.81	26.22	−	0.59	26.94	0.54	18.24	−
Public & Cultural	6.41	14.90	7.31	16.20	+	0.16	7.31	0.20	6.76	−
Parking (Public)	NA	−	−	−	−	0.00	0.00	0.17	5.74	+
	43.01	100.00†	45.04	100.00†		2.19	100.00†	2.96	100.00†	

* Areas in millions m².
† Totals may not add to 100 due to rounding.

N.A. = not available

Sources: Perth: 1953—Stephenson & Hepburn 1955; 1968—Perth City Council, land-use survey data. London: Greater London Council Records.

The changing functional composition of the central areas over the time span also illustrates this process; in general terms there has been an increase in the significance of activities high in the rent-paying hierarchy at the expense of those of lower rent-paying ability. Thus offices have increased considerably in relative importance in both cities, whilst public, wholesaling and industrial activities have declined in importance (though some show absolute increases). The space devoted to residential establishments has also decreased considerably over the period, in both relative and absolute terms. Retailing provides something of an exception to the general trend: this is an activity of high rent-paying ability generally (as shown in Chapter 3), and yet it experienced a relative decrease in significance in both cities over time. This is symptomatic of the decentralization of certain types of retailing establishment, particularly those handling heavy goods, from the area. It is this phenomenon that has caused the lateral contraction of Perth's core in recent years (see Chapter 3).

In general terms, however, there appears to be a process of land-use succession operating, which is gradually diminishing the areal importance of activities that have a low productivity/space ratio and cannot afford to continue occupying expensive central-area sites. Analogical trends were discovered in Toronto by Bourne (1967) and by Ratcliff (1953) in Madison. Indeed it is an expected outcome of the competition for land that occurs between activities in the land market. Whether it is a desirable trend seems open to serious question, for the importance of certain economic activities of low rent-paying ability and of non-profit oriented uses in the city centre has already been demonstrated. The costs and benefits of methods of protecting such activities are discussed in § 5-4.

Observations concerning the changing functional composition of the centre are substantiated in Perth's case by reference to the relative importance of various types of building (commenced) in the central area over the time period 1954-72. As shown in Table 5-2 and Fig. 5-4, offices are the leading activity (in terms of floorspace) in all years except five: on an overall basis they account for over half (59%) of the floorspace constructed over the time period. In recent years this proportion reaches as high as 80% (see Table 5-2). On the other hand, other uses—manufacturing, wholesaling, retailing and residential—show a decline in importance over the years, the trend particularly marked since 1960.

Economic competition between activities for space within the city centre, then, is clearly an important factor contributing to the trends of change and increasing specialization. With regard to office development, however, exogenous factors must also be considered. In the case of Perth, an upsurge of economic growth during the 1960s was an important spur to the redevelopment of offices in the central area. Development in northern Western Australia, mainly in the form of mineral extraction, processing and export, led to an upsurge of investment in building activity throughout the metropolitan region. The demand for office space has grown particularly rapidly, as most new companies established their headquarters in Perth, invariably in the centre, where locational advantages were perceived to be greatest. This led to an increased demand for office-based service activities such as banking

Table 5-2

BUILDING CONSTRUCTION, PERTH CENTRAL AREA 1954-72 (INCLUSIVE)

Year	Residential area*	%	Retail service area	%	Office area	%	Wholesale area	%	Manufacture area	%	Public-cultural area	%	Total area	%
1954	43	14.9	24	8.4	118	40.8	53	18.5	43	14.8	8	2.6	289	100.0
1955	52	18.6	37	13.1	37	13.2	72	25.5	68	24.3	15	5.3	281	100.0
1956	9	2.2	70	17.1	184	44.9	76	18.5	63	15.5	8	1.9	410	100.0
1957	22	9.6	35	15.4	47	20.6	49	21.5	75	32.9	—	—	228	100.0
1958	47	6.0	24	3.0	371	47.0	46	5.8	48	6.1	253	32.1	789	100.0
1959	40	12.6	32	10.1	123	38.7	42	13.2	47	14.8	34	10.7	318	100.0
1960	86	14.9	76	13.1	139	24.0	24	4.1	12	2.1	241	41.7	578	100.0
1961	47	7.8	12	2.0	233	38.5	14	2.3	15	2.5	284	46.9	605	100.0
1962	56	23.2	17	7.1	12	5.3	54	22.6	23	9.6	77	32.2	239	100.0
1963	55	6.6	187	22.3	511	61.0	55	6.5	20	2.3	10	1.3	838	100.0
1964	107	35.6	19	6.3	79	26.3	54	18.0	15	5.0	26	8.7	300	100.0
1965	76	16.8	141	31.1	171	37.6	53	11.7	6	1.3	7	1.6	454	100.0
1966	27	4.3	22	3.5	405	63.7	30	4.7	20	3.7	132	20.8	636	100.0
1967	41	2.6	10	0.6	1 123	72.0	35	2.3	31	2.0	319	20.5	1 559	100.0
1968	216	12.8	60	3.6	1 168	69.3	114	6.8	40	2.4	93	5.5	1 686	100.0
1969	231	10.7	86	39.6	1 281	59.5	83	3.9	119	5.6	354	16.5	2 154	100.0
1970	241	9.4	147	5.7	1 660	64.5	62	2.4	50	1.9	412	16.0	2 572	100.0
1971	144	14.1	29	2.8	682	66.6	106	10.4	29	2.8	34	3.3	1 024	100.0
1972	—	0.0	39	3.4	916	79.1	39	3.4	18	1.5	146	12.6	1 158	100.0
Total	1 540	9.55	1 067	6.61	9 255	57.42	1 061	6.58	742	4.60	2 453	15.21	16 118	100.0

Source: Perth City Council Building Surveyor's records extracts.

* In hundreds m² (gross floorspace).

Fig. 5-4 *Construction activity, Perth central area 1954-72*

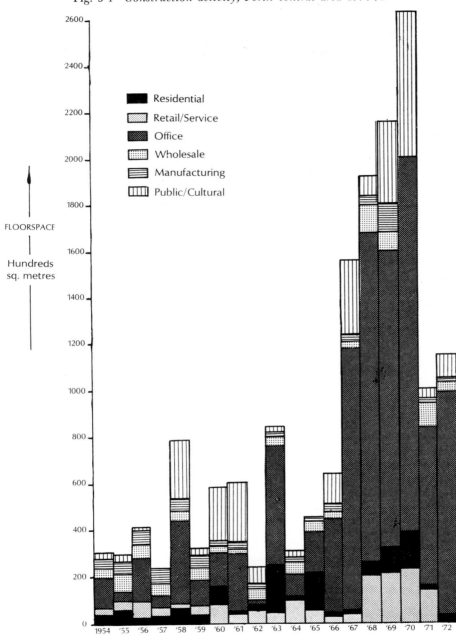

and insurance, stockbroking, legal advice, accounting and government services. The spectacular rise of the graph during the late sixties is indicative of the far-reaching effects of the economic boom; the impact on the skyline of the city has been dramatic (see Plates XII, XIII). However, by 1970 many of the new offices were finding it difficult to lease space, and a temporary over-supply still prevailed at the time of writing.

It would be incorrect to imply, however, that Perth is unique in experiencing an office boom in recent years. The general trend towards increased office development in many city centres has received attention earlier (Chapter 1), and recent studies have shown that other Australian capital cities are also undergoing considerable central office expansion (see Linge 1967, Whipple 1970, Manning 1967, Johnston 1967). This points to the operation of factors at a national level (as suggested by Archer 1967:279) as also relevant to an explanation of the boom. This hypothesis receives some confirmation from a comparison of the cycle of office building completed over the period 1954-70 in Perth and Sydney (see Fig. 5-5).* Although the gross amount of space constructed in Sydney is well above that for Perth in most years, the two cities show some correlation over time. Such evidence places some doubt on the contention that the completion of office space in Sydney has been 'random' over the period (Whipple 1970:5.32). This renders the possibility of constructing a predictive model of office construction, taking into account both local and national factors, at least worthy of further investigation.

A recent attempt in this direction is reported in Cowan et al. (1969). These workers were able to construct a relatively accurate simulation of the spatial and temporal pattern of office development in London over the period 1957-62; probabilistic procedures were used as a base. However, the model took no direct account of external economic factors or of the operation of the land market, simply assuming that the pattern of construction was related to the existing distribution of office space, the relative accessibility of various locations and the availability of planning permissions. The authors recognize that other factors are at work, but their failure to account for them renders the model a particularly dubious base for predictive purposes. Nevertheless, it is an advance on purely notional procedures, and in combination with other approaches could prove a useful tool in the future. These points are taken up in § 5-3.8.

Apart from such considerations, the trends of building activity also have spatial manifestations, and attention is now turned in that direction, with each major activity being examined in turn. An attempt will be made to assess the implications of such trends for the planning of the area's future structure; too often analyses are content to accept the patterns examined without stopping to question their desirability. Small wonder that much planning of such development to date has often been on a completely *ad hoc* basis.

---

* For purposes of these calculations in Perth, it was assumed that the average time period for the construction of new office buildings was eighteen months. Fig. 5-4, on the other hand, refers to commencement dates.

Fig. 5-5   *Office construction, Perth* vs *Sydney 1954-70*

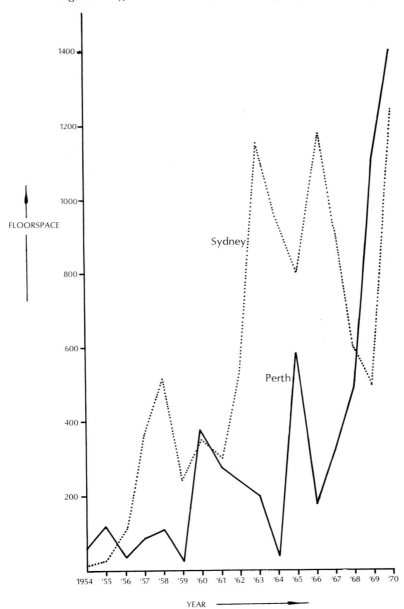

5-3.2   OFFICE DEVELOPMENT

The expansion of offices in central Perth over the period 1954-72 has taken place predominantly as redevelopment of existing office areas in the core; however, there has also been considerable invasion of formerly non-office areas to the east and west of the core. In terms of the area's structure, these trends have resulted in the intensification of land use within the core, the extension of core boundaries, and the establishment of an office node within the frame.

Redevelopment of existing office areas

The predominance of the St George Terrace area as an office zone in the core has been reinforced by redevelopment since 1953: approximately 60% of all office construction in the central area was located in the Terrace. Whilst the number of projects has not been so great as in other sections of the area, those office blocks that have been constructed have invariably been over ten floors in height, with leasable areas of well over 10 000 m² being common. This type of development has drastically altered the appearance of the areas involved, and the central sections of the area are rapidly becoming canyon-like in character to the ground-level observer, although they afford their occupants unrivalled views over the river. Indeed, the proximity of the Terrace axis to the river has undoubtedly been a factor encouraging office development to concentrate there. The developers are also aware of the prestige of a Terrace address—this could perhaps be likened to the kudos attached to a City address in London. Planners have endorsed such desires in zoning the Terrace area as the core's primary office zone (see Fig. 5-3), and allowing bonus plot ratios (of up to 20%)* if certain concessions such as the provision of public space on the site are made by the developers. Such ratios have meant that it has generally been more than economic for developers to rebuild on a site-by-site basis. This is in contrast to London and Sydney, where amalgamation is becoming increasingly common (Cowan *et al.* 1969, Archer 1967). However, Perth may soon also witness this process as redevelopment moves into the mixed-use areas north of the Terrace, where sites are smaller.

Redevelopment has centred on the hub of the office area, rather than to the west, and this is reflected in differential rises in land values over the period—50%-70% in the hub area, as against 25%-50% in western sections (see Fig. 5-6). Much of the more recent development, however, has been concentrated first in the western sections of the core and then in the eastern segments of the Terrace and beyond. Latest projects have again centred on the hub area. The spatial development of offices has, therefore, tended to move in definite cycles. This contrasts with the situation in central Sydney, where redevelopment within the core has exhibited 'few spatial shifts since 1964' (Whipple 1970:3.48). However, Bourne (1967:174) found spatial clustering of redevelopment over time in Toronto, which he attributes

---

* Plot ratio is an expression relating the maximum allowable floor area of a building to the area of the site upon which it is constructed. In the Terrace the current plot ratio is 5.0 plus 1.0 bonus (see § 5-3.7).

Fig. 5-6 *Land value changes, Perth central area 1954-68*

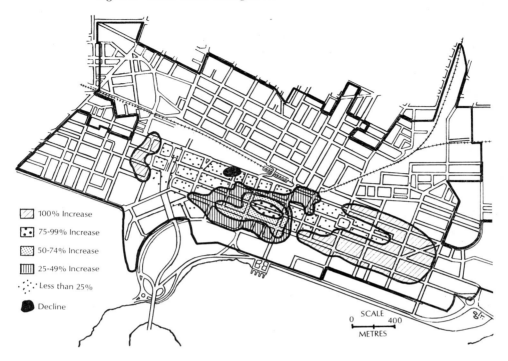

to the 'catalytic reaction of one major redevelopment project in attracting others'. He also notes that

> once selected, an area receives the concentrated efforts of developers until its relative potential is exhausted. Activity then shifts to another location and the process is repeated. [Bourne 1967:175]

Extension of the core

At the time of the 1953 land-use survey, offices within Perth's central area were mostly confined to the central sections of the core (see Fig. 5-1). It was noted at that time, however, that offices were already beginning to spread eastwards along the Adelaide Terrace axis (Stephenson & Hepburn 1955:182). As predicted, this trend has continued, particularly strongly since 1960, and by 1972 faceless office towers occupied much of the frontage of both Adelaide and St George Terrace, east of the estimated 1953 core boundary (at Pier St., Fig. 5-1). This phenomenon of the spread of offices into formerly non-core areas has been noted in other cities including Sydney; here Whipple (1967:262) has rather weakly commented that it 'implies certain trends in the evolution of central area structure'. More specifically it shows that the core may still be in process of extending its boundaries laterally by way of office expansion. This is contrary to the claims of Preston and Griffin

(1966) who suggest that lateral expansion of the core is a thing of the past. As indicated earlier, the process confirms the existence of a 'zone of assimilation' or advancing front of the core. Murphy and Vance (1955) propounded that this zone is characterized by prestige retail and office outlets. Whilst this does not appear to be the case in Perth or Sydney, there is no doubt that the zone is advancing into former residential areas.

The above process commences with the piecemeal conversion of single-family dwellings, duplexes and terrace housing, and other uses of lower rent-paying ability, into temporary office accommodation. As the demand for more 'economic' use of these sites rise, such a course gives way to demolition and rebuilding on a scale typical of other core office areas; this completes the process of land-use succession that has already been noted as the main cause of the altering functional composition of the core over time.

Perth's zone of assimilation takes the form of a definitely linear axis, and it might be suggested that this is an example of axial development as outlined by Hoyt (1939; see Chapter 1). There is no doubt that the Terrace spine has acted as a magnet to new office developments; however, it must also be noted that other encouraging factors have also been at work. The nodes of public/cultural activities to the north-east and south of the core have acted as barriers to expansion in these directions; thus, easterly expansion was almost bound to be channelled along the Terrace axis. Such trends, once initiated by the land market, have also been encouraged by zoning ordinances which have restricted offices to specific areas as shown in Fig. 5-3. Another factor that has advanced the linear development of offices is the apparently repelling effect of the core's wholesaling and heavy-retailing area to the north-west; as hinted earlier, this area can be regarded as the core's 'zone of discard'. The current environment of this area is clearly not attractive to developers seeking to create 'prestige' accommodation, and the zoning of the area is primarily for retailing. The logic of this will be questioned further in § 5-3.3. Suffice it to say here that the continuing march of office towers along the Terrace axis has had the effect of creating a somewhat elongated office zone that may not be in the best interests of either the tenants of the peripheral blocks or their employees: the tenants are placed away from the major concentration of offices in the core's central sections, whilst the employees are no longer within easy walking distance of the shopping zones of the core.

Given this, the proposed Perth City Council policy of extending the office zone 'over the whole length of the Terrace' (Perth City Council 1971b:98) seems rather questionable. A consolidation of the zone might not pander to the developer's desires to extract maximum returns from so-called prestige developments (that more often than not turn out to be architectural horrors in the interests of economy— Plate X). But it would recognize the requirements of accessibility to other core functions, and would appear to be in the best interests of centre as a whole. The linear extension policy will only further encourage the fragmentation of development caused by the site-by-site redevelopment process; if there is to be any hope of co-ordinating these developments, it would be considerably more feasible within a consolidated office zone.

The rise of the professional office zone

The migration of offices from the core to the frame of the central area is a process noted in many cities in recent years. Horwood and Boyce (1959) suggested that a node of special services—they cite medical services as an example—was typical of frame areas (as illustrated in Fig. 1-1); subsequent investigations by McNair (1960) in Seattle, Merriman (1967) in Christchurch, Pain (1967) in Auckland, Johnston (1967) in Melbourne, Cowan *et al.* (1969) in London, Alexander (1970) and Kemp (1972) in Perth have confirmed this hypothesis.

It has already been shown that the major proportion of recent office development in Perth has taken place within the core and its extensions. However, office development in the western frame area, mainly in the form of professional offices (particularly since 1960), has also been a significant feature of the area's evolution. Although this only accounts for 5% of total constructions since 1954, it amounts almost to 15% of new *office* space within the centre. In any case, this understates the strength of the invasion of the area by offices, for the predominant process has been conversion rather than redevelopment. Where redevelopment has occurred, new office buildings are limited to three or four floors at the most: this is largely a response to the limiting plot ratio of 1.33 that has been imposed by the Perth City Council, but the development seems typical of the frame rather than the core. As already noted, the invasion has had the effect of fragmenting the previous land-use pattern: in 1953 the area was almost purely residential, but by 1972 offices occupied almost half of the zone's floorspace (see Figs 5-1, 5-2a). Zoning of the area for 'flats and professional chambers' ensures the continued development of the area for these purposes.

The move of offices into the area has been by no means constant over time; prior to 1960 only twenty projects involving conversion, extension or construction of new premises occurred; since that time, however, a further 114 projects (involving forty-five new office blocks) have been carried out, reaching a peak in the 1969-71 period (see Fig. 5-7).* Such a fluctuation over time has been observed in similar locational shifts of offices. It was noted by McNair (1960) that the movement of medicos into the emerging medical-service area in Seattle's frame tended to accelerate over time. A similar trend has occurred in Christchurch, where Merriman (1967) analysed the move of professional offices from the core to the frame over the 1955-65 period. These accelerations appear to be the result of a 'snowballing' effect: the movement grows stronger as the advantages of the receiving area become more widely known and as tenants complete end of lease negotiations in the core. Kemp 1972:71) suggests that there is a 'take-off-point' after which relocation is drastically

---

* Recent research (carried out by Kemp 1972) has shown that the annual number of firms locating in the area has dropped from a peak in 1970; this is held to be due to rising diseconomies in the area.

Fig. 5-7   *Construction of professional offices, West Perth 1954-72*

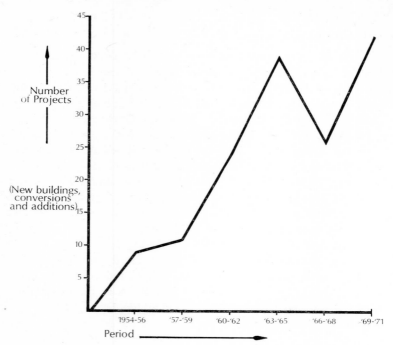

accelerated. This point appears to have been reached in 1960 in Perth's case (see Fig. 5-7).

In Perth the main professionals involved in the move have been doctors, accountants, architects and engineers, and surveyors. A sprinkling of footloose general offices has also been involved, although the type of offices allowed to locate in the area is now fairly strictly defined in the council zoning regulations. Most have migrated from the core, but some have commenced operations within the zone and some have originated from outside the study area.*

A recent survey of a similar office movement in Christchurch (Merriman 1967) found that the major reasons causing relocations were lack of parking space in the core, congestion and rising land values, as well as the pull of functional linkages exerted by the relocating firms on those remaining in the core. Such reasons would also seem applicable in Perth, particularly in view of the fact that professional offices also constituted a large proportion of the movers in Christchurch. However, the recent detailed survey carried out by Kemp (1972) in Perth showed that while parking stress was the 'most substantial' push from the core, increasing space

* Substantiated from reference to registers of Australian Medical Association and Institute of Architects (W.A. chapter), and by recent questionnaire survey (Kemp 1972:26).

requirements were also significant and, contrary to popular opinion, accommodation costs were generally an insignificant 'push factor'. As Kemp points out, this
finding illustrates the danger of leaping to false conclusions on the basis of superficial analysis: a cursory examination of changing land values in Perth's central
area over the time period (see Fig. 5-6) could suggest that rising rents in the core
were an important relocation factor for firms moving to the frame. Thus the suggestions of Cowan *et al.* (1969:90) that offices of lesser rent-paying ability are
constantly being forced from the central area core to peripheral locations are clearly
not applicable in this case. Nevertheless, offices invading frame areas are themselves
universally replacing activities of lower rent-paying ability (predominantly residential), thus contributing to the declining significance of such activities within the
centre. Furthermore, core areas vacated by decentralizing offices are being gradually
redeveloped for more intensive office uses.

Implications for planning

Office expansion within Perth's central area in recent years has been shown to be
occurring in three distinct ways: through redevelopment of existing office areas,
extension of the core into former frame areas, and the relocation of certain types
of offices from the core to the frame. Such trends have also been identified in
several other cities and thus appear symptomatic of generally increasing intensity
of office functions within the city centre (as suggested by Cowan *et al.* 1969). This
is not to deny that some offices are also leaving the centre in favour of outlying
locations: this tendency has been shown to be increasing in strength in many United
States and British cities (see e.g. Horwood & Boyce 1959, Hoyt 1964, Location of
Offices Bureau 1964, 1969). However, redevelopment is ensuring the continuance
of offices as an important central function in most cities. This process is occurring
at the expense of less-intensive activities, and whilst it does not point to their demise,
it does illustrate that competition between uses has an effect upon the functional
composition of the centre. Such trends have often been abhorred by planners, but
their remedies have proved ineffective. Intervention has either taken the form of
arbitrary zoning that tends to sterilize the land-use pattern, or attempts at comprehensive redevelopment that have often produced apparently worse solutions than
would have occurred through 'non-planning'. Such points are discussed further in
§ 5-4.

5-3.3   RETAIL-SERVICE DEVELOPMENT

In contrast to the manifestations of office development, few changes in the
overall distribution of retail-service activities within the Perth central area are
evident from a comparison of 1953 and 1968 land-use patterns (see Figs 5-1, 5-2a).
This no doubt partly reflects the declining importance of these activities within the
city centre; over the time period (to 1972) only 1.0 million m² have been added
to the stock of retail-service premises, and to 1968 the nett space increase was 36%
(see Table 5-1). In all, the retail-service space constructed over the time accounts

for 16% of the total (Table 5-2, Fig. 5-4).* Offices, on the other hand, account for over half the new space, and show a nett space increase of 66% to 1968.

One of the few changes in the locational pattern of retail-service activities that is discernible over the time span is the establishment of groups of automotive-oriented and heavy-retail establishments on the northern, eastern and western peripheries of the central area. These nodes (whose composition has already been analysed in Chapter 2), appear to have originated partly through the relocation from their former positions close to the core (as illustrated in Fig. 5-1), and partly from the establishment of new premises (in response to rising car ownership) at strategic locations on major traffic arteries leading to the core. The relocation appears to have been due partially to the relative lack of rent-paying ability of the activities (according to Stephenson & Hepburn 1955:160). However, it must also be noted that the area to the west of the core from where they originated has been zoned for 'shopping' purposes since 1964; this designation excludes car sales and service establishments. The city council has taken little direct action against existing non-conforming uses (indeed provision is made for them to be recognized as 'legal' under new zoning provisions). But the mere existence of this zoning and the difficulty of gaining permission for expansion or rebuilding, clearly increases the pressure on such uses. This, coupled with the zoning of peripheral areas for 'showrooms', will have encouraged outward movement of these premises. As with offices therefore, relocation has resulted from a combination of pressures at existing sites (centrifugal forces in Colby's terms; see § 1-2.4) and attractive conditions at peripheral sites. These movements well illustrate the dynamic nature of the central-area land-use pattern.

Apart from the building activity associated with these peripheral nodes, the bulk of retail-service development has occurred within a limited tract of the central-area core in the IRZ (cf. Chapters 3, 4), where new variety and departmental stores and three new shopping arcades have been erected. These projects represent approximately 65% of all retail-service construction over the time span, and account for the bulk of large-scale redevelopment within the IRZ. In this respect, however, it must be recognized that redevelopment is not the only structural improvement that occurs in city-centre buildings. Retailers have preferred in the main to carry out minor internal improvements (e.g. the installation of escalators in department stores) and renew frontages only, in preference to wholesale rebuilding, which is in any case a difficult operation given the continual trading process and the problems of temporary relocation. Office tenants are much more mobile in this respect; furthermore, most office-based firms have been able to locate in speculatively-built office premises, the equivalent of which is much rarer for retailers.

Thus the lack of rebuilding activity in the retail sections of the central area does not necessarily signify decline, although the trade transacted in the centre has

---

* However, it must be pointed out that this figure for retail-service activities undoubtedly under-represents the true total since the Building Surveyor's records do not include certain 'automotive' activities (see footnote on p. 131). Moreover, there have been a large number of improvements, as opposed to redevelopment projects, in retail premises over the period.

shown a relative decline in recent years (as shown in Appendix IV). An analysis of the spatial distribution of shop-front renewals over the time period, similar to that carried out in Utrecht by Buissink and de Widt (1967), shows that renewal has been concentrated in particular areas, and this gives some indication of the state of these components in terms of their viability. As shown in Fig. 5-8, the frontages that have received most attention in terms of renewal are concenrated in the IRZ, where the core's specialist retail and departmental facilities are located. On the other hand, the frontages receiving little or no attention correlate with the outer sections of the retail area. The changes in land values over the time period (Fig. 5-6) reflect these trends for they have risen by up to 75% in the IRZ, whilst those in the outer segments have shown more moderate increases of a maximum 25%. The areas on the periphery (many of which have seen no renewal activity and land-value increase at all) coincide with the portions of the core that have been suggested as its zone of discard through the static analysis. This area was seen to have higher than average vacancy rates and poorly-maintained structures housing marginal and 'low-grade' retail concerns such as disposal shops, auction rooms and second-hand bookshops. The fact that little or no renewal activity has occurred in the area confirms that the area is in a state of decay and this together with the contraction of core boundaries, labels the area as a true 'zone of discard'.

This spatial differentiation in renewal activity corresponds to the situation in Utrecht, where it was found that renewal activity increased towards the central sections of the retail area (Buissink and de Widt 1967:255). In Perth, the retailing area has undergone contraction and has become blighted in its western and north-eastern sections; renewal has concentrated on the prime locations of the IRZ. These trends are in contrast to those claimed to be operating in the early 1950s, when it was suggested that the retailing area was *expanding* in a westerly direction and predicted that this was likely to continue (Stephenson & Hepburn 1955). Significantly, these judgements were made on the basis of a purely subjective analysis and hence are suspect. This renders the recommendation of the zoning of a large area to the west of the retail core for shopping purposes doubly questionable, and the incorporation of this recommendation in 1963 and 1971 zoning ordinances completely inappropriate. In total, this zoning makes an allowance for some 1.1 million m² of retail space within the core, a figure which is clearly excessive in the light of the generally declining significance of retailing within the central area. The retailing space within the core grew from 0.33 million to 0.45 million m² between 1953 and 1968 (Table 5-1), still well under half of the allowed space; furthermore, as we have seen, this expansion had generally occurred within the existing retailing areas rather than in the north-west, where spatial *contraction* occurred.*

Another unfortunate by-product of the zoning of this area for shopping purposes is that it threatens the future of the existing wholesaling premises. This activity is

---

* As noted in § 5-2, however, future core retailing development seems likely to occur to the south-west of the existing IRZ. This may eventually 'regenerate' the entire western sector of the core.

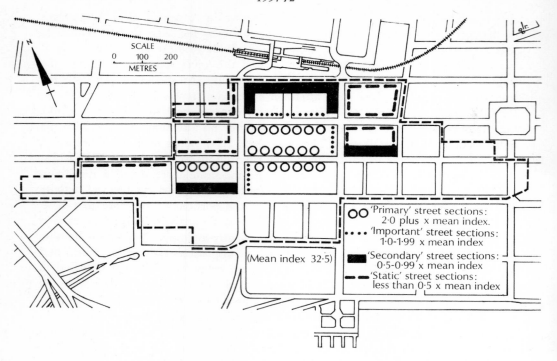

Fig. 5-8   *Classification of renewal activity in retail segments of Perth core*
1954-72

SCALE
0   100   200
METRES

(Mean index 32·5)

OO 'Primary' street sections:
2·0 plus x mean index.

···· 'Important' street sections:
1·0-1·99 x mean index

■ 'Secondary' street sections:
0·5-0·99 x mean index

▬ ▬ 'Static' street sections:
less than 0·5 x mean index

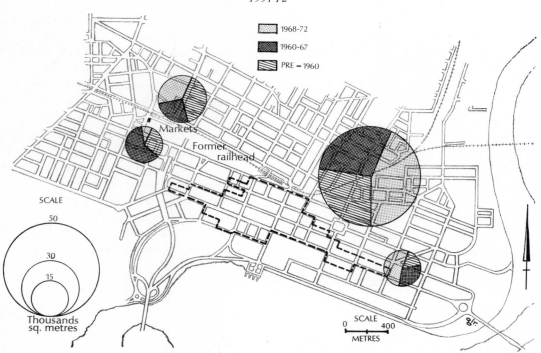

Fig. 5-9   *Spatial movement of wholesaling construction, Perth central area*
1954-72

1968-72
1960-67
PRE — 1960

Markets
Former
railhead

SCALE
50
30
15
Thousands
sq. metres

SCALE
0   400
METRES

currently spatially dominant in this zone although in theory it is only permitted as a subsidiary use. Although no action is contemplated against non-conforming uses, the zoning precludes large-scale redevelopment for wholesaling purposes. The Perth City Council (1971*b*) argues that there is in any case declining demand for whole-saling space within this portion of the central area, and it is certainly true that most central wholesaling development in recent years has occurred in outer portions (see § 5-3.4). It is also true that a number of wholesalers have vacated the area recently because of the unsuitability of the area and its environment (Wolinski 1970; see Plate VIIb). However, few structures have been left vacant after such moves, and in any case some firms cited unsuitable zoning as a reason for moving. Thus inappropriate zoning, based on imperfect understanding of the nature of changes affecting the area, has contributed to its stagnation. There may be a need for some redevelopment in this area, but since the incentive for the construction of retailing premises is clearly lacking, rezoning is a necessary prerequisite to the regeneration of the area.

But the stagnation of the area and its gradual blighting should not necessarily be regarded as undesirable *per se*. Areas of decline within city centres, whilst often in need of physical restructuring—and here it must be admitted that the zone in question in Perth has a layout that makes access difficult—may in fact house a rich diversity of activities that have adapted the premises to suit their needs. Firms seeking a central location (because of links with other central-area activities) and low-cost premises are naturally attracted to older buildings, that for various reasons have been abandoned by their original users. An excellent example of this process of building adaptation is found in the Covent Garden area of central London: here a host of small firms operating on limited budgets (and thus priced out of new premises) have located in older buildings that have been abandoned by their former occupants, mainly wholesalers and small-scale industries. Many of the new occupants are of an experimental or 'arts-oriented' nature, such as film studios, small galleries, theatrical suppliers and agents, and small publishing firms. Together with the area's more traditional uses (mainly connected with the wholesale vegetable and fruit market which is being relocated in 1974), these activities add diversity and character not only to the immediate area, but also to the total central-area activity mix. Redevelopment of such areas threatens these activities with extinction, for they cannot afford to rent space in newer buildings and, given their close links with nearby activities, suitably located alternative premises are almost impossible to find. Perth has not yet reached a size where the diversity of activities evident in London's central area could be expected; yet it may be that in seeking to 'regenerate' or redevelop all the so-called blighted areas, these activities will never be given the opportunity to develop. Significantly, one of Perth's most diverse activity mixes is found in the retail-service area to the north of the core (see Chapter 2), where, from a design point of view, redevelopment might be perceived as an urgent need.

In the case of Perth's zone of discard and the adjacent wholesaling area, rezoning should take account of the necessity for maintaining and encouraging the develop-ment of a variety of building stock within which activities can develop. Thus rezoning should not be for any one use, for whilst single-use zoning has the advantage of simplicity, it encourages a somewhat sterile environment. The city council states in its latest plan proposals (1971*b*) that it wishes to avoid 'the complexites that mixed development inevitably brings', an incredibly narrow argument, for mixed development is precisely the factor that gives the central area its unique flavour and excitement. Admittedly private profit-oriented redevelopment is eroding this aspect of the area's character, but for the planning authority to encourage the trend is criminal, particularly when one of its stated goals is 'promotion and maintenance of a healthy, safe and pleasant environment' (Perth City Council 1971*b*:1).

It should be noted that the criticisms of the zoning of the Perth central area for future retail-service expansion have been based on an analysis of the processes of change that are constantly at work, shaping the land-use pattern. It appears that the planning authorities have ignored these processes and have relied too heavily on outdated projections of space requirements and rather unimaginative zoning ordinances in producing their proposals. This has contributed to the stagnation of certain sections of the central area, and is clearly at odds with both the planners' intentions and the public interest.

5-3.4 WHOLESALING DEVELOPMENT

It has already been noted that wholesaling is amongst those activities that are declining in significance as a central-area function, as the competition for space intensifies. It was pointed out in Chapter 2 that by nature many wholesalers require large premises with abundant ground-level floorspace to handle bulky goods: this renders them unsuitable activities for areas of intense land use, which are in any case becoming increasingly congested. Thus many wholesalers are relocating away from the centre completely; others, however, still find the outer areas of the frame a suitable location since it continues to retain the advantages of centrality and easy access to the core, whilst offering more spacious and cheaper sites. For those handling less-bulky goods, such as clothing and textiles, a core or inner-frame location may still be suitable—as seen earlier, a node of such wholesalers is found in close proximity to the core in many cities.

These factors help to elucidate the spatial distribution of wholesaling construction in the Perth central area since 1954. New construction has been confined largely to the outer-sections of the frame,* particularly in locations north of the railway-Wellington Street axis (see Fig. 5-9); this indicates the contemporary inability of wholesalers to compete for sites for new or replacement buildings in prime sites. However, as already noted, the zoning of the centre precludes new construction in the inner portions of the area (see Fig. 5-3), particularly from the existing zone of concentrated wholesaling close to the core. This provides a partial explanation for the lack of wholesaling construction in these areas; yet it must be

---

* A considerable amount of wholesaling space has been constructed recently along major traffic arteries close to the outer frame. Such sites combine the advantage of accessibility, public display and advertising with relative cheapness.

pointed out that the sites available there for redevelopment are somewhat unsuitable for large-scale extensive developments in any case and the land values are such as to render this type of construction uneconomic. These factors have contributed clearly to the lack of construction close to the core even before the introduction of the 1963 zoning regulations (Fig. 2-7).

In similarity to the pattern on office development, the locus of wholesaling construction in the frame area has shifted over time. Initially, the area around the markets (see Fig. 5-9) was favoured, with a good deal of construction also occurring in the north-eastern sections of the frame. After 1960, however, the western flank of the frame predominated in terms of the number of projects and the area constructed. Since 1968 the centre of gravity of development has again shifted back to the north-east flank, particularly in the area between Wellington Street and the railway, where residential development had gradually been taken over and redeveloped as small-scale warehousing facilities. This process illustrates again the nature of the land-use succession occurring in the frame. It also reiterates the tendency for redevelopment to move in definite spatial concentrations over time.

In general terms, it is evident that the pattern of wholesaling development over time in the central area contrasts strongly with that of retail-service facilities. There has been decentralization of both activities over the period, decreasing their relative strength in terms of the total central land-use mix (as one would expect both from the trends produced through land-use competition and the growth of the city). However, retailing activities have dispersed over a wider area of the city than wholesaling: in the former case suburbanization has been the rule, whilst many relocating wholesale facilities have shifted shorter distances to the frame (see Wolinski 1970). Within the centre, rebuilding and extension of retailing facilities has been strongly centralized, whereas wholesaling construction has been more widespread. These differential trends point to the variable locational rationale between the two activity sets.

5-3.5 MANUFACTURING DEVELOPMENT

In similarity to wholesaling, the construction of manufacturing plants within the Perth central area has declined in recent years: this fits in with the general trend towards the decreasing significance of space-extensive activities within the centre. Between 1954 and 1959 (inclusive) a total of 106 construction projects for manufacturing purposes occurred within the central area; these constituted 34 400 m^2 of floorspace (Table 5-2), which accounts for an average 13% of the total floorspace constructed over that period. Since 1960 a further 141 manufacturing building projects have occurred, amounting to 39 800 m^2 floorspace, but in terms of an annual increment these account for an average of only 3% of total space constructed. Furthermore, most of these projects were in the form of extensions to existing premises rather than being new buildings; on an average only 1.5 new manufacturing premises per annum have been erected within the central area since 1960, as compared with 7.9 in the pre-1960 period.

Almost 90% of the manufacturing construction over the total period has occurred in the area north of the Wellington Street-railway axis (as opposed to 67% of wholesaling construction). Zoning ordinances have again been an influencing factor in this pattern, for the only areas where manufacturing development is permitted within the centre are north of this axis in the outer frame (see Fig. 5-3). Even before these regulations took effect (in 1963), however, very little construction for manufacturing purposes occurred in the southern sections of the area. Comparison of 1953 and 1968 land-use maps (Figs 5-1, 5-2a) shows that a considerable number of industrial plants formerly located within the now stagnating area to the north-west of the core have shifted over the period. Various factors have been at work encouraging this trend; it seems likely that the relocation process has been another contributing factor to the decline of the zone.

Most of the new plants constructed in the frame have been relatively small concerns (averaging *c.* 740 m² in area) of a semi-intensive nature, such as printing works, clothing factories, and auto-repair establishments. This is indicative of the restructuring of manufacturing composition in the central area that has already received some attention; the rising values of land and non-availability of large sites precludes more extensive industries from establishing there. Many plants of the latter type have moved to suburban areas in recent years, where more extensive, cheaper and less-congested conditions are still available. These trends are by no means unique to Perth; in general, central-area manufacturing is becoming increasingly oriented towards small labour-intensive plants and away from more extensive types (see e.g. Pred 1964). According to Preston (1966:258), 'Most lines of heavy industry with their increasing space demands will eventually leave the transition zone.' In any case, it should be noted that in Perth zoning ordinances now prevent many types of 'heavy industry' (particularly noisy and noxious types) from locating within the frame. But this is once again only reinforcing existing trends; as Scott (1963) has shown, the suburbanization had reached considerable proportions before the introduction of the ordinances.

Manufacturing premises locating in these areas over the period (1954-72) have invariably displaced single-family, duplex or terrace housing, the only uses that are below manufacturing in the central-area hierarchy of rent-paying abilities. However, there is now less than 5% of these areas under residential coverage; the situation is exacerbated by uncertainties over freeway routing and timing. This precludes the occupation of further large tracts of land (see § 2-5), whilst the existing freeway has itself absorbed many acres of former industrial land. Such forces are bound to contribute to the continuing decline of manufacturing within the central area, a trend that must, however, be regarded as a natural part of the city's evolution.

5-3.6 DEVELOPMENTS OF PUBLIC AND CULTURAL FACILITIES

It has already been suggested that non-profit generating (essentially non-commercial) activities are coming under increasing pressure in the central area as the city grows and the land values increase. Redevelopment tends to concentrate on such uses as offices, hotels and specialist retailing that show the greatest return to their developers. Tetlow and Goss (1965:229) point out that:

> Few public buildings and amenities have been provided [in the centre] because they provide no observable revenue; it is . . . very difficult to measure the value of civic offices, concert halls and open spaces.

Moreover, the market exerts pressure on such uses already existing, and as was discovered in Chapter 3, institutional bodies such as Churches are finding it increasingly difficult to maintain central facilities.

In the light of these considerations, it appears surprising at first sight that over 0.1 million m² of floorspace have been added to the stock of so called public and cultural activities within Perth's central area since 1954. This represents 16% of the total floorspace constructed over the period, and in certain years these facilities have accounted for considerably larger percentages of the annual total (see Table 5-2). Two points are of relevance in resolving this apparent paradox. The first is that governmental authorities have not been completely oblivious to the need for public facilities in the city centre. Consequently they have intervened in the free-market processes that determine land use, by providing, for example, open space and also by introducing special measures to protect existing public areas (e.g. protective zoning or special designation of recreational facilities). Secondly, however, it should be noted that the bulk of the construction that falls into the 'public and cultural' category has in Perth's case been for quasi-public activities, such as governmental transport depots, radio and TV studios, police stations, hospital extensions, telephone and mail exchanges and multi-storey car parks. In combination, facilities of this type account for over 90% of the central-area 'public' activity construction over the period. The erection of these facilities emphasizes that the centre still plays an important rôle as a focus for public services in the city.

Turning to the spatial distribution of this construction, most of it (95% floorspace) has occurred in the frame areas, where these facilities are traditionally concentrated (see Chapter 2). This has reinforced the 1953 land-use pattern, as shown by a comparison of land-use maps (Figs 5-1, 5-2a). Although not recorded in the building statistics, comparison of the maps also shows that a number of car parks have been constructed on the peripheries of the central area over the period. It is these facilities that are largely responsible for the large increase in car-parking space from 0.003 m² in 1953 (0.17% of central-area space) to 0.16 million m² in 1968 (5.6% of total space; see Table 5-1). The need for such space was emphasized in the Stephenson Report (Stephenson & Hepburn 1955) and many of the parking areas subsequently established along the reclaimed river foreshore are in line with the report's recommendations. Unfortunately, suggestions that 'the aim of such car parks should be to enhance the visual attraction of the area' have been lost in the translation (as illustrated in Plate XV). But the space is invariably used to capacity; this reflects the growing dependence on car transport as a means of travel to work in the central area (see § 2-5, 3-7). The users appear to be mainly core office and service workers. Thus developments in one section of the central area (in this case employment increase in the core) can affect the spatial arrangement of other sections.

In overall terms, therefore, there has been an increase in the significance of the public facilities in the frame; the core has seen little construction activity of this type. Indeed some quasi-public facilities, such as clubs, have relocated from the core to the frame in response to the increasing centrifugal forces operating in the core—these have already been seen to have affected the location of a considerable number of other former core activities. Little complementary movement of activities from frame to core is discernible—this is predictable, given the spatial distribution of land values within the central area and the gradient of activity intensity observable in a cross-section of the area. The combination of static structure and the dynamic response and feedback effect on this structure are the essential elements in the conceptual model of the city centre that is discussed in the next chapter.

5-3.7 RESIDENTIAL DEVELOPMENT

The processes of commercial redevelopment described in earlier sections have had an important effect upon the pattern of residential land use within the city central area, for much of this redevelopment has displaced residential premises. This was noted even in the case of activities such as wholesaling and manufacturing that are declining in a total central-area context. These factors help to explain the considerable nett decline in space occupied by housing in the Perth centre since 1954: despite lateral extension of boundaries residential space declined by 9% to 0.54 million m² in 1968 (see Table 5-1). The strength of the decline is emphasized when it is noted that some 0.1 million m² of new residential space were added to the stock over the period; on an annual basis this construction accounts for an average of 13% of total.

These gross figures, however, disguise the real nature of the changes that have occurred, for the new construction that falls into the 'residential' category is all accounted for by hotel, motel and high-density residences. No single-family dwellings have been involved; on the contrary, a considerable number of these structures have fallen victim to the continuing expansion of other activities within the frame area. This process has been facilitated in recent years by ordinances that have zoned most areas of the frame for commercial purposes. The residential areas designated to the east and west of the core are all for flats at high densities (see Fig. 5-3). This zoning philosophy has no doubt been influenced by the sentiments expressed in the Stephenson Report (upon which the 1963 zoning was based) :

> It is unlikely that anyone would desire to build or occupy a dwelling within the Central Area, for all social and financial forces are against this eventuality. [Stephenson & Hepburn 1955: 187]

Certainly the existence of these 'financial forces' cannot be denied: land values are such as to make the construction of low-density central-area housing a somewhat uneconomic proposition especially when demand exists for commercial premises.

The transition processes at work within the frame are largely a result of these forces; indeed here is the crunch, for the forces are allowed free reign by the permissive zoning. Hence the existing stock of low-density residential accommodation —and at 1968 this accounted for 5% of central-area floorspace and housed some *c.* 5 000 people—comes under increasing pressure from other uses. It may be argued that this trend is justifiable given the economic competition from apparently more viable uses and the continuing decline of central-area population that has been recognized the world over (see Preston & Griffin 1966 for United States examples, Johnson 1967 for United Kingdom evidence, and Davies 1965 for a South African case).

In Perth the population of the central area, in line with these trends, declined from nearly 26 000 in 1954 to 16 000 in 1966 (a decrease of 37%),* against a total metropolitan-area population increase of over 40%. The strength of this trend suggests that regardless of economic pressures people are showing an increasing preference for living in suburban as against city locations. But such preferences are bound to be influenced by local environmental considerations as Daly (1970) has found. From this point of view the frame, with its creeping blight, increasing commercial activity, mounting congestion and impending freeway construction is becoming a less and less desirable environment to live in. Were the existing residential areas given greater positive protection however, the demand for such facilities might well increase. The case for the construction of new low-density accommodation close to the city core does not seem particularly strong, but on the other hand there is a case for protection of existing accommodation. This affords one avenue of restoring vitality to the increasingly sterile city centre.

High-density accommodation constructed within the central area in Perth since 1954 has led to the development of two nodes flanking the core; as suggested in Chapter 2, these are characteristic of a large number of frame areas. A third node, to the north-east of the core, is now developing, with two large blocks having recently been erected in that locality, now specifically zoned for the purpose (see Fig. 5-3). These nodes have developed in sequence, once again illustrating the tendency for new development to shift its locus over time. The blocks developed to the immediate south of the recent eastern expansion arm of the core were mostly constructed in the 1950s on former vacant land (see Fig. 5-1). Unfortunately, the aesthetics of this development leaves much to be desired (Plate III) and they can hardly be said to 'enrich the urban scene', as was envisaged in the original recommendations (Stephenson & Hepburn 1955:187). Even so, they undoubtedly fulfill an important need in providing a ready pool of low-cost accommodation close to the core—indeed, this has apparently influenced their aesthetics. This point is substantiated by the recent (post-1960) developments to the west of the core; whilst

---

* These figures are inflated by the inclusion of population residing in transient accommodation (hotels, etc.) at the time of the census. Given the increase in hotel facilities over the period, the actual decline of permanent population is probably stronger than the above figures indicate.

architecturally more pleasing, they are catering largely to the high-income market (Plate XIV).

Residential development within the core of Perth's central area over the period is confined to hotels; apart from preventitive zoning, the high land values prevailing in the area clearly preclude permanent residences from locating therein. The construction of this transient accommodation has been accompanied by the disappearance from the core of a large number of private hotels and boarding houses. Some remain in the eastern sections of the core as seen earlier, but the majority have been forced out through the expansion of other commercial activities more typical of the core (offices in particular). Thus these premises can be added to the list of functions that are vacating the core. As in other cases, their loss has partly been compensated by developments in the frame, where a number of motels have established in recent years, a trend noticed in the United States cities as long ago as 1959 (see Horwood & Boyce). Such a process underlines the dynamic nature of the central area and its continually altering structure.

5-3.8   THE PATTERNS SYNTHESISED

The analysis of building patterns within the Perth central area and the comparisons with other cities has shown that each activity type behaves in different ways in its evolution within the area. Yet together the differing patterns produce the changes in central-area structure that were referred to in § 5-3.1, namely: the intensification of land use and the increasing dominance of activities of high rent-paying ability at the expense of financially less-viable uses. Furthermore, the development of one activity pattern both affects and is conditioned by the balance. The evolution of the location pattern of many activities has been seen to involve a centrifugal movement (cf. Colby 1933) from a predominantly core (or near-core) location to a more peripheral one within or beyond the frame. This is associated with the increasing intensity of space use within the core, and thus it would appear that the core sheds various functions as it grows and hence becomes more specialized.

Financial forces appear to be an important agent of change: rising land values, centred on the core, are clearly correlated with the outward movement of various activities. Thus in explaining the patterns of change within the central area it seems that the models of city structure (discussed in Chapter 1) have little applicability. However, certain trends towards axial development have been noted in the case of offices and highway-oriented activities (such as car-sales rooms), and to this extent Hoyt's (1939) notions have relevance. Furthermore, it can be argued that the centrifugal trends of activities which relocate from inner to outer segments of the central area are a logical response to the structure of the area in terms of bands of decreasing activity intensity and land values away from the focus (Chapter 3)—this will lead to a radial expansion of the area as a whole (cf. Burgess 1925) and to relocation within the area as growth continues. Finally, it may be seen that the gradual decline in the significance of certain central functions will favour the development of Harris and Ullman's (1945) multiple-nuclear city.

Moreover, the locational forces of agglomeration and spatial competition these authors referred to, are clearly one factor leading to the creation of a poly-nuclear central area marked by functional zonation.

But the models take no account of institutional forces, such as zoning, which are also significant catalysts in the processes of change. But zoning often reflects 'natural' processes in any case, and thus tends to reinforce rather than initiate change. This is the case with the continued decline of the residential function of the centre, the decentralization of wholesaling and industrial premises (particularly those of an extensive type), and the movements from core to frame of automotive-service activities, professional offices, clubs, and those wholesaling and industrial activities that still seek a central location.

But in certain cases, zoning can act to stagnate the land-use pattern. This is particularly so if it is based on an imperfect understanding of the processes of change occurring within the centre as in the case of zoning of the 'zone of discard' within Perth's central area. And even if zoning acts to reinforce so called 'natural' trends, it may be doing positive harm to the structure of the centre if the change is undesirable in the first instance. Clearly, the planning authorities should not only possess greater knowledge of the processes of change at work within the centre, but should also evolve a set of goals and priorities so that this change can be controlled and guided in the best interests of all those concerned.

These forces of change are not acting evenly throughout the entire expanse of the centre: when the total areal distribution of change is examined, it is immediately noticeable that certain sections are undergoing very rapid change whilst others are being only moderately affected, and still others virtually remaining stagnant. The comparison of land-use patterns within the Perth central area at 1953 and 1968 reveals certain of these trends, but the composite picture of building-construction activity and change of use within existing structures clarifies this coarse image a good deal. This picture is presented in Fig. 5-10, whilst Fig. 5-11 breaks the pattern down to a finer level. In overall terms, it is evident that the core is dominant, accounting for 40% of space constructed over the period (in total the core accounted for only 20% of central-area space in 1968). By type, offices constitute 79% of this amount, with retail-service and residential expansion covering the bulk of the balance (8% each). The concentration of office development along the Terrace axis and the rapidity of change in the eastern 'zone of assimilation' identified in the spatial analysis is strongly evident in Fig. 5-11. The axial nature of the expansion was seen to be the result of a combination of forces: the natural attraction of developers to the area because of its prestige rating and its opportunity to boost rents with river views; the influence of the pattern of location and consolidation of public land use to the north and south of the axis; the repelling effects of the core's zone of discard; the availability of redevelopment sites; and zoning ordinances. Some of the loss of residential space in this area has been compensated for by expansion of high-density facilities to the north and south of the axis in the western sections of the frame (see Fig. 5-10), whilst there has been similar expansion recently to the west of the core. However, these new constructions have

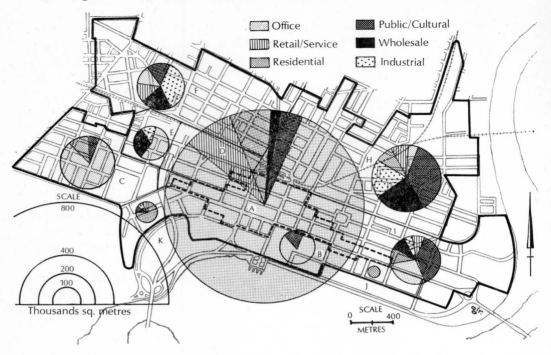

Fig. 5-10 *Distribution of construction activity, Perth central area 1954-72*

Office
Retail/Service
Residential
Public/Cultural
Wholesale
Industrial

SCALE
800

400
200
100

Thousands sq. metres

SCALE
0   400
METRES

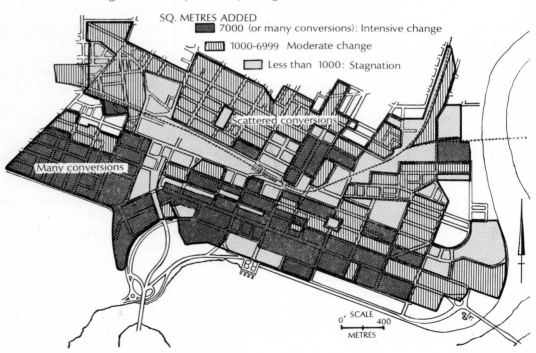

Fig. 5-11 *Classification of change, Perth central area 1954-72*

SQ. METRES ADDED
7000 (or many conversions): Intensive change
1000-6999 Moderate change
Less than 1000: Stagnation

Scattered conversions

Many conversions

SCALE
0   400
METRES

failed to arrest the trend towards the decline of residential space and population within the centre, largely because of the strength of the transition processes at work elsewhere in the area.

These transition processes have been noted to be at work particularly strongly in the western sections of the frame, where professional offices (largely emanating from the core) are invading the former purely residential area; together with new flat construction in this area the new floorspace constitutes 7% of the total increment (see Fig. 5-10). As shown in Fig. 5-11, most blocks there have also been functionally altered through a large number of conversions from housing to professional offices.

Transition processes to the north of the railway-Wellington Street axis have not been due to office expansion, thus reflecting both the ready availability of space to the south and the differing environment to the north, where industry and wholesaling are predominant. These activities have, in fact, been the main agents of change in the area, particularly in the north-east and north-west segments, where transition processes have been strongest (see Fig. 5-11). Over 75% of the total wholesaling and industrial construction since 1954 has occurred in these areas. Public and cultural activities, mainly in the form of government depots, have also contributed to the processes of change, especially in the north-west sections, where they constitute 42% of new floorspace. The pace of development has slowed down in recent years in these northern segments of the frame, and has become increasingly focussed on new office and retail-service expansion in the core. This is partly a reflection of the declining relative significance of frame-type activities in a total central-area context, and is also no doubt influenced by impending freeway construction. It is of significance that in studying the frame areas of several United States cities, Preston and Griffin (1966:349) point to a similar decline of these extensive frame activities, though their conclusions must be treated with caution, since they are based on a purely static analysis. Thus Pain (1967) found from a directory study of the evolution of Auckland's central area that many manufacturing and wholesaling activities appeared to be increasing in significance.

In overall terms, then, there has clearly been considerable change both in the intensity and relative importance of the various activities that comprise the central-area mix over the period 1954-72. The location patterns of certain of these has also been altered considerably. This conclusion does not concur with the apparent situation in Melbourne, where Johnston (1967:189) found that from 1859 to 1964 there was 'little overall change in the organisation of land uses'. But the differing time scales and resolution levels of the two studies make comparisons of results difficult; and in any case, Johnston did find, in similarity to the pattern in Perth, an expansion of core activities at the expense of those of frame.

Finally, it is of interest to compare the overall pattern of change within Perth's frame area with that postulated for the 'transition zone' by Preston and Griffin (1966; see § 1-3.4). In their model of the zone (Fig. 1-5) the authors identify three zones: (1) a zone of active assimilation, where non-residential uses are rapidly invading areas of older, but high-quality housing; (2) a zone of passive assimilation, whose growth is based upon slower rates of change and invasion of housing areas; and (3) a zone of general inactivity which is relatively stable in comparison, containing several activities that have successfully resisted assimilation (Preston & Griffin 1966:347-8). It was noted earlier that the classification is highly subjective in nature, for no analysis of change was undertaken by the authors. Even so, with areal statistics at our disposal, the pattern of change within Perth's central area can be classified in line with Preston and Griffin's framework according to the amount of change. Thus in Fig. 5-11, three different areas of change have been identified:

1. *Zones of intensive activity* (areas where over 7 000m² of new floorspace have been added to the floorspace of each block, or where there have been a large number of conversions). These areas are largely confined to office development areas in the Terrace, the zone of assimilation to the east of the core, the emerging professional node to the west and isolated pockets north of the railway. Conceptually these correspond to Preston and Griffin's zones of active assimilation; whereas, however, these authors suggest that such areas will be limited to one flank of the core, they are found on all flanks in Perth's case. This situation corresponds with that in Auckland as identified by Pain (1967). Furthermore, the expansion is not necessarily into areas of former high-quality residences (a trend also suggested by Dickinson 1964) although West Perth was a relatively high-income residential area, and some portions of the Terrace evidence a once prestige residential enclave. Certainly residential areas are the main victim of transition processes in these zones.

2. *Zones of moderate activity* (1-6 999 m² added). These are widespread over the balance of the area, and follow no logical pattern as do the model's zones of passive assimilation to which they correspond. The predominant process occurring is the transition from low-density residential premises to commercial uses such as wholesaling, light industry and retail-service activities of low rent-paying ability. Areas involved are marked by a considerable mixture of uses and a relatively low space-use intensity, this indicating the gradual nature of change occurring.

3. *Stagnant zones* (less than 1 000 m² added). These occur in and around the identified 'zone of discard'; in zones spatially dominated by semi-permanent public uses or government depots; and in small pockets throughout the industrial-wholesale areas of the frame, some of which are affected by freeway construction. No correspondence to the suggested location of the model's 'zones of general inactivity' is apparent, but the fact that definite zones are identifiable does suggest that certain areas within the central area become 'dead pockets' as far as change is concerned. It is in such pockets that blight develops most rapidly and externalities inhibit redevelopment (see Davis & Winston 1961, Parsons 1967). Preston and Griffin (1966:349) suggest that these areas have 'resisted' change, but it appears that the pressures for redevelopment are in fact absent in these zones and thus the blight becomes cumulative (Richardson 1971:133).

Such a classification of change reveals certain similarities with Preston and Griffin's model; however, in itself it cannot be regarded as providing any sort of definitive statement concerning central-area dynamics, for as Bourne (1968) has so usefully pointed out, it reveals little concerning the causes of the processes it attempts to depict. The analysis undertaken in this chapter, on the contrary, has shown that the major causes of structural change in the city centre lie in the *modus operandi* of the land market, and the continuing competition between activities for central locations. Change is most rapid where this competition is strongest, and the overall pattern of change corresponds well with land-value increases (these are sharpest in the zones of intense activity as shown by comparison of Figs 5-6, 5-11). The pattern of change is modified (or sometimes encouraged) by external factors such as zoning, the pattern of public-owned property, the existing land-use distributions and age of buildings, and the whims of developers. The patterns of development will also be influenced by the differing space and locational requirements of the activities involved, and the locational attributes of the various segments of the area. This complex of factors renders the construction of a model of property redevelopment particularly hazardous at the present time.

But certain attempts have been made in this direction in recent years: the model of office construction in London devised by Cowan *et al.* (1969) has already received mention. Although this model may not have great predictive reliability by itself, owing to its reliance on very few 'causative factors', it has the potential for development into a more rigorous framework. Bourne (1971) has shown that, given a suitable data base, it is possible to predict (within certain limits of probability) the amount and type of change likely to occur within certain segments of the central city area. This suffers from obvious limitations as an explanatory device for change since it does not incorporate any variables likely to affect change. However, if the locational variables suggested by Cowan *et al.* (1969), together with ownership and leasehold data suggested as relevant by Parry-Lewis *et al.* (1971) were incorporated, the model might have greater explanatory powers. But clearly many other variables, including property condition and age, land values and site attractiveness, and the differing locational requirements of the various activities also need to be considered. But first the exact importance of these variables needs to be more precisely established. A reliable model will only be a feasible proposition when the forces of change discussed in this chapter are more fully understood. This appears to be a fruitful avenue for further research. In the meantime, however, the implications and desirability of the changes deserve consideration.

5-4 PLANNING FOR CENTRAL-AREA CHANGE AND REDEVELOPMENT

5-4.1 THE NEED FOR PLANNING

The processes of change within the central area examined in the previous section have been largely brought about by the gradual piecemeal redevelopment of the city's building stock. This process is controlled largely by private companies or individuals—property developers and insurance companies have been responsible for most of Perth's new office space for example. The process has clearly been modified by external factors and supplemented by government building projects; yet private profit-oriented redevelopment remains the predominant process, as indeed it does in most capitalist-oriented economies. This explains the emphasis of core-redevelopment projects on prestige offices, hotels and luxury residences, and specialist retailing facilities. Such uses provide the highest returns on the expensive sites within the area. The land values thus influence the type of development that occurs; at the same time the development pattern has a reciprocal effect on land values (see Fig. 5-6). In the frame, development concentrates on activities of lesser rent-paying ability such as wholesaling and industrial premises; but despite their relatively low financial capacity, these uses undoubtedly provide a healthy return on capital investment in this location. The nett result of redevelopment in the core and frame is increasing emphasis on activities of high rent-paying ability at the expense of those lower on the scale. This is in accord with the theories of the land market as has already been pointed out; but whether it is desirable seems open to question, for the element of social benefit contributed by the less financially-viable activities is being lost, whilst social costs are being generated by new development. Other disbenefits arising from piecemeal redevelopment have also emerged: in particular the lack of coordination between building projects and the difficulty of keeping pace with increased parking and transport demands.

5-4.2   THE LIMITATIONS OF CONVENTIONAL PLANNING CONTROLS

Planning can intervene in these processes to obtain a possibly more desirable form of redevelopment and avoid other disadvantages of the piecemeal approach. Certain controls over development are available to local planning authorities: thus planning permission can be refused for developments that do not accord with provisions laid down in a statutory plan. In Perth, the statutory plan has taken the classical form of a zoning schedule which limits each activity type to a certain section of the central area (as illustrated in Fig. 5-3), accompanied by plot-ratio controls. However, it has been seen that in fact many of these zoning provisions have merely reinforced existing trends of change (as in the case of office development for example) or have been based on false assumptions concerning the likely future form of the area (as in the case of the provision of excessive shopping space). Moreover plot ratios have been particularly generous, especially to office developments, where a standard of 5:1 (plus bonuses of up to 20%) has been adopted even in the latest plan proposals (Perth City Council 1971b). Thus the Terrace axis has gradually been built out despite (cynics might say because of) planning. Latest Perth City Council proposals do suggest a lowering of the plot ratio in other sections of the centre in order both, to maintain an 'acceptable environment' and to limit the eventual central-area workforce to the current regional proposals of 90 000 (see Perth Regional Transport Study Group 1970). Under the existing blanket ratio of 5:1 (in all areas except West Perth, where 1.33 is the rule) the workforce could reach 350 000 if the total development potential were taken up (Perth City Council 1971b:101).

However, the council has yet to approve these proposals, and latest reports indicate that they are likely to reject them and allow a 5:1 ratio (plus bonuses) over the entire area.* This attitude is apparently justified by suggestions that lower ratios would remove incentives for redevelopment: undoubtedly they would afford more control over redevelopment, but surely this is in the best interests of both the environment of the central area, and the transport capacity of the projected and existing arteries serving the area.† One suspects that the council might be bowing to the short-term interests of those wishing to use the redevelopment process purely as a vehicle for profit.

In any case it is clear that planning controls in the form of zoning and plot ratios have done little to alter the processes of redevelopment at work within the central area. This has been the experience in other cities such as London, where despite the existence of strong planning regulations since World War II, private profit-oriented redevelopment appears to have proceeded almost at will (see Marriot 1967), and the symptoms of structural change are similar to those discerned in Perth (see § 5-2). This apparent failure of planning controls to guide the redevelopment process more closely, reflects the unhappy compromise that planners are often forced into for fear of destroying private developer's hallowed 'incentive': too stringent a set of controls would possibly prevent the construction of much-needed central business premises and the like. However, it also results from the inherent negative nature of such controls: the initiative remains in the hands of the developers. It is for these reasons that government intervention is necessary to procure the construction and maintenance of public facilities. Furthermore, such factors have also often encouraged planners to proceed with more positive intervention in the land market.

5-4.3   COMPREHENSIVE REDEVELOPMENT AS AN ANSWER?‡

Comprehensive redevelopment as a planning tool originated in Britain after World War II, mainly as a response to war damage to British cities: large tracts of many cities, particularly the central sections, were damaged beyond repair and thus needed to be completely reconstructed. The legislation, covering the comprehensive approach, allowed local authorities to acquire such tracts of land through compulsory purchase and coordinate redevelopment in accordance with a previously

---

* This situation prevailed in mid-1973.
† One of the main justifications put forward for limiting the central area workforce to 90 000 is that any excess would mean unacceptable peak-hour delays on road transport entries to the area (Metropolitan Regional Planning Authority 1972). This results from the high dependence of commuters on private transport: currently 60% of all peak-hour trips to the central area are undertaken by private car.
‡ Much of the material in the ensuing section is based on research carried out for an M. Phil. thesis in town planning presented to University College London in 1972 under the title 'Alternative approaches to city-centre redevelopment: an evaluation'. The study has recently been published (in revised form) by Pergamon Press as part of the *Progress in Planning* series (see Bibliography).

determined plan.* This was seen both as a method of quickly restoring the fabric of the areas concerned, and as a means of incorporating improvements to street layout and controlling land use. These two aspects could not be achieved so readily (if at all), were the redevelopment left to private initiative, unless the property were under single ownership—an extremely unlikely situation in a formerly built up central area. As time went on, the latter two aims of comprehensive redevelopment became increasingly important, especially once most war-damaged areas had been restored; planners turned their attention to the comprehensive reconstruction of inner city and central areas considered in need both of structural improvement and improved amenity and layout. The basic principles were simple: large-scale clearing of the existing fabric and complete reconstruction along lines considered in accordance with good planning practice, i.e. improved housing with all basic facilities provided, generous provision of open space, shopping areas closed to traffic if possible, and major traffic arteries routed around rather than through the residential enclaves or neighbourhoods. In general, high-density housing was favoured as a replacement to terrace housing in residential areas.

In central areas the public acquisition of land allowed the incorporation of public facilities, which would otherwise have been squeezed from the area. The segregation of pedestrian and vehicular traffic became a higher priority, and ring roads were often proposed to relieve traffic congestion in the centre and to facilitate the segregation. Schemes of this type became increasingly popular, and by 1965 comprehensive development areas were evident in the centres of all large British cities and a host of others besides (see Tetlow & Goss 1965, Hart 1968). Small wonder that by this time the practice had become accepted as a partial if not full cure for the central-area's ills, and had passed into the annals of good planning practice as witnessed by its promulgation in handbooks produced by the Ministry of Housing and Local Government (1963, 1963a, 1963b).

This approach to central-area redevelopment was linked to the problem of increasing traffic congestion by the Buchanan Report (1964). The report comes to the conclusion that the best method of accommodating the conflicting interests of increasing volumes of traffic and pedestrians in city centres is 'through the introduction of traffic architecture'. This envisages the creation of a multi-level segregated circulatory system overlain by a reconstructed activity fabric (as illustrated in Fig. 5-12a); it is noted that such a system could only be created in existing cities through massive redevelopment:

> unless the public accepts that there has to be *comprehensive redevelopment* over large areas, then the opportunities for dealing with traffic will all be lost.† [Buchanan 1964:69]

Similar 'design oriented' solutions to city-centre problems have been advocated by many architects seeking to evolve blueprints for the utopian-city centre devoid of

---

* As incorporated in the British Town and Country Planning Act 1971 (originally part of the 1947 act of the same name).
† My italics.

congestion, pedestrian-vehicular conflict, domination by commercial functions and, one might suggest, character (see Figs 5-12a, 5-12b; Gruen 1965).

Even so, it appears that comprehensive redevelopment has many potential benefits to offer the central area, particularly where planners are seeking to improve the environment for central activities, traffic and pedestrians, balance the provision of privately-developed space with public facilities, and coordinate the fragmented pattern of redevelopment currently occurring. From this point of view it is perhaps surprising that little if any such comprehensive redevelopment has been attempted in the central areas of Australian cities. This can probably be accounted for, how-ever, by the lack of suitable powers given to planning authorities, which no doubt partly stems from the faith of Australian authorities in private enterprise solutions. But this may, in the long term, have proved to be a fortunate attitude, for whilst private redevelopment activity has undoubtedly created many problems and a deteriorating environment in the Australian city centres, comprehensive redevelop-ment does not necessarily provide a solution. This stems from the fact that the

Fig. 5-12 *The concept of comprehensive redevelopment.* After Richards 1966:47; from a project by J. Weber 1965.

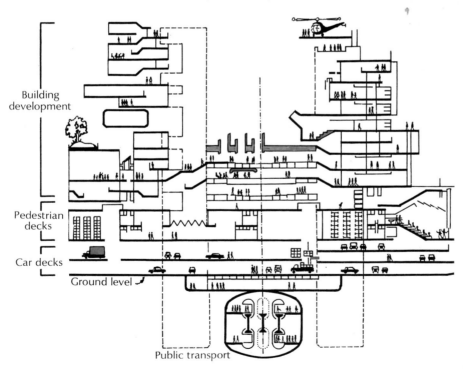

5-12a The general concept of multi-level development

Fig. 5-12 Contd

Section through Bow Street Concourse to the Strand

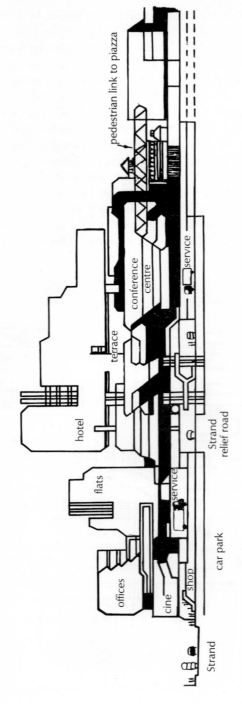

5-12b   Plans for Covent Garden, London. Adapted from Greater London Council 1971.

benefits referred to above are offset by the extra costs incurred. The approach is relatively simple, the effects complex and far-reaching.

Comprehensive redevelopment generally speeds up renewal by dealing on a co-ordinated and complete basis with areas that would normally be only partially renewed by private developers on a fragmented basis in space and time. One result of this is the destruction of a greater proportion of the existing fabric and hence the displacement of a great number of existing activities than would normally be the case. Heavier costs inevitably arise, and whilst correspondingly greater benefits may accrue to incoming tenants of the redeveloped fabric, other externalities created in the process (e.g. extra traffic leading to increased congestion costs) may help outweigh these benefits.* Such factors have consistently been ignored by planners in the past; only recently has the wisdom of the comprehensive approach been questioned.

The comprehensive approach, therefore, must be applied with caution. At first sight it appears an apparently viable answer to problems of planning redevelopment and change in the central area, but this may not always be the case. In this situa-tion, claims that the method offers considerable benefits for Australian city centres (see Winston *et al.* 1965) must be treated with scepticism. Before any redevelop-ment scheme of this sort is adopted, it must be thoroughly evaluated against the possible alternatives. Only if it then proves a better solution should it be adopted. This applies equally in the opposite direction: too often in the past have planners stood by and allowed piecemeal redevelopment to proceed without considering alternative approaches. In the final analysis it may be that neither option offers a desirable solution to the problem; thus a compromise that combines the benefits of both approaches whilst minimizing costs becomes not only inevitable but essential to the future of the city centre.

* For elaboration of these arguments and a case study of costs and benefits see Alexander 1974.

6

Central-area structure and dynamics:
a synthesis

6-1 TOWARDS A MODEL?

6-1.1 PARALLELS AND PRECEDENTS

The city centre has for long been seen as an important and distinctive component of urban structure although its significance and function alter over time and with growth, leading to a diminishing but more specialized rôle.

Our study has focussed on the internal structure of the city centre and it has shown that activities within the area are arranged in patterns that exhibit considerable order. But because the centre is, like the entire city it serves, a 'dynamic organism' (to borrow the phrase first coined by Colby some forty years ago), these patterns of structure cannot be regarded as static in nature. Past studies of individual cities, and indeed of the area in general, have tended to fall into this trap; but clearly the static structure is only a framework within which the processes producing the patterns, and the forces of change are occurring. Previous chapters have demonstrated that such processes are an important controlling influence over the locational patterns of activities, and the direction and nature of change affecting the area. Thus to analyse patterns but not processes is clearly inadequate; a meshing of the two leads to the emergence of a broader and more complete image of the area's structure and its rationale.

The preceding analysis has been undertaken within a framework as suggested by Horwood and Boyce's (1959) core/frame concept. This framework is clearly a valid one within which to view the overall arrangement of land use. The analysis has confirmed the existence of sub-regions within the area as hypothesized in the core/frame model, later modified by Preston and Griffin (1966). Certainly this framework turns out to be eminently more suitable than that based on the narrow premises of Murphy and Vance (1954a) in that it makes allowance for a much wider range of central activities. But the framework as it stands is only that; it provides little in the way of explanation for observed patterns, it overlooks important aspects of the area's structure, it does not refer to processes of change and it does not analyse the important three-dimensional structure of the inner segments of the area.

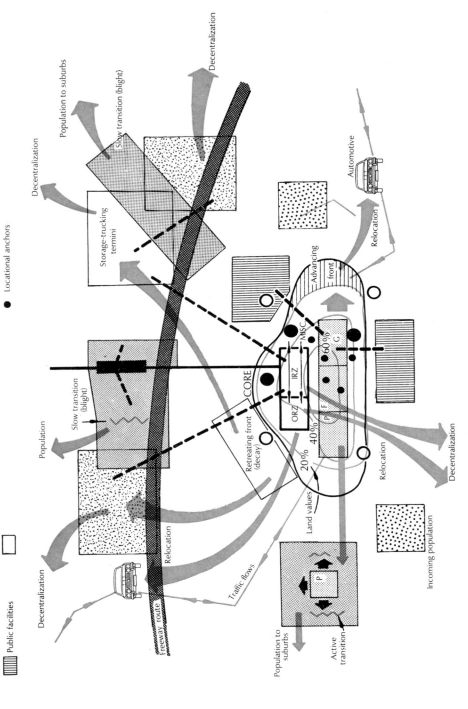

Fig. 6-1 *Conceptual model of the central area*

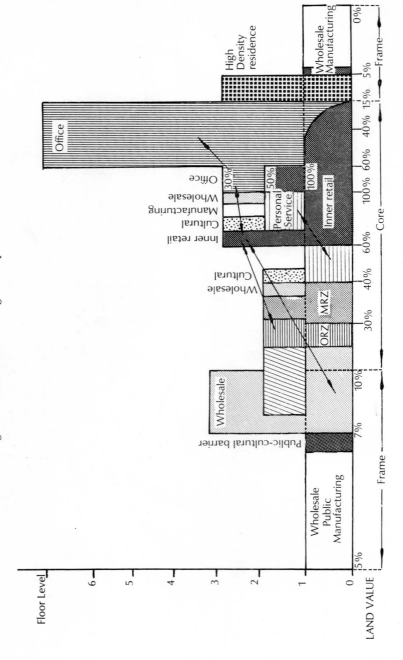

Fig. 6-2 *Cross-section through conceptual model*

Taking account of such considerations, and of the light thrown on these neglected aspects by the preceding analysis, an attempt has been made to construct a more refined conceptual model of central-area structure (Figs 6-1, 6-2). This model refers not only to major aspects of the area's structure in both a horizontal (Fig. 6-1) and vertical (Fig. 6-2) context, but also to the processes at work and the major variables controlling the patterns as well as the dynamic aspects of structure. It is thus an elaboration of the core/frame connotation that seeks to overcome the 'disarming simplicity' (Archer 1969) of that concept by reference to the true complexities of structure and change that characterize the area.

The model thus reflects the structural zonation of the central area and also refers to individual activity clusters. Furthermore, explicit reference is made to the relationship between land usage and land values within the area, and particularly within the core in a vertical context. This illustrates the tendency towards decreasing intensity and specialization of space use away from central peak-value sections in a horizontal and vertical plane. It is also suggested that functional linkages are an important influence on locational behaviour within the area as a whole and between the various segments of it. The analysis of dynamic aspects has allowed the inclusion of positively-identified zones of expansion, discard, transition and stagnation, as well as processes of land-use succession that are constantly occurring as the core continues to shed its activities. But such aspects deserve to be dealt with in more detail; attention is firstly focussed on the core.

6-1.2 THE CORE

The land use and activity intensity within the core, the orientation to pedestrian traffic and the land-value peaking have long been recognized as salient characteristics of the area (Table 3-1), but to supplement such properties several further observations can be made.

1. In terms of space occupied, office and retail activities dominate the area, and these appear to grow and decline respectively in relative significance with increasing city size. But the spatial dominance of these activities should not be taken to mean, as certain workers have, that these are the only rightful tenants of the core. Certainly they are most able to survive the competition for space within the area, but the attitude that regards other equally valid core components as 'anachronistic' must be abandoned before it is too late (see § 6-2). Core activities are characterized by intensity of space use and orientation to pedestrian traffic, and in this respect certain civic and residential facilities have equal claim to a continued location in the core.

2. All activities within the core arrange themselves in a distinctive manner in both the horizontal and vertical plane. The peak-value areas occur in the central sections of the core at ground level, where pedestrian flows are at a maximum as a response to the rich intermixture of specialist retail elements located within a framework of transportation termini and multi-storey department stores (the latter are key elements within the structure). Whilst this area is losing strength

in comparison to the total city retail mix, it retains its viability as the most significant mixture of elements within the core and forms a definite IRZ. However,
redevelopment within this area is at a minimum, and is generally restricted to
renewal and arcade construction in conjunction with office developments. As Buissink and de Widt (1967) suggest, the number of improvements over time correlates
clearly with the importance of the street in terms of its shopping intensity and
pedestrian generating capacity.

(The whole of the city's retail zone is becoming increasingly dependant upon the
office workforce for its trade.) The activities of this zone are, however, complemented by a set of personal-service activities, small intensive manufacturing plants,
wholesaling premises and offices, at upper-floor levels (and, in the case of services,
towards the periphery) of the IRZ.) These activities have both a lesser need for a
prime location and a lower rent-paying capacity than the specialist retailers, but
because they are either functionally linked to the activities of the IRZ, or are
dependant on them for trade, a nearby location is essential. This differential arrangement of activities in a horizontal and vertical plane gives the inner segments of the
core an overall profile akin to a series of overlain enclosed hemispheres (Fig. 6-2).

This structure is similar to, though more sophisticated than the internal structure
of non-central retail-service nucleations observed by Garner (1966) in Chicago.
However, the main variable affecting the core patterns appear to be rent-paying
ability, accessibility requirements, and nature of merchandise or service offered
rather than threshold level proposed in Garner's model. Nonetheless, the high
threshold specialist-goods stores are the most viable within the core, as retail sales
and outlets continue to decentralize.

3. Away from peak-value areas (the locus of which appears to be shifting towards the increasingly important office areas) the specialist retail areas give way
to office zones on the one hand and to miscellaneous and household retail areas
on the other. The latter elements, which have a lower rent-paying ability and
greater space requirements than the specialist stores, are declining particularly
rapidly within the central area, whilst office areas are at the forefront of the core's
redevelopment and expansion. The zone of discard and zone of assimilation
(respectively) are found on these opposite flanks of the core (Fig. 6-1).

4. In general, the pattern of pedestrian flows within the retail areas of the core
is both linked to and affected by the structure of the retailing elements. Levels of
flow correlate closely with land values, and are a particularly significant variable
for new shops entering the system. By the same token large groups of new shops
in multi-level arcades are themselves capable of altering patterns of pedestrian flow.

5. Distinct sectors of activity are evident within the office areas, their homogeneity strengthening with city size. The strongest and most viable area appears to
be the financial office zone: this 'hub' area is characterized by high land values
and is strongly linked to institutional establishments such as the stock exchange, law
courts, government centres and so on. These anchors appear to exert strong locational pulls on the offices of the set, although recent research (e.g. Goddard 1971)
suggests that contact patterns between offices of similar and differing functional

persuasion is also an important locational factor binding the set together. However, the true significance of these contact patterns has yet to be established, and in any case only affects executive levels within firms. Moreover, prestige and inertia factors also appear to be at work in maintaining such clusters. But the advent of more efficient telecommunication media and information storage and transaction procedures will undoubtedly act to loosen such forces.

6. Apart from the financial office set, a professional area is another widely recognized component of core structure. However, in many instances linkages to other office functions (such as between legal, financial and business offices) mean that such premises are often more attracted to these areas than to each other. Furthermore, the strength of the professional office set within the core has been considerably weakened in recent years in many cities by the migration movement to frame and suburban areas. Contrary to popular opinion, this particular move is not only due to financial factors; considerations of congestion and decreasing amenity within the core in comparison to the attractions of nearby residential areas also come into play (Kemp 1972).

7. Government services show equal propensity to concentrate in particular segments of the office zones, in general towards the periphery of the area. Offices of other types appear to be less sensitive to location at the micro-level and are relatively footloose elements within the core. It is offices of this sort (and those of manufacturers and distributors in particular) that are located on upper floors of the older premises within retail areas, and in older office structures elsewhere.

8. The vertical location of offices is correlated with their relative needs for public contact, advertising and prestige locations. Those at ground level show the strongest need in this direction, whilst those locating predominantly at upper levels are less directly tied to public contact and more to other central-area business concerns. Direct accessibility is therefore of less concern.

9. Despite some decentralization of certain office functions in recent years, particularly in larger cities, continuing redevelopment is strengthening the concentration of offices in many city centres. This redevelopment can cause the lateral expansion of core boundaries in small and developing cities. This suggests that the core is not so 'internally conditioned' in extent as Horwood and Boyce (1959:16) hypothesized; nonetheless, it does appear that the peripheral location of many new office developments is one cause of the initially high vacancy rates.

10. The continued redevelopment and expansion of office sectors within the core places increasing pressure on non-commercial and other activities of lower rent-paying ability as land values continue to rise. Churches, halls, cultural facilities and private hotels and clubs are among the activities affected, and without positive intervention from planning authorities such activities will eventually be forced to relocate in a sub-optimal frame location; this process can in turn cause the displacement of frame activities to suburban locations (Fig. 6-1).

In overall terms it is clear that the core is an exceedingly complex structure characterized by a wide but generally distinctive set of activities, and also that it is a dynamic sub-system within the central area. Many of the activities within the core are functionally linked to one another and this affects their locational behaviour. Similarly many are linked to non-core activities, and this is reflected in the composition of the frame area. The overall arrangement of elements within the core is conditioned by many factors: land and rental values, pedestrian flows, need for display and accessibility, and the nature of the activities themselves. The dynamic character of the area renders this structure a fluid one, in which the processes assume particular significance as controls on structural composition. There is a clear need for further research into these processes, but in the meantime the conclusions which emerge from this study have certain important implications for planning (see § 6-2).

6-1.3 THE FRAME

The differing general character of the frame in comparison to the core has been clear from the commencement of this study and this aspect needs no further emphasis here. But to a certain extent it is artificial to view the two major components of the central area as distinct from one another, for despite their characteristic differences, the two areas are clearly linked to one another in functional and dynamic terms. Indeed the analysis and synthesis in the previous two chapters demonstrated that the transition zones between the two areas that arise from the dynamic processes of change render any boundary between them both arbitrary and temporary in nature. Furthermore, changes occurring in one segment often cause changes in the other.

Nonetheless, a number of conclusions relating to the frame area emerge from the model:

1. The composition of the frame reflects its character through extensive activities such as industrial establishments, warehouse and wholesaling premises, and storage depots. Yet other activities, such as automotive services and labour-intensive industries are becoming increasingly important in spatial terms—these are attracted to the area by its central location, by functional links to core activities and by the relatively cheap land available in comparison to the core. Indeed, some of these activities emanate from the core, replace in their turn the more extensive premises, and also contribute to the continuing transition of the remaining residential premises. There is thus an active process of land-use succession occurring within the area. But the new activities entering the frame system are not the only catalytic agent in this process; the traditional frame activities are in any case actively seeking alternative (suburban) locations. Nonetheless, insofar as the increasing congestion, rising land values and lack of space for expansion within the frame are inducing this behaviour, these activities are being 'forced out' from the area by economic competition.

2. Despite the importance of economic competition as an arbitrator of the content of the frame, non-economic activities remain an important sector of the area's structure. As in the case of the core, the overall significance of these activities cannot be measured purely in terms of their rent-paying ability. But in the frame, non-commercial activities are (in keeping with the area's character) more extensive

than their core counterparts. Public and service facilities including hospitals, police stations, courts and other government services tend to form a ring around the core and are important controls on the spatial patterns of change. These are complemented by a growing number of car-parks for employees and shoppers predominantly bound for the core. Thus developments within the core (such as rising office employment and/or use of cars as a mode of travel to work, lack of parking space for shoppers and/or falling retail sales), influence the structure of the frame.

On the outskirts of the frame, public activities reappear in the form of extensive regional sporting facilities and open spaces.

The other major non-commercial activities in the frame are high-density residential establishments. These are on the increase in many cities, and are partially compensating for the continuing loss of population, resulting from the displacement of other residential facilities.

3. The activities of the frame arrange themselves in definite nodes and clusters, with the result that a functional zoning of activities is identifiable. Objective classificatory techniques assist in this task and show that definite associations of activities occur within the area in contrast to the pattern proposed by Horwood and Boyce. The most significant of these at a broad level are: wholesaling and manufacturing, storage depots and transport termini, residential and invading professional offices. In all these areas transition processes are at work, reducing the residential component to insignificance. Remnant residential areas remain in proximity to retail-service clusters.

4. The location patterns of individual frame activities shows considerable variation, and in general activities are much less clustered than their core counterparts. However, certain activities do exhibit clustering tendencies: these reflect linkages to locational anchors in certain instances, or a strong degree of internal linkage. The most significant anchors within the frame are in the form of transportation termini (rail originally, now being replaced by road) and wholesaling markets. These attract manufacturing and wholesaling establishments that are functionally linked to them. Certain types of industrial activity such as printing works and associated industries gain agglomeration economies from clustering together and also have direct links to the core; others exhibit only the latter linkage type and are, therefore, more scattered over the frame. In general, the more extensive types of manufacturing and wholesaling plants that are gradually decreasing in significance within the frame are those with the lowest degree of linkage to other frame or core activities, and are in addition the least able to compete for space within the area as land values rise.

Another significant activity cluster commonly found within the frame is composed of automotive sales (and associated service) establishments. As shown in Fig. 6-1, these tend to be located along major traffic routes passing through the frame, and are similar in form to the 'automotive rows' identified elsewhere within the city's structure (Berry *et al.* 1963).

5. The dynamic aspects of frame structure can be classified on a more objective basis than provided by Preston and Griffin (1966) in their transition-zone concept.

This can be achieved through an analysis of the actual patterns of change occurring within the area, and a grouping of areas of like intensity of change. Through such a process it becomes evident that areas of active and passive assimilation are indeed evident within the area as Preston and Griffin suggest. But it is also clear that the redevelopment of the frame is (as Bourne 1967 discovered for the inner city as a whole in Toronto) a sporadic process both temporarily and spatially, and that the locus of change shifts considerably over time. Furthermore, there are considerable areas of stagnation within the frame not identified by Preston and Griffin's concept, and these appear to be self-perpetuating in the sense that blight encourages a downward spiral of values and property condition, thus further discouraging redevelopment.

6. The models of city structure proposed by early ecologists and geographers (Burgess 1925, Hoyt 1939, Harris & Ullman 1945) are of some assistance in explaining the patterns and nature of the expansion and change within the area, as are the long-standing notions of Colby (1933). However, by themselves these models give little more than a superficial explanation of change, and it is clear that a large range of variables is relevant to a fuller understanding of process.

7. Freeway construction in the inner city often poses a threat to the stability and character of the frame area, at least in the short-term. Freeway routes are often planned without sufficient attention being paid to the costs of impact on the activities and people displaced and those in the immediate environs. These costs include: disruption of commercial linkages within the frame and from frame to core; removal expenses and loss of established goodwill; interference with patterns of pedestrian and vehicular movement; loss of amenity of areas destroyed and open spaces absorbed by the route; and short-term planning blight along and around proposed routes in advance of construction. Evidence suggests that if such costs were to be taken into account, the case for many freeways would have to be re-examined, and routes planned in such a way as to minimize these costs.

6-1.4 OVERALL CONSIDERATIONS

This conceptual model of central-area structure and change hopefully provides the basis of a more complete comprehension of the organization of the centre, and of the processes at work within. The central-area activity-mix is never fully replicated elsewhere within the city structure, yet the principles governing its operation and structure are evident throughout the urban fabric. The processes are, however, at work on a much grander and more concentrated scale within the central area.

Nonetheless considerable ignorance of the patterns and causes of change within the urban fabric still prevails. Models constructed in recent years (Cowan *et al.* 1969, Bourne 1971) have had some success in simulating past patterns of change; but a sound base of knowledge concerning the operation of the land market is still lacking. Hence any predictions in this direction must be viewed with some caution. However, it is hoped that the analysis of change as undertaken in this study has thrown some light on the processes and that it might form the basis of a probability model of change as suggested by Bourne (1971) for the inner city as a whole. But since the probability of change within a particular segment of the frame—or the central area as a whole for that matter—varies over time, this is a somewhat complex task.

In this situation it may be safer and more reliable to attempt predictions which incorporate variables that are clearly relevant to an explanation of change—such as age of buildings, current and anticipated rental values, zoning regulations and demand trends—as suggested elsewhere (Alexander 1974).

The analysis of change undertaken in this study has confirmed that the continued redevelopment of the central area causes increasing intensification of space use and specialization in activities of high rent-paying capacity at the expense of more-extensive and less-economic activities. The city centre is, therefore, becoming more oriented to the former activities over time. In this situation the likely changes in structure and activity-mix can be predicted and allocated spatially, provided sufficient information is available concerning land values, property ownership and condition, past patterns of change, and the relative attractiveness of various portions of the central-area fabric. This procedure would form an invaluable guide to planners seeking to control and direct this change.

6-2 IMPLICATIONS FOR PLANNING

It was suggested at the outset of this study that many attempts to plan the future structure and form of the city's central area have foundered because of a lack of knowledge concerning the organization and operation of the area. Obviously this does not apply universally, but nonetheless there is little doubt that a greater knowledge of the nature and dynamic structure of the central area would be of immense assistance to planners. Our study has concentrated on investigating these aspects of the city centre. It has not provided, and could not claim to be a guide to the planning of the area. But the analyses and conclusions of preceding chapters and the synthesis presented in § 6-1 nonetheless bear certain important planning implications.

The first relates to the overall structure of the area, that emerges as a logical arrangement of activities within a confined space in response to a number of factors summarized in § 6-1 and in Figs 6-1, 6-2. The logicality of the structure, and in particular the functional zoning of the core and the frame, suggest that efforts should be made to protect the existing structure and to ensure its maintenance as the area develops. Indeed, this is often attempted through zoning ordinances that use the existing 'natural' zoning and trends of change as its basis.

But there are dangers in applying this approach as a rule of thumb, since in allowing for the 'natural' expansion of certain existing activities, planners are prone to accelerate the trend towards the dominance of the area by 'highest and best' uses. Thus activities of a high rent-paying ability are given precedence for space over others; clearly there are some grounds for this since the high-value land of the central area warrants efficient use. But it must be stressed again that the efficiency or worth of an activity cannot and should not be measured purely in terms of its rent-paying ability (particularly in the case of non-commercial activities). Thus space must be allowed for all activities that require and benefit from a central location. Efforts should be made to protect areas comprised of those activities of low rent-paying ability that are otherwise squeezed out from the central-area system. It is simply not sufficient or realistic to allow profit to determine the entire composition of the city centre; social values must also be recognized.

Currently, most city centres are still characterized by a wide range of activity types, but there is a danger that this range will be detrimentally reduced if market forces are allowed too great a reign over the direction and nature of change within the area. In this respect, residential activities (in particular) would appear to have a greater claim to space within the area that many plans recognize. Current efforts to expand residential space availability within the area tend to concentrate on the provision of luxury appartments and the like that are clearly only accessible to the high-income sections of the community. Meanwhile the traditional lower-income housing areas close to the core are undergoing rapid transition, as commercial activity and employment are allowed to expand unchecked; thus the resident population of the central area continues to decline rapidly. There is clearly a case for the protection and rehabilitation of such housing areas before the population dwindles to insignificance.

Similarly there seems to be a need for greater recognition of the function of certain sections of the frame as 'seed-bed' locations for new enterprises entering the city system. These activities not only benefit from a central location, but also are attracted to the area by the reservoir of low-rent accommodation available within the area. Thus, some areas of so called 'blight' may warrant protection as much as 'regeneration'.

Protective zoning is one method of achieving this end; but in itself zoning is a rather sterile tool, since it is often applied on a single-use basis. This results in many cases from the excessive zeal of planners desirous of creating an orderly and neat land-use pattern. But it fails to recognize the interconnections between activities that cause different types of premises to locate in close proximity to one another. The functional zoning of the central area is marked, it is true, and in broad terms differentiation of space use is evident across the area, but the functional zones are in many instances characterized by association rather than segregation of activity types. Thus zoning must allow for the continued development of areas of mixed use.

Furthermore, the zoning applied to an area should be constantly monitored to take account of altering conditions; inappropriate zoning can lead to the unnecessary stagnation of patterns of change and hence blight. On the other hand provision should be made in certain areas for the encouragement of the filtering down process, whereby structures no longer required by their original tenants, but still possessing useful economic life, are adapted for another purpose rather than being prematurely redeveloped. In this way, space can be made available to those activities of lower rent-paying ability referred to above. There are many small-business activities operating on low overheads, and public and cultural facilities that could benefit from the application of such policy. These activities help add diversity to an otherwise increasingly sterile city centre.

Such an approach to the control of change within the city centre implies that redevelopment should be steered to particular areas in order to protect certain segments of the fabric and to encourage positively the redevelopment of others, where alternative uses are not viable. Differential plot ratios are a useful weapon in this regard, as developers will naturally seek out the areas of highest plot ratio first, particularly when constructing high-rent premises such as offices and hotels. Areas for application of such differential ratios should be chosen not simply on the basis of the physical condition of buildings, but on the basis of an evaluation of the alternative uses for the area, taking social as well as financial considerations into account.

This implies that no redevelopment scheme should be adopted without a full consideration of alternatives. As shown in Chapter 5 this applies particularly in the case of comprehensive redevelopment schemes which are a popular planning 'solution' to the regeneration of the so called obsolete section of central-area fabric. Such schemes may offer the city certain benefits, but in many cases the costs of disruption to the existing fabric, as well as the extra congestion costs incurred through excessively intensive redevelopment proposals will outweigh such benefits. The planning balance sheet (Lichfield & Chapman 1970) provides one method of evaluating the full spectrum of cost and benefits flowing from alternative schemes.

In contrast to the traditional cost-benefit framework, the balance sheet explicitly recognizes the value of intangible items and includes them in the calculus; this means that the true costs and benefits of any scheme are at least recognized. Furthermore, costs and benefits are assessed in terms of individual groups within the community and by reference to their objectives. It has been shown elsewhere in detail (Alexander 1974) that such factors make it possible to evaluate the impact of alternative redevelopment strategies in relatively realistic terms.

Similarly the balance-sheet framework would appear to have potential for the assessment of the impact of freeway construction programmes on the central area. Although it is possible to use the pure cost-benefit framework for these purposes (as shown by Pearce & Nash 1973), the balance-sheet framework allows a wider spectrum of costs and benefits to be considered, allows their incidence on various community groups to be traced, and by explicitly taking account of intangible items allows some consideration of their relative significance. It is hoped that planning authorities will recognize the potential of these techniques, for in the past they have been prone to adopt a planning strategy without full consideration of its possible impact on the existing fabric of an area, and without due evaluation against a wide range of alternatives.

In the case of freeway systems, the alternatives should not only include differing routes within the area, but also possibility of providing the same function through new public transport facilities or upgrading of existing facilities. Current thinking in many cities is to allow the car virtually free reign: new roads and new parking areas are constructed to and within the city centre, with the result that the tendency towards the use of cars is further encouraged. This not only leads to increased congestion and decreased amenity within the area, but also to the loosening of the fabric of the inner frame, where new parking facilities progressively consume more and more existing space. This trend only serves to exacerbate the difficulties of the smaller and less-profitable activities within the central area.

Meanwhile, the increased congestion causes the deterioration of the environment within the core areas in particular, where space use and pedestrian flows are at a peak. The conflict between vehicles and pedestrians has been overcome within shopping areas of many cities by the exclusion of vehicular traffic and the creation of shopping malls. But this programme is often accompanied by an expansion of the capacity of roads elsewhere within the city centre to allow freer traffic flow, and also by the construction of the by-pass freeway loops or ring roads referred to above. As noted, the need for these facilities is often assumed rather than proven; but even if it is justifiable, care must be taken to plan the route of the facility so that it causes minimum disruption to the existing pattern of activity arrangement and linkages. Otherwise, the programme will, in solving one problem, simply create another.

Thus it is clear that in planning the future structure and composition of the city's central area greater account should be taken of the existing fabric, its patterns of organization, the processes producing these patterns and the dynamic character of the area. Patterns within the area have resulted from a complex of forces that is now only beginning to be comprehended. Certainly some of the processes produce undesirable results if allowed free reign; but planners must exercise caution in applying design-oriented prognoses to the solution of non-design problems. On the other hand, planners have a responsibility to attempt to redistribute the benefits of redevelopment projects more evenly through the community—currently the costs appear to impinge on the poorer sections of the community, with the benefits flowing almost exclusively to the richer sections. Unfortunately, many planning projects designed to correct such trends have only aggravated the problem. The community deserves better treatment than this.

6-3 CONCLUSION: DIRECTIONS FOR FURTHER RESEARCH

In attempting to unravel the complex structure of the city's central area, this study has concentrated upon the patterns in one particular city. But comparisons have been made with patterns in other cities wherever possible, and these indicate that the arrangement of activities, and hence the processes operating within different cities, are consistent. It is recognized that some of the conclusions and generalizations presented in the preceding pages must be viewed with a certain amount of caution. On the other hand, this study has been in the fortunate position of being able to draw on a wealth of data, and it is believed that insofar as the broad structure and character of the area and its rationale are concerned, a reasonably valid general picture has emerged. Nonetheless, it is clear that a good deal of research remains to be done in certain fields, particularly in connection with dynamic character of the city centre and the processes operating within.

In particular, further investigation is needed into the actual significance of the many linkages that have been identified as existing between central-area activities. Multivariate techniques help to identify the statistically significant spatial groupings of activities, and are particularly helpful within the core area, where these group-ings are at their most complex. In many cases these groupings appear to have functional significance, as shown by the investigations of Goddard (1971, 1973). But the mere existence of a rich pattern of interlinkages between central activities does not mean either that the activities, *prima facie*, require spatial proximity, or even that the linkage patterns are vital to the functioning of these activities. Thus a measure of the relative importance of the linkages is required. Furthermore, since likely or feasible decentralization programmes are of concern as central congestion grows, some indication of the 'stretchability' of the linkages over space is required (as noted by Goddard 1971).

Another aspect of the processes operating within the central area that requires further research is that of change and redevelopment. This study has shown that it is possible to trace the mechanics of change and infer some of the causes thereof, and it has pointed to the futility of considering the central area as a static phenomenon. But it is evident that the mechanics of change require a good deal of further study in order both to elucidate the nature and causes of the changes themselves, and more importantly to lay the foundations of a more reliable method of predicting change that now exists.

Such research will assist in bridging the gap between present knowledge and a full understanding of the organization of the city centre and the processes operating therein. But this target is within reach; indeed it must be achieved if the planning of the area is to be placed on a firmer footing. For too long planners have operated from within a vacuum of ignorance to the detriment of the city's structure and population. It is to be hoped that this study might assist in the removal of this vacuum.

Central-area delimitation

(a) Frame delimitation criteria

The following rules were adopted in drawing the outer boundary of the frame:

1. In the outer margins of the central area (hereinafter CA), each establishment was examined individually and excluded from the CA if judged *not* to serve a central function (i.e. serving the entire city rather than a section of it) or *not* functionally linked to a central establishment.

2. Areas of land use which could be considered central in character under the terms of rule 1, but which originally developed spatially separated from the balance of the CA, and now happen to abut on to it because of CA expansion, were excluded.

3. In the case of permanent dwellings, the boundary was drawn to exclude areas of solid or continuous residential development which mark the edge of the city's inner residential zone. Any block composed of a mixture of residential development and other activities (considered to be central in nature) was included. Remnant residential areas in the inner parts of the frame and high-density residential development were both regarded as a valid part of the area.

4. Areas of *pure* ribbon or strip commercial development were excluded on the grounds that they are a distinctive type of development within the city's commercial structure rather than a part of the central area. For these purposes ribbon development was defined as commercial premises lining one side of a block only, facing a major traffic artery and backing on to non-central area development.

5. Where other criteria did not apply, natural barriers (e.g. rivers, areas of cliffs etc.), were taken as forming the outer boundary. The tendency for the central area to be limited by such barriers has been noted in several studies (e.g. Horwood & Boyce 1959, Pain 1967, Preston 1966).

(b) The classification of activities into 'core' and 'frame' categories

Certain points of the classification call for comment. Firstly, certain retail activities (automotive, machinery and builders' hardware) have been classified as frame activities. Murphy and Vance (1954a:203) did recognize that such activities (they name automotive agencies, service stations and supermarts) are rare within the CBD (cf. core). Yet, because of 'practical difficulties' and their desire not to split broad land-use categories, the authors include them as CBD activities (Murphy & Vance 1954a:204). It was not on the basis of other observations, however, that such activities were classified as frame in nature, but rather on the basis of their location characteristics in Perth (definitely peripheral); furthermore their inherent characteristics (extensive space occupiers) are definitely more akin to the frame than to the core. It is interesting to note that Horwood and Boyce (1959) also find automotive sales and service a frame activity. Similar reasons exist for the classification of certain types of heavy services (contractors and repair services) as frame activities. In location, character, and functional linkages, such land-use types belong clearly to the frame.

Professional offices are not allocated to either category, since they occur in concentrations in both the core and the frame. This dual location pattern results from a steady movement of these office types from the core into the frame in recent years. This phenomenon, which has been noted in several studies (e.g. Merriman 1967, McNair 1960) is discussed in Chapter 5.

Wholesaling is regarded as a frame activity. While wholesalers situated in the central area may gain considerably from a central location, they cannot afford to pay the high rents of the core, and in any case probably do not require a core location. Moreover, wholesaling is generally an extensive activity, generating vehicular rather than pedestrian traffic, and contact with the public is at a minimum. It is true that in Perth, as has been noted in Auckland (Pain 1967:83), some small wholesaling establishments do occur in the core on floors above the central retailing area; this, however, is the exception rather than the rule.

Similar reasons are advanced for the classification of most manufacturing establishments as frame activities. Their extensive nature is even more marked than is the wholesaling, and thus the location pattern even more peripheral. The exceptions are women's clothing- and jewellery-manufacturing establishments, both of which cluster above or at the rear of the relevant retail sectors of the core.

In the case of 'public' land uses, most are classified as frame activities. This may seem something of a paradox since one of the criteria for the classification of an activity as core-type in nature is contact with the public (Table 2-2). Under the land-use coding system adoped in this study, however, it is evident that many of the so-called public land uses are actually only semi-public or service-type activities not requiring general contact with the people at large. Those that do (e.g. hospitals) tend to be extensive in nature and therefore occur in outer portions of the central area—an exception is provided by the central post office which is clearly a core activity.

The classification of parking activities caused some problems. It was finally decided that private parking should be placed in that category into which its associated land use fell: thus a private parking area used by tenants of a central multi-storey office building becomes core in nature, whereas parking associated with a large manufacturing establishment is considered frame in nature. Public parking, on the other hand, is classified as a frame activity on the basis of its location (a ring around the intensive core area) and its extensive nature. Horwood and Boyce (1959:15) claim that Murphy and Vance's decision to classify commercial parking as a *core* activity is incorrect since they hold that parking areas are 'disfunctional' within the core. This contention seems questionable, since it is often suggested that short-term car parks built in the frame are located too far outside the core to be of any service to the area. Nevertheless, on the basis of their present location in Perth, commercial parking lots were classified as frame activities.

Business colleges and associated training schools, cinemas and central churches or cathedrals are the main 'cultural' facilities classified as core in nature. Certain authors (e.g. Horwood & Boyce 1959:15, Pain 1967:71) claim that central churches are 'anachronistic' structures within the city centre. This view seems extremely narrow, for while it may be true that such establishments would not be able nowadays to afford a core location, clearly the function of a cathedral is central in nature, and it is an activity having direct contact with people. On these grounds, and since three major denominational cathedrals are located in the central sections of Perth's central area, it was decided to classify them as core activities.

Finally, offices under construction are classified as a 'core' activity, where they are of an intensive multi-storey nature. This was necessary owing to the office-building boom currently affecting Perth (see Chapter 5). Buildings under construction result in the lateral extension of the core, and thus it seems only logical to include them.

The land-use code

The code used by the Perth City Council in their 1968 land-use survey is listed below. The code has been applied in a few other studies (see City of Hobart 1968) in recent years, and was devised by Clark Gazzard and Associates of Melbourne. In this listing a few modifications have been effected.

Any land-use classification system has certain merits and faults. The major positive and negative attributes of the Perth City Council code are:

1. ADVANTAGES

1. It is a flexible three-digit code, and thus can be viewed at three levels.
2. It is much more detailed than codes often employed in central-area studies (e.g. Murphy & Vance 1954b, 1955, Davies 1965); this enables a fine level of scrutiny of activity patterns.
3. It is easily adaptable for computer programming.
4. The classification system is generally fairly well categorized with minimum overlap. It is based on conventional activity-sets, and thus makes comparisons with previous studies easier.

2. DISADVANTAGES

1. Many classifications are questionable. The most notable are: (a) the 'public' category—in many cases the activities included are not public at all, but are rather government-owned service facilities of a restricted access nature (e.g. utilities, military). Others are more akin to commercial establishments than to 'public facilities' and are only included in this category because of government ownership—e.g. government depots (714) should really be included under 'wholesale and storage facilities'; (b) in the 'cultural and recreational' category certain uses, e.g. lottery sales (856), billiard saloons (867), etc. are operated on a commercial basis and thus display functional linkages and location patterns more akin to retail-service premises than to recreational facilities; (c) the 'office' category: many uses in this category in fact perform services. That the activities are carried out in an office is really incidental, for their major function is more akin to service activities (e.g. professional offices). The 'service' category is as it stands, somewhat unsatisfactory since it is not really complete. On the other hand it could be argued that certain activities, e.g. 'personal service' are in fact quasi-retail activities and should thus be included in other categories.
2. The above points raise the question of the code's basis. It is, generally, based on the conventional activity-sets, i.e. residential, retail etc. As mentioned above, this facili-

190

tates some comparisons (although quirks frustrate others). However, some attempt
has apparently been made to incorporate the *functional* basis of activities (cf. Rannells
1957) into the system—witness the 'service' classification. As plausible as this goal may
be, it has resulted in a somewhat confusing system, since the two approaches do not
readily coincide and thus some ambiguities are evident.

---

0   RESIDENTIAL

00   *Dwellings*

   001   Single-family house
   002   Semi-detached house
   003   Terrace houses

01   *Flats and Home Units*

   010   Investment flat blocks 2-6 units
   011   Investment flat blocks 7-14 units
   012   Investment flat blocks above 15 units
   013   Bed sitting-rooms
   015   Home units 2-6 units
   016   Home units 7-14 units
   017   Home units above 15 units

02   *Transient residence*

   020   Private hotel, boarding house, etc.

   021   Licensed hotel, guest rooms
   022   Monasteries, convents
   023   Orphanage
   024   Motel
   025   Nurses' home
   026   Halls of residence
   027   Old-people's home
   028   Other commercial residential buildings

03   *Flats associated with commercial premises*

   030   Flats behind shops
   031   Flats over shops
   032   Flats with offices
   033   Caretaker's flat
   034   Flats with other commercial uses

---

1   RETAIL

10   *Food*

   100   Grocery
   101   Meat
   102   Fruit & vegetables
   103   Bread & cakes
   104   Confectionery
   105   Delicatessen
   106   Fish shops
   107   Snack bar
   108   Drinks (non-alcoholic)
   109   Food shops (NEC) *

11   *Supermarkets*

   110   Food only
   111   Variety store—food

   112   Variety store—clothing
   113   Variety store—other

12   *Clothing*

   120   Men's clothing
   121   Women's clothing
   122   Drapery
   123   General footwear
   124   Men's footwear
   125   Women's footwear
   126   Children's & baby's wear incl. shoes
   127   Women's lingerie
   128   Women's hats
   129   Clothing shops (NEC)

* Not elsewhere classified

13 *Department Store*

  130 Food
  131 Clothing & drapery
  132 Footwear
  133 Hardware
  134 Appliances & hardware
  135 Furniture & furnishings
  136 Books & stationery
  137 Chemists
  138 Personal service
  139 Goods (NEC)

14 *Variety Store*

  140 Variety food store
  141 Variety clothing store
  142 Variety store household

15 *Household Goods*

  150 Domestic hardware & paint
  151 Appliances & electrical
  152 Furniture & floor covering, antiques
  153 Newspapers & books
  154 Chemist
  155 Sporting, incl. bicycles
  156 Jewellery & gifts
  157 Disposal, second hand, pawn shops
  158 Toys
  159 Handbags & travel goods

16 *Miscellaneous*

  160 Tobacconist
  161 Florist
  162 Photographic equipment
  163 Stationery

  164 Office machines, etc.
  165 Garden shop
  166 Pet shop
  167 Music & musical instruments
  168 Sewing machines
  169 Retail (NEC)

17 *Liquor*

  170 Hotels—bars & other facilities
  171 Liquor stores
  172 Wine shops

18 *Automotive and Machinery*

  180 Motor-vehicle dealer (in buildings)
  181 Car-sales lot
  182 Motor accessories, parts
  183 Petrol filling station
  184 Agric. implement dealer
  185 Motor tyre service
  186 Motor cycles, mowers, chain saws
  187 Marine craft & accessories
  188 Industrial equipment
  189 Machinery (NEC)

19 *Heavy Hardware*

  190 Builders' hardware
  191 Produce stores
  192 Timber yards
  193 Builders' supply yards
  194 Glass merchants
  195 Building materials show-rooms
  196 Wood yard

2 SERVICE

20 *Personal*

  200 Restaurant, cafe
  201 Milk bar
  202 Barber
  203 Beauty salon
  204 Dry cleaner, laundrette
  205 Photographer
  206 Tailor
  207 Dressmaker, milliner

  208 Shoe repair, bootmaker
  209 Health & slimming studio

21 *Personal Business*

  210 Real estate agents
  211 Travel agents
  212 Stockbrokers
  213 Auction rooms & auctioneers
  214 Enquiry agents

215 Hire cars, rent-a-car
216 Undertakers, funeral parlours
217 Caterers
218 Opticians
219 Watch, jewellery repairs

22 *Business*

220 Typing, duplicating service
221 Employment agencies
222 Computation centre
223 Plan printers
224 Drafting service
225 Telephone answering service
226 Business service (NEC)

23 *Banks, Financial*

230 Branch bank
235 Debt collectors
236 Credit reference bureau

24 *Contractors*

240 General building contractors, office & yard
241 Electrical contractors
242 Plumbing- draining- gas-fitting contractors
243 Painting contractors

244 Roofing contractors
245 Plastering & tiling contractors
246 Flooring contractors
247 Pest exterminators
248 Cleaning contractors
249 Special trade contractors (NEC)

25 *Automotive/Machinery*

250 Motor-vehicle repair garages, mechanical & electrical
251 Motor-vehicle repair garages, panel beating, spray painting
252 Motor-vehicle repair work (NEC)
253 Machinery repair

27 *Repair and Miscellaneous*

270 Electrical repair incl. TV & radio
271 Upholstery & French polish repair
272 Dental mechanics
273 Refrigerator repair
274 Furniture removals
275 Service (NEC)
276 Hire service

3 OFFICE

30 *General and Financial*

300 Manufacturers, wholesalers, distributors
301 General business offices
302 Unions, lodges, charity, religious, political, co-operative
303 Medical benefits, hospital funds
304 Insurance companies
305 Banks, finance companies
306 Shipping, airline, transport companies
307 Importers, customs agents
308 Business offices (NEC)

31 *Professional*

310 Accountants
311 Architects

312 Engineers
313 Surveyors
314 Doctors
315 Dentists
316 Other health services; chiropractors, optometrists
317 Veterinary surgeons
318 Legal (barristers, solicitors)
319 Professional offices (NEC)

32 *Governmental*

320 Commonwealth government
321 State government
322 Quasi government
323 Local government
324 Consuls, legations
325 Public utilities

33 *Business Advisory*
   330 Management consultants

331 Advertising agents
332 Commercial artists

---

4 WHOLESALE AND STORAGE
   400 Sales offices without stocks*

41 *Wholesale—Sales and storage*
   410 Food
   411 Textiles, softgoods
   412 Building materials, hardware, paint
   413 Spirits
   414 Tobacco
   415 Crockery/glass/silver/jewellery
   416 Clothing
   417 Footwear
   418 Leather goods
   419 Sporting goods

42 *Wholesale—Sales and storage*
   420 Stationery/paper/books
   421 Machinery/hospital equipment/steel
   422 Pharmaceutical, cosmetics
   423 Chemicals
   424 Furnishings, furniture
   425 Scientific/musical/photographic/surgical/optical instruments
   426 Electrical
   427 Produce, fruit & vegetable markets
   428 Domestic appliances, baths, sinks
   429 General wholesalers (NEC)

43 *Storage*
   430 Foods
   431 Textiles, softgoods
   432 Building materials, hardware, **paints**
   433 Spirits
   434 Tobacco
   435 Crockery/glass/silver/jewellery

436 Clothing
437 Footwear
438 Leather goods
439 Sporting goods

44 *Storage*
   440 Stationery, drawing & printing, paper, books
   441 Machinery, heavy equipment, steel
   442 Pharmaceutical, cosmetics
   443 Chemicals
   444 Furnishings, furniture
   445 Scientific/musical/photographic/surgical/optical instruments
   446 Electrical
   447 Produce, fruit & vegetables
   448 Domestic appliances, etc.
   449 General storage (NEC) & bond

45 *Bulk Storage*
   450 Wool stores

46 *Bulk Storage*
   460 Petroleum & petroleum product tanks
   461 Grain silos
   462 Stockyards & saleyards
   463 Cold stores

47 *Open Storage*
   470 Coal
   471 Sand
   472 Mineral ores
   473 Scrap yards & motor wreckers
   474 Open storage (NEC)

* Reclassified as 300 in all calculations

48 *Construction Yards*

  480 Heavy construction contractor offices/yards
  481 Ready-mixed concrete yard
  482 Road-paving contractors

---

5 and 6 MANUFACTURE

50 *Mineral Processing*

  500 Coke & coal processing
  501 Lime, plaster, fibrous plaster
  502 Bitumen, asphalt products
  503 Stone & slate processing
  504 Portland cement & cement goods
  505 Asbestos cement
  506 Bricks & tiles
  507 Earthenware, china, porcelain
  508 Glass, bottles, etc.
  509 Other mineral processing (NEC)

51 *Chemical Products*

  510 Industrial, heavy chemicals, acids
  511 Drugs, disinfectants, detergents
  512 Pharmaceutical & toiletries
  513 Explosives & fireworks
  514 White-lead paints, varnishes
  515 Chemical fertilizers
  516 Inks, polishes, etc.
  517 Matches
  518 Chemical products (NEC)

52 *Soaps and Oils*

  520 Vegetable oils
  521 Mineral oils, by-products
  522 Animal oils
  523 Boiling down works, tallow
  524 Soap & candle manufacturer

53 *Engineering and Metal Working*

  530 Iron & steel smelting, rolling
  531 Iron foundries
  532 Heavy machinery, structural steel
  533 Machinery, motors, steel furniture, nuts, etc.
  534 Jobbing engineers
  535 Non-ferrous metal refining
  536 Non-ferrous metal rolling
  537 Non-ferrous metal casting/processing
  538 Electrical/machinery cables
  539 Radio & electronic equipment

54 *Metal Working*

  540 Construction & repair railway rolling stock
  541 Vehicle, accessories, construction & assembly
  542 Aeroplane & parts manufacturing
  543 Shipbuilding & maintenance
  544 Cutlery and small hand tools
  545 Agricultural machines and implements
  546 Sheet metal working, galvanizing
  547 Pipes, tubes & fittings
  548 Wire, wire working and nails
  549 Metal works (NEC)

55 *Textiles*

  550 Cotton, spinning & weaving
  551 Wool, spinning & weaving
  552 Hosiery & knitted goods
  553 Silk
  554 Synthetic fibres
  555 Rope & cordage
  556 Canvas, goods, tarpaulins, tents
  557 Bags & sacks
  558 Textile printing
  559 Textile (NEC)

56 *Clothing*

  560 Readymade clothing
  561 Waterproof clothing

562   Women's clothing
563   Millinery
564   Shirts, underclothing, ties, etc.
565   Foundation garments
566   Hats, caps
567   Footwear manufacturers
568   Dry-cleaning plants, laundry, dyeing
569   Apparel (NEC)

57   *Food Processing*

570   Flour milling, cereals & starch
571   Animal & bird foods
572   Bakeries
573   Sugar mills & refining
574   Canning & freezing
575   Dairy & related products
576   Pickles, sauces, vinegar, etc.
577   Meat & fish preserving
578   Margarine, shortening, etc.
579   Tea, coffee, spices, etc.

58   *Food Processing*

580   Soft drinks
581   Breweries
582   Distilleries
583   Wineries
584   Other drinks
585   Bottling plants
586   Confectionery, chocolates, etc.
587   Tobacco, cigarettes, etc.
588   Dehydrated fruits & vegetables
589   Food processing (NEC)

59   *Leather Goods*

590   Wool scouring
591   Furriers
592   Tanning
593   Saddling, harness & whips
594   Machine belting
595   Bags, trunks, leather goods (NEC)
596   Goods of leather substitutes

60   *Sawmills and Furniture*

600   Sawmills
601   Plywood, wallboard, etc.
602   Joinery, boxes, cases
603   Wood turning & carving
604   Basketware, cane furniture
605   Perambulators
606   Woodwork (NEC)

61   *Furniture*

610   Cabinet & furniture making
611   Bedding & mattresses
612   Furnishings, drapery
613   Picture frames
614   Blinds
615   Furniture, etc. (NEC)

62   *Printing and Publishing, Paper*

620   Newspapers & periodicals
621   Printing general
622   Printing & bookbinding
623   Stationery manufacture
624   Stereotyping & electrotyping
625   Process & photo-engraving
626   Paper making
627   Cardboard boxes, cartons etc.
628   Paper bags
629   Pencils, crayons, paper treatment (NEC)

63   *Rubber Goods*

630   Rubber goods
631   Tyre retreading, etc.

64   *Miscellaneous*

640   Gramophones & records
641   Pianos, musical instruments, etc.
642   Jewellery
643   Watches, clocks, etc.
644   Linoleum & related products
645   Plastic mouldings & plastic products
646   Brooms & brushes
647   Surgical & scientific instruments
648   Photographic materials & processing
649   Spectacle makers

65 *Miscellaneous*

    650   Toys & sporting goods
    651   Manufacturing (NEC)
    655   Ice production

66 *Mines and Quarries*

    660   Underground mines
    661   Open cut mines
    662   Clay pits
    663   Sand & gravel pits
    664   Quarries

    665   Ore concentrating
    666   Oil wells
    667   Natural gas wells
    668   Salt pans

67 *Meatworks*

    670   Abattoirs
    671   Knackeries

68 *Railway Workshops*

    680   Railway workshops

---

7   PUBLIC

70 *Public Utilities*

    700   Electricity-generating station
    701   Electricity sub-station
    702   Gas works
    703   Gasometer & sub-station
    704   Water-supply dam
    705   Water-supply reservoir
    706   Water-supply pumping station
    707   Sewage-treatment works
    708   Sewage-pumping station
    709   Power easements, water pipes, etc.

71 *Special Public Uses*

    710   Telephone exchange
    711   Radio & T.V. station
    712   Fire station
    713   Ambulance station
    714   Govt. works depot
    715   Municipal govt. works depot
    716   Garbage incinerator, dump, etc.
    717   Sanitary depots
    718   Other special uses (NEC)
    719   Public conveniences, change rooms

72 *Public Service Facilities*

    720   Police station
    721   Court house
    722   Post office
    723   Baby health centre

73 *Hospitals*

    730   General hospital
    731   Private hospitals
    732   Rest home
    733   Special clinics
    734   Mental hospital
    735   Hospitals (NEC)
    739   Animal health

74 *Prisons*

    740   Prisons
    741   Prison farm
    742   Children's correction home
    743   Correction establishments (NEC)

75 *Military*

    750   Army camp & barracks
    751   Air force base
    752   Military aerodrome
    753   Naval station
    754   Naval dockyard

76 *Cemeteries*

    760   Cemeteries
    761   Lawn cemetery
    762   Crematoria

77 *Transport Termini*

    770   Bus station
    771   Railway station
    772   Railway passenger terminal
    773   Airways terminal
    774   Ferry wharves

775 Heliport
776 Airports

78 *Transport Termini*

780 Railway-goods terminal
781 Ocean wharves
782 Truck-freight terminals
783 Bus garage
784 Truck garage & depot
785 Railway lines
786 Railway marshalling yards
787 Parcels office

79 *Car Parking*

790 Car park open, free & public

791 Car park open, free & private
792 Car park in building, commercial public
793 Car park in building, private
794 Car park open, commercial public
795 Roads, streets, lane
796 Car parks open, commercial private
797 Car park in building, commercial private
798 Car parking in association with residential building

8 CULTURAL AND RECREATIONAL

80 *Educational: Primary and Secondary*

800 Kindergarten, nursery school
801 State primary school
802 State secondary school
803 Rom. Catholic primary school
804 Rom. Catholic secondary school
805 Other primary schools
806 Other secondary schools
807 Schools for handicapped children
808 Coaching colleges

81 *Educational: Tertiary*

810 Technical colleges
811 Universities
812 Teachers' colleges
813 Seminaries
814 Business and commercial colleges
815 Other tertiary establishments
816 Government research establishments

82 *Educational: Special*

820 Music schools
821 Dancing schools
822 Dressmaking school
823 Driving schools
824 Cookery school

825 Other training schools
826 Drama school
827 Modelling school

83 *Worship*

830 Church of England
831 Roman Catholic
832 Methodist
833 Presbyterian
834 Congregational
835 Baptist
836 Seventh Day Adventist
837 Salvation Army
838 Synagogue
839 Other churches

84 *Entertainment*

840 Art galleries
841 Theatres
842 Concert halls
843 Church halls
844 Other public halls
845 Commercial library
846 Public library
847 Cinemas
848 Tourist information centres
849 Museums & historical societies

85 *Private Clubs*

850 Licensed clubs

851 Reception homes
855 Indoor amusement centre
856 Lottery-sales kiosk
857 TAB betting shop
858 Gaming house
859 Brothel

86 *Indoor Amusement*

860 Club rooms
861 Gymnasium
862 Stadium
863 Dance halls, ballrooms
864 Bowling alleys
865 Skating rinks
866 Squash & indoor court games
867 Billiard rooms, table tennis, etc.
868 Indoor sports (NEC)

87 *Outdoor Entertainment Facilities*

870 Amusement parks
871 Drive-in theatres
872 Show grounds
873 Sports fields, ovals
874 Race track
875 Speedway
876 Outdoor cultural entertainment

88 *Outdoor Recreation Facilities*

880 Tennis courts
881 Public swimming pools
882 Restricted swimming pools
883 Bowling greens
884 Golf driving ranges, mini-golf
885 Playgrounds
886 Basketball courts
887 Trampolines
889 Open space among freeways

89 *Public Open Space*

890 Public golf course
891 Private golf course
892 Beach reserves
893 Parks & reserves
894 National park
895 Botanical gardens
896 Zoological gardens
897 Rifle range

---

9   VACANCY AND CONSTRUCTION*

9/26 *Vacant Premises*

9/260 Vacant flat in commercial premises
9/261 Vacant shop
9/262 Vacant office space
9/263 Vacant warehouse space
9/264 Vacant factory space
9/265 Vacant house
9/266 Vacant flat
9/267 Vacant space (NEC)
9/268 Vacant showrooms

9/28 *Vacant Land*

9/280 Vacant commercial land
9/281 Vacant industrial land
9/282 Vacant residential land
9/283 Vacant govt. land
9/284 Vacant educational land
9/285 Vacant institutional land

9/29 *Buildings under Construction*

9/290 Flats under construction
9/291 House under construction
9/292 Shop under construction
9/293 Office under construction
9/294 Warehouse under construction
9/295 Factory under construction
9/296 Institutional building under construction
9/297 Recreational building under construction
9/298 Educational building under construction
9/299 Other building under construction

* Appears in Perth City Council code as categories 26, 28, 29. Reclassified for computational purposes.

Retail and service establishments

VERTICAL LOCATION, PERTH CORE

Establishment type	base	% Establishments at each floor level (by area)						
		ground	1st	2nd	3rd	4th	5th	6th
Food stores	0.2	90.5	9.3	—	—	—	—	—
Men's clothing	4.3	75.1	17.4	3.2	—	—	—	—
Women's clothing	6.1	69.6	24.3	—	—	—	—	—
Drapery	21.7	70.7	7.6	—	—	—	—	—
Shoe stores	0.8	81.3	10.1	7.9	—	—	—	—
Children's/baby wear	—	89.5	10.5	—	—	—	—	—
Clothing accessories	—	88.7	—	11.3	—	—	—	—
Stationery/books	4.9	75.6	17.0	2.5	—	—	—	—
Chemists	0.7	99.3	—	—	—	—	—	—
Sporting goods	—	65.6	34.4	—	—	—	—	—
Disposals	43.9	56.1	—	—	—	—	—	—
Toys	15.7	54.6	29.7	—	—	—	—	—
Jewellery, gifts	5.8	64.8	20.6	4.4	4.4	—	—	—
Tobacconists	6.1	50.2	21.9	21.9	—	—	—	—
Florists/garden shops	11.6	88.4	—	—	—	—	—	—
Photographic equipment	—	79.0	21.0	—	—	—	—	—
Office machinery	14.7	34.0	30.0	6.7	14.7	—	—	—
Musical instruments	39.7	39.4	20.9	—	—	—	—	—
Miscellaneous	20.6	40.7	24.9	13.8	—	—	—	—
Household goods	21.2	52.6	26.2	—	—	—	—	—
Hotel bars/wine shops	20.6	79.4	—	—	—	—	—	—
Restaurant/cafe	9.6	82.5	7.9	—	—	—	—	—
Men's hairdresser	4.0	77.0	9.5	9.5	—	—	—	—
Beauty salon	8.9	33.0	42.3	6.2	0.8	4.1	2.9	1.9
Photographer	—	36.1	30.0	33.9	—	—	—	—
Dry cleaner	—	100.0	—	—	—	—	—	—

Establishment type	base	% Establishments at each floor level (by area)						
		ground	1st	2nd	3rd	4th	5th	6th
Tailor	3.0	16.2	<u>62.2</u>	18.6	—	—	—	—
Dressmaker	—	15.4	<u>56.3</u>	22.4	2.6	3.3	—	—
Boot repair	—	<u>81.9</u>	12.5	5.6	—	—	—	—
Optician	5.9	<u>66.3</u>	17.4	5.2	5.2	—	—	—
Jewellery repair	9.5	<u>26.2</u>	<u>47.6</u>	16.7	—	—	—	—

Note: Leading floor underlined for each use
Source: Perth City Council, land-use survey data

Retail and service establishments

CHANGES IN NUMBERS, PERTH CORE 1957-68

Establishment type	Numbers		Increase/ decrease
	1957	1968	
Department stores	7	7	0
Variety stores	5	4	— 1
Women's clothing	58	60	+ 2
Men's clothing	22	24	+ 2
Footwear	14	18	+ 4
Jewellery/gifts*	38	49	+ 11
Coffee lounges	4	8	+ 4
Cinemas	9	9	0
Chemists	15	20	+ 5
Food stores (including supermarts)	52	43	— 9
Restaurant-cafes	65	65	0
Bootmaker*	7	11	+ 4
Hotel (bars only)	15	15	0
Hardware	13	6	— 7
Furniture	18	10	— 8
Electrical goods	35	26	— 9
Dry cleaning	16	16	0
Tobacconists	11	7	— 4
Men's hairdresser	20	22	+ 2
Florists	9	12	+ 3

* These figures cannot be guaranteed accurate since Scott's analysis covered ground floor establishments only. A few establishments (single-floor) above ground level existed in these categories at the 1968 survey.

Note: Core boundaries as at 1968 survey

Sources: 1957—Maps published in Scott (1959) ; 1968—Perth City Council, land-use survey data.

Retail-sales trends and regional significance

PERTH INNER CITY AREA 1957-69*

| | 1957 | | 1969 | | Trends | |
Commodity	Value ($'000)	Proportion metropolitan sales† %	Value ($'000)	Proportion metropolitan sales %	Absolute value change ($'000)	Relative % change
Groceries	5015	12.80	5213	6.41	+ 198	− 6.39
Meat	1682	8.84	1446	4.44	− 236	− 4.38
Fruit/vegetables	1308	13.65	754	4.90	− 554	− 8.75
Confectionery	2082	25.17	2991	15.26	+ 909	− 9.91
Tobacco	2376	21.12	2395	11.74	+ 19	− 9.38
Beer, spirits, etc.	4676	17.57	4791	9.15	+ 115	− 8.42
Men's clothing	9093	72.23	13223	58.44	+ 3130	− 13.81
Women's clothing	15265	76.16	22737	58.26	+ 7472	− 17.90
Drapery	7180	71.69	9662	59.15	+ 2482	− 12.54
Electrical goods	7203	56.98	13441	38.43	+ 6238	− 18.55
Hardware	3848	67.39	5051	42.68	+ 1203	− 24.71
Furniture & floor coverings	6060	57.07	7894	27.89	+ 1834	− 29.18
Total (including other goods)	134538	37.69	141398	20.79	+ 6860	− 16.90

* Values in constant (1969) dollars; 1957 figures adjusted by reference to consumer price index (as published by Commonwealth Bureau of Census and Statistics, W.A. Office).
† Metropolitan sales figures refer to Perth Statistical Retail Division (as defined in 1969).

Source: 1957 figures: *Census of retail establishments and other services,* year ended 30 June 1957, bull. 6—W.A. (Canberra: Commonwealth Bureau of Census and Statistics). 1969 figures supplied by Commonwealth Bureau of Census and Statistics, W.A. Office.

Bibliography

Abler, R. *et al.* (1972). *Spatial Organisation: the geographers view of the world.* London: Prentice Hall.

Alexander, I. (1970). Land use structure and change in the central area of a city. M.A. thesis, Uni. of Western Australia.

———(1972*a*). Multivariate techniques in land use studies: the case of information analysis. *Reg. Stud.* **6**, 93-103.

———(1972*b*). Alternative approaches to city centre redevelopment: an evaluation. M.Phil. thesis, Uni. College, London.

———(1974). *The evaluation of city centre redevelopment.* In *Progress in Planning,* **3** (1). Oxford: Pergamon.

Allpass, J. *et al.* (1966). *Urban centres and change in centre structure.* Copenhagen: Copenhagen Institute for Centre Planning.

Alonso, W. (1960). A theory of the urban land market. *Papers Reg. Sci. Ass.* **6**, 149-59.

Andrews, L. (1962). *Urban Growth and Development: a problem approach.* New York: Simmons-Broadman.

Archer, R. (1967). Market factors in the redevelopment of the central business area of Sydney. In *Urban Redevelopment in Australia* (Ed. P. Troy). Canberra: A.N.U. Press.

———(1969). The efficiency of the Sydney CBD: the public authority contribution. *Aust. Plan. Inst. J.* **7**, 77-86.

Bachi, R. (1963). Standard distance measures and related measures in spatial analysis. *Papers Reg. Sci. Ass.* **10**, 83-132.

Baker, L. & Goddard, J. (1972). Inter-sectoral contact flows and office location in central London. In *London Studies in Regional Science* (Ed. A. Wilson), **3**. London: Pion.

Beaujeau-Garnier, J. (1965). Methodes d'etudes pour le centre des villes. *Annls de Geogr.* **406**, 694-707.

Berry, B. (1967). Grouping and regionalising: an approach to the problem using multivariate analysis. In *Quantitative Geography* (Eds W. Garrison & D. Marble), pt 1, 219-51. Evanston, Illinois: Northwestern Uni. Dept of Geography.

Berry, B. *et al.* (1963). *Commercial Structure and Commercial Blight.* Chicago: Uni. of Chicago Dept of Geography Research Paper 85.

Berry, B. & Horton, J. (1970). *Geographic perspectives on urban systems.* New York: McGraw-Hill.

Bonhert, J. & Mattingley, P. (1964). Delimitation of the CBD through time. *Econ. Geogr.* **40**, 337-47.

Bourne, L. (1967). *Private Redevelopment of the Central City*. Chicago: Uni. of Chicago Dept of Geography Research Paper 112.

────(1968). Comments on the transition zone concept. *Prof. Geogr.* **20**, 23-35.

────(1971). Physical adjustment processes and land use succession: a conceptual review and central city example. *Econ. Geogr.* **47**, 1-16.

Bowden, M. (1971). Downtown through time: delimitation, expansion and internal growth. *Econ. Geogr.* **47**, 121-36.

Buissink, J. & Widt, D. de (1967). The shopping centre of Utrecht. In *Urban Core and Inner City*. Leiden: E. J. Brill.

Buchanan, C. (1964). *Traffic in Towns*. Harmondsworth: Penguin Books and H.M.S.O.

Burgess, W. (1925). The growth of a city: introduction to a research project. In *The City* (Eds E. Park & W. Burgess). Chicago: Chicago Uni. Press.

Caroe, L. (1968). A multivariate grouping scheme: association analysis of East Anglian towns. In *Geography at Aberystwyth* (Eds E. Bowen *et al.*). Cardiff: Uni. of Wales Press.

Carol, H. (1960). The hierarchy of central functions within the city. *Annals Ass. Am. Geogr.* **50**, 419-38.

Carter, H. (1972). *The Study of Urban Geography*. London: Arnold.

Carter, H. & Rowley, G. (1966). The morphology of the central business district of Cardiff. *Trans. Inst. Br. Geogr.* **38**, 119-34.

Chadwick, G. (1971). *A Systems Approach to Planning*. Oxford: Pergamon.

City of Adelaide (1968). *Land Use Survey 1967*. City Engineer's Office.

────(1973). *Land Use Survey 1972*. City Engineer's Office.

City of Hobart (1968). *Land Use Survey—Central Business District 1967-68*. City Engineer's Dept, Development Section.

City of Johannesburg (1967). *Central Area Land Use Survey*. City Engineer's Dept.

Coddington, A. (1970). Hard numbers, soft facts. *New Society*, Oct. 1st issue.

Colby, C. (1933). Centripetal and centrifugal forces in urban geography. Repr. in *Readings in Urban Geography* (Eds H. Mayer & M. Kohn), 287-98. Chicago: Chicago Uni. Press.

Cole, J. (Ed.) (1969). *Numerical Taxonomy*. London: Academic Press.

Cooper, C. (1960). The Industrial Function of the CBD. M.A. thesis, Georgia Institute of Technology.

Cowan, P. (1971). Communications. *Urban Studies*, **6**, 436-46.

Cowan, P. *et al.* (1969). *The Office—A facet of urban growth*. London: Heinemann.

Crosby, T. (1968). *Architecture: city sense*. London: Studio Vista.

Dale, M. *et al.* (1971). Extensions of information analysis. *Aust. Comput. J.* **3**, 29-34.

Daly, M. (1970). Residential land use. In *The Analysis of Urban Development* (Ed. N. Clark) Proceedings of the Tewkesbury Symposium. Melbourne: Dept of Civil Engineering, Uni. of Melbourne.

Davies, D. (1965). *Land use in central Cape Town: a study in urban geography*. Johannesburg: Longmans.

Davies, D. & Rajah, H. (1965). The Durban CBD: boundary delimitation and racial dualism. *South Af. Geogr. J.* **47**, 45-58.

Davis, O. & Winston, A. (1961). The economics of urban renewal. In *Urban Renewal* (Ed. J. Wilson). Cambridge, Mass.: M.I.T. Press.

De Leuw Cather (1967). *Perth Metropolitan Region Inner Ring Freeway Studies. Phase II Geometric Design Studies*. Perth: Main Roads Dept.

Diamond, D. (1962). The CBD of Glasgow. *Lund Stud. Geogr.* (series B) **24**, 525-34.

Dickinson, R. (1964). *City and Region.* London: Routledge and Kegan Paul.

Eades, D. (1965). The inappropriateness of 'r' as a taxonomic measure of resemblance. *Syst. Zool.* **14**, 98-100.

Economic Geography (1971). Supplement: Factorial ecology. *Econ. Geogr.* **47**, (2).

Edwards, K. (1962). Trends in central area differentiation. *Lund Stud. Geogr.* (series B) **24**, 519-24.

Garner, B. (1966). *The internal structure of retail nucleations.* Studies in Geography No. 12. Illinois: Northwestern Uni. Press.

General Register Office (1966). *Census Report—England and Wales: Country Report for London.* London: H.M.S.O.

Getis, A. & Getis, J. (1968). Retail store spatial affinities. *Urban Studies*, **5**, 317-32.

Goddard, J. (1967). The internal structure of London's central area. In *Urban Core and Inner City*, 118-37. Leiden: E. J. Brill.

———(1968). Multivariate analysis of office locations patterns in the city centre: a London example. *Reg. Stud.* **2**, 69-85.

———(1970). Functional regions within the city centre: a study by factor analysis of taxi flows in central London. *Trans. Inst. Br. Geogr.* **49**, 161-82.

———(1971). Office communication and office location: a review of current research. *Reg. Stud.* **5**, 263-80.

———(1973). Office linkages and location. In *Progress in Planning*, **1** (2) (Eds D. Diamond & J. McLoughlin). Oxford: Pergamon.

Goodall, B. (1972). *The economics of urban areas.* Oxford: Pergamon.

Greig-Smith, P. (1964). *Quantitative plant ecology.* London: Butterworth.

Griffin, D. (1963). A central commercial area fringe on the basis of valuation data. Ph.D. thesis, Clark Uni.

Gruen, V. (1965). *The heart of our cities.* New York: Thames and Hodson.

Haig, R. (1926). Towards an understanding of the metropolis. *Q. Jl Econ.* **40**, 179-298; 402-34.

Hall, P. (1966). *The world cities.* London: World Uni. Library.

———(1970). *London 2 000.* 2nd edn. London: Faber and Faber.

Harris, C. & Ullman, E. (1945). The nature of cities. *Annals Am. Ac. Pol. Soc. Sci.* **242**, 7-17.

Hart, T. (1968). *The comprehensive development area.* Edinburgh: Oliver and Boyd.

Hartenstein, W. & Stack, A. (1967). Land use in the urban core. In *Urban Core and Inner City*, 35-52. Leiden: E. J. Brill.

Harvey, D. (1969). *Explanation in geography.* London: Arnold.

Hill, M. (1968). A goals achievement matrix for evaluating alternative plans. *J. Am. Inst. Plan.* **34**, 19-29.

Horwood, E. & Boyce, R. (1959). *Studies of the central business district and urban freeway development.* Seattle: Uni. of Washington Press.

Horwood, E. & McNair, M. (1961). The core of the city: emerging concepts. *Plan (Canada)*, **1**, 108-14.

Hoyt, H. (1939). *The structure and growth of residential neighbourhoods in American cities.* Washington, D.C.: U.S. Govt. Printing Office.

———(1964). Recent distortions of the classical models of urban structure. *Land Econs.* **40**, 199-212.

Jacobs, J. (1958). Downtown is for people, *Fortune* **41**, 133-40.

———— (1964). *The death and life of great American cities: the failure of town planning.* Harmondsworth: Pelican Books.

Johnson, L. J. (1954). The coincidence of certain types of establishment with the edge of the CBD. M.A. thesis, Clark Uni.

Johnson, J. (1967). *Urban geography: an introductory analysis.* Oxford: Pergamon.

Johnston, R. (1967). Land use changes in Melbourne's CBD 1857-1962. In *Urban Redevelopment in Australia* (Ed. P. Troy), 177-201. Canberra: A.N.U. Press.

———— (1968). Choice in classification: the subjectivity of objective methods. *Annals Ass. Am. Geogr.* **58**, 575-89.

Jones, M. (1970). Urban renewal—the role of public housing authorities. In *Analysis of Urban Development* (Ed. N. Clark), 3.79-3.95. Proceedings of the Tewkesbury Symposium. Melbourne: Dept of Civil Engineering, Uni. of Melbourne.

Kemp, D. (1972). Factors affecting the location of professional offices in West Perth. Hon. thesis, Dept of Geography, Uni. of Western Australia.

Kenyon, J. (1967). Manufacturing and sprawl. In *Metropolis on the Move* (Eds J. Gottman & R. Harper). New York: Wiley.

Kerr, D. & Spelt, J. (1958). Manufacturing in downtown Toronto. *Geogr. Bull.* **10**, 4-20.

Lance, G. & Williams, W. (1967). A note on a new information statistic classificatory programme. *Comput. J.* **9**, 195.

———— (1968). Mixed-data classificatory programmes. II: divisive systems. *Aust. Comput. J.* **1**, 82-5.

Lambert, J. & Williams, W. (1966). Multivariate methods in plant ecology. IV: comparison of information analysis and association analysis. *J. Ecol.* **54**, 635-64.

Lichfield, N. (1971). Cost-benefit analysis in planning: a critique of the Roskill Commission. *Reg. Stud.* **5**, 157-83.

Lichfield, N. & Chapman, H. (1970). Cost-benefit analysis in urban expansion: a case study: Ipswich. *Urban Studies,* **7**, 153-88.

Linge, G. (1967). Building activity in Australian metropolitan areas: a statistical background. In *Urban Redevelopment in Australia* (Ed. P. Troy), 403-41. Canberra: A.N.U. Press.

Lister, F. (1972). Movements within and extensions of the central office area in Perth. B.A. Hons thesis, Uni. of Manchester.

Logan, M. (1966). Locational behaviour of manufacturing firms in urban areas. *Annals Ass. Am. Geogr.* **56**, 451-66.

Losch, A. (1933). *The Economics of Location.* New Haven: Yale V.P.

Location of Offices Bureau (1964). *A survey of the factors governing the location of offices in the London area.* London: Economist Intelligence Unit.

———— (1969). *Offices in a Regional Centre.* London: L.O.B.

Mabogunje, A. (1964). The evaluation and analysis of the retail structure of Lagos, Nigeria. *Econ. Geogr.* **40**, 304-23.

McNair, D. (1960). The medical services area of Seattle. Ph.D. thesis, Uni. of Washington.

McNaughton-Smith, P. (1965). *Some statistical and other numerical techniques for classifying data.* Home Office Research Unit, Report 6. London: H.M.S.O.

Manning, H. (1967). The effects of land valuation and property tax on CBD redevelopment. In *Urban Redevelopment in Australia* (Ed. P. Troy). Canberra: A.N.U. Press.

Marriot, O. (1967). *The property boom.* London: Pan.

Masser, F. (1967). Car-parking in central Liverpool. In *Liverpool Essays in Geography* (Eds R. Steel & R. Lawton), 513-24. London: Longmans.

May, A. (1967). A geographical analysis of the development along the Albany Highway, Victoria Park, W.A. Hon. thesis, Dept of Geography, Uni. of Western Australia.

Merriman, R. (1967). Office movement in central Christchurch 1955-65. *N.Z. Geogr.* **23**, 117-32.

Metropolitan Regional Planning Authority (1970). *Report on the Corridor Plan for Perth*. Perth.

Ministry of Housing and Local Government (1962). *Town Centres: approach to renewal*. Planning Bull. 1. London: H.M.S.O.

———— (1963a). *Town Centres: cost and control of redevelopment*. Planning Bull. 3. London: H.M.S.O.

———— (1963b). *Town Centres: current practice*. Planning Bull. 4. London: H.M.S.O.

Mika, P. (1965). A comparative study of English and American CBD's. Ph.D. thesis, Clark Uni. (Microfilms Ltd).

Morgan, W. (1961). The two office districts of central London. *J. Tn Plan. Inst.* **47**, 161-6.

Morris, A. (1966). The internal differentiation of a type area: the CBD. Ph.D. thesis, Uni. of Wisconsin.

Murphy, R. (1962). Central business district research. *Lund Stud. Geogr.* (series B) **24**, 525-34.

———— (1966). *The American city*. New York: McGraw-Hill.

———— (1972). *The Central Business District*. London: Longmans.

Murphy, R. & Vance, J. (1954a). Delimiting the CBD. *Econ. Geogr.* **30**, 189-222.

———— (1954b). A comparative study of nine CBD's. *Econ. Geogr.* **30**, 301-36.

———— (1955). The internal structure of the CBD. *Econ. Geogr.* **31**, 21-46.

Murphy, R. *et al.* (1960). *The effect of freeways on CBD's*. Worcester: Clark Uni. Studies in Economic Geography.

Nelson, R. (1958). *The selection of retail locations*. New York: McGraw-Hill.

Outwater, R. (1967). The edge of the CBD: a comparative study in urban geography. M.A. thesis, Uni. of Oklahoma.

Pain, S. (1967). The changing functions of the CBD of Auckland 1954-66. M.A. thesis, Auckland Uni.

Parry-Lewis *et al.* (1971). Towards a comprehensive urban simulation model. Paper presented to Urban Economics conference, University of Keele, July 1971.

Parsons, H. (1967). Urban blight: a problem. In *Analysis of Urban Development* (Ed. N. Clark). Proceedings of the Tewkesbury Symposium. Melbourne: Dept of Civil Engineering, Uni. of Melbourne.

Pasdermadjan, H. (1954). *The department store: its origin, evolution and economics*. London: Newman.

Pearce, D. (1971). *Cost-benefit analysis*. London: Macmillan.

Pearce, D. & Nash, C. (1973). The evaluation of urban motorway schemes: a case study. *Urban Studies*, **8**.

Perth City Council (1963). *Zoning By-laws—The Municipality of the City of Perth— By-law 65*.

———— (1968). Freeways Area Survey. Analysis of questionnaire results.

———— (1971a). *Central Area Survey 1967/68*. Planning Dept.

———— (1971b). *City of Perth planning scheme*. Planning Dept.

Perth Regional Transport Study Group (1970). *Perth Regional Transportation Plan.* Perth: Govt. Printer.

Plowden, S. (1972). *Towns against Traffic.* London: Andre Deutsch.

Poole, M. & O'Farrell, J. (1971). The assumptions of the linear regression model. *Trans. Inst. Br. Geogr.* **52**, 145-58.

Pred, A. (1964). The intra-metropolitan location of manufacturing. *Annals Ass. Am. Geogr.* **54**, 165-80.

Prest, J. & Turvey, R. (1965). Cost-benefit analysis: a survey. Repr. in *Surveys on Economic Theory.* Vol. III: *Resource allocation,* 155-207. New York: Macmillan.

Preston, R. (1966). The zone in transition: a study of land use patterns. *Econ. Geogr.* **42**, 236-60.

————(1968). A detailed comparison of land use in three transition zones. *Annals Ass. Am. Geogr.* **58**, 461-83.

Preston, R. & Griffin, D. (1966). A restatement of the transition zone concept. *Annals Ass. Am. Geogr.* **56**, 339-50.

Rannells, J. (1957). *The core of the city.* New York: Columbia Uni. Press.

Rapkin, C. & Grigsby, W. (1959). *Residential renewal in the urban core.* Philadelphia: Uni. of Philadelphia Press.

Ratcliff, R. (1949). *Urban land economics.* New York: McGraw-Hill.

————(1953). The Madison central business area: a case study of functional change. *Wisconsin Commerce Papers,* **1** (5).

Richardson, H. (1971). *Urban economics.* Harmondsworth: Penguin Books.

Rimmer, P. (1969). *Manufacturing in Melbourne.* Canberra: A.N.U. Research School of Pacific Studies Research Paper.

Robinson, P. (1965). Land use in the CBD of Hamilton. M.A. thesis, Victoria Uni. of Wellington.

Rose, A. (1967). *Patterns of cities.* Sydney: Nelson.

————(1972). Australia as a cultural landscape. In *Australia as Human Setting* (Ed. A. Rapoport), 58-74. Sydney: Angus and Robertson.

Scott, D. (1963). An examination of the localisation factors affecting metropolitan area industries. M.A. thesis, Uni. of Western Australia.

Scott, P. (1959). The Australian CBD. *Econ. Geogr.* **35**, 290-314.

————(1970). *Geography and Retailing.* London: Hutchinson Uni. Library.

Sendut, H. (1965). The structure of Kuala Lumpur, Malaysia's capital city. *Tn Plan. Rev.* **36**, 125-38.

Simons, P. (1966). *Sydney's wholesaling district.* Research Paper 10, Dept of Geography, Uni. of Sydney.

Smeed, R. (1970). The intensity of traffic movement in towns. In *Analysis of Urban Development* (Ed. N. Clark), 4.3-4.76. Proceedings of the Tewkesbury Symposium. Melbourne: Dept of Civil Engineering, Uni. of Melbourne.

Smith, L. (1961). Space for the CBD's functions. *J. Am. Inst. Plan.* **26**.

Sokal, R. & Sneath, P. (1963). *Principles of numerical taxonomy.* San Francisco: Freeman.

Spence, N. & Taylor, P. (1970). Quantitative methods in regional taxonomy. *Progress in Geography,* **2**, 1-64.

Stafford, H. (1972). The geography of manufacturers. *Progress in Geography,* **4**, 181-217.

Stephenson, G. & Hepburn, J. (1955). *Plan for the Metropolitan Region of Perth and Fremantle 1955.* Perth: Govt. Printer.

Stewart, J. & Warntz, W. (1958). Macrogeography and social science. *Geogr. Rev.* **48**, 167-84.

Stimson, R. (1970). Hierarchical classificatory methods: an application to Melbourne population data. *Aust. Geogr. Studies*, **8**, 149-72.

Tacoma City Planning Commission (1959). *Central Business District Studies*. Pt I: *The Central Core*.

———— (1962). *The Central Business District Studies*. Pt II: *The Frame*.

Taeuber, H. (1964). Population redistribution and retail changes in the CBD. In *Contributions to Urban Sociology* (Eds W. Burgess & D. Boyce), 163-77. Chicago: Chicago Uni. Press.

Tetlow, T. & Goss, A. (1965). *Homes, Towns and Traffic*. London: Faber and Faber.

Thompson, J. (Ed.) (1969). *Motorways in London*. London: Duckworth.

Thorngren, B. (1970). How do contact systems affect regional development? *Envt. and Planning*, **2**, 409-27.

Thunen, J. von (1826). *The Isolated State* (Ed. P. Hall). Oxford: Pergamon 1966 (trans. by C. Wastenburg).

Varley, R. (1968). Land-use analysis in the city centre with special reference to Manchester. M.A. thesis, Uni. of Wales.

Weaver, J. (1954). Crop combination regions in the Middle West. *Geogr. Rev.* **44**, 195-200.

Webber, M. (1964). The urban place and the non-place urban realm. In *Explorations into urban structure* (Ed. M. Webber). Philadelphia: Uni. of Pennsylvania Press.

Weber, A. (1929). *Theory of the location of industries*. Chicago: Chicago Uni. Press (trans. by C. J. Freidrich).

Weber, D. (1958). *A comparison of two oil city centres: Odessa-Midland Texas*. Chicago: Uni. of Chicago Dept of Geography Research Paper 60.

Weiss, S. (1957). The central business district in transition. *City and regional planning studies*. Research Paper 1. Chapel Hill: Dept of City and Regional Planning, Uni. of N. Carolina.

Whipple, R. (1967). Redevelopment and the real estate market. In *Urban Redevelopment in Australia* (Ed. P. Troy). Canberra: A.N.U. Press.

——— (1970). Office space development. In *Analysis of Urban Development* (Ed. N. Clark), 3.35-3.57. Proceedings of the Tewkesbury Symposium. Melbourne: Dept of Civil Engineering, Uni. of Melbourne.

Williams, W. (1971). Principles of clustering. *Annual Rev. Ecol. Systematics*, **2**, 303-26.

Williams, W. *et al.* (1966). Multivariate methods in plant ecology. V: similarity analyses and information analyses. *J. Ecol.* **54**, 427-45.

Winston, D. *et al.* (1965). *Urban redevelopment in inner city areas*. Sydney: Planning Research Centre.

Wolinski, J. (1970). Locational rationale of the wholesaling structure of the Perth Metropolitan Region. Hon. thesis, Dept of Geography, Uni. of Western Australia.

Index

Accessibility, 36, 50, 72, 81-2, 89
Activity clusters, *see* Clusters
Agglomeration economies, 4, 15-16, 74, 87, 95, 161
Analysis problems, 32-3, 68-9, 83-4, 101, 130-1
Assimilation
   process, 19-21, 145-7
   zone of, *see* Zone
Australian cities, 4-6, 8, 12, 34, 37, 46, 62, 75, 83-5, 89, 91, 94, 105, 131, 169
Automotive activities, 36-9, 150
   effect on central area, 36-7, 50-7, 150
   expansion, 36-7, 150
   rows, 37

Banks, 48, 74, 85, 92-3
Basic activity, 3
Blight, 19, 49, 53-5, 92, 99, 151, 153, 159, 164-5, 173, 180, 182
Boundary 24-9
   core-frame, 27-9, 45, 97, 102, 123-4, 128
   delimitation, 24-9, 101-30
   movement, 128, 133, 145-6
British cities, 23, 36-7, 81, 91, 106-7, 149

CBD, 1-3, 8-12
   inappropriateness of term, 2, 8
   core-frame concept, 8-12
   Murphy/Vance concept, 1-8
Centrifugal forces, 20, 97, 150, 156, 160-1
Centripetal forces, 4, 20
Centrality, 2-8, 39, 44, 85-7, 91
Central place theory, 3, 95
Change in the CBD, 19-21, 83, 91, 130-72
   and redevelopment, 130-72
   models of, 16-21, 116, 161-5
   study of, 19-21, 130-3, 160-5
City size, 3, 61-3, 66, 68

Classification
   of activities, 1-2, 27-9, 83-5
   procedures, 116-23, 129
Clothing stores, 84-9, 125
Clusters, 3-34, 37, 42, 45-8, 69-75, 82, 85-97, 125-9
Congestion, 4, 15, 21, 50, 154, 171
   costs of, 15, 171, 183
Core, 10, 59-100, 124-9, 144-7, 151, 175-8, 167-71
   activity patterns, 66-98
   composition of, 59-63
   extension of, 145-6
   properties of, 10, 59-60
   redevelopment, 144-5, 151, 167-71
   vertical structure, 63-5, 124-9, 168-9
Core-frame concept, 8-12, 31-2, 104, 172-3
   history, 10
   utility, 12
Correlation coefficient, 120
Cost-benefit analysis, 171, 183
Commuting, 36, 50, 59, 166
Court house, 74-5
Cultural facilities, 2, 4-5, 33, 97, 156-8, 177, 182

Decentralization, 3-4, 7, 41, 74, 91, 149, 155-6, 177
Delimitation techniques, 3, 23-9
Department stores, 84-9, 94, 109, 125-9, 150, 175
Discard, zone of, *see* Zone
Dispersal index, 68-9, 72, 74-5, 78, 81-2, 87, 89, 91-2, 94

Ecology, 116-18
Economic forces, 13-15, 33-4, 66, 87, 91, 95-8, 144, 146, 149, 153, 158-9, 167-71, 175-6, 178

213

Entertainment facilities, 48, 89
Entropy, 121-3
Environment, value of, 57, 144, 167-71
European cities, 61, 64, 149
Evaluation, 56, 167-71, 182-3
Externalities, 15, 50-9, 72-5, 144, 164, 166-71, 183-4

Factor analysis, 118-20
Financial offices, *see* Offices
Frame, 10, 12, 19, 23-58, 102-8, 178-80
  activity patterns, 32-49
  character, 23-29
  composition, 29-32
  delimitation, 24-9
  redevelopment in, 144-56, 158-160
Freeways, 21, 36, 50-7
  impact of, 50-7
Function of city centre, 1-8, 15-16
Functional zones, 66-7, 83, 85, 99, 101-16, 123-30
  links and relationships, 15-16, 33, 43-5, 58, 72-5, 87, 176

Goals, 154, 171, 183
Government offices, 5, 33, 78-9, 81
Ground floor
  patterns, 12, 64-5, 83, 125-8
  activities, 72, 78, 81-92, 125, 174
Grouping techniques, 116-23
Groupings, 32; *see also* Clusters

Hay Street, Perth, 47, 66, 87, 89, 97-8
Hard core, 117
Household-goods stores, 84-5, 91-2, 94, 96, 109, 125, 128, 150

Index of dispersal, *see* Dispersal index
Industrial, *see* Manufacturing
Information analysis, 121-9
Information flows, 72-5
Information statistics, 121-3
Inner retail zone (IRZ), 83, 85-91, 94, 109, 111-16, 150-1, 175-6
Insurance companies, 72
Insurance offices, 72
Intensity of land use, 2, 10, 13-17, 19, 133, 136, 139, 149, 160-1, 175-6

Land market theory, 13-15, 44-5, 66, 87, 89, 91-2, 95, 97, 139, 149, 155-6, 158-9, 165, 175, 181-2

Land use
  succession, 13-15, 19, 41, 133-9, 146, 148-50, 153, 155-6, 158-65, 171, 181-2
  regions, 66, 83, 94-7, 104-16, 123-9
Land value
  and land use, 13-16, 18, 33-4, 39, 41, 49, 66, 78, 83-7, 89-91, 94-7 123, 128, 133-42, 144-6, 148-51, 169-71, 178-8, 181-2
  changes, 37, 100, 144-5, 148-9, 151, 164
Linkages, 4, 15-16, 24, 37, 41-2, 45, 47-8, 57, 60, 66, 72-5, 78, 82, 87, 89, 94, 97, 118-19, 148, 170, 177-80, 182; *see also* Offices, Manufacturing, Wholesaling
Location factors, 13-16, 37, 39-42, 44-8, 72-99, 144, 149-50, 154, 156-7, 176-80
London, 46, 54, 60, 68-9, 74, 106, 129, 144, 153, 176

Manufacturing activities
  central function, 7-8
  decentralization, 39, 41-2
  heavy manufacturing, 40-1, 156
  in the core, 39
  in the frame, 39-44
  light manufacturing, 39-40, 156
  location patterns, 42-4, 155-8
  redevelopment, 155-8
Market, *see* Land market, Rent-paying ability, Land values
Market, food, 41, 43, 45, 153
Medical offices, 47-8, 69, 77-8, 147-9
Models
  concentric ring, 10-12, 16-18, 160, 180
  multiple nuclei, 17-18
  of central-area structure, 13-21, 172-80
  of city structure, 16-19, 120, 146, 160, 180
  of land-use change, 19-21, 142, 163-5, 167-71, 185
  sectoral, 17-19, 146, 160, 180
Motorways, *see* Freeways
Multivariate analysis, 116-29, 185

Objectivity, 116-19
Office activities, 4, 15-16, 66-82, 99, 109-12, 124-9, 133-49, 166-7, 176-9
  financial offices, 68-75, 109-16, 125-9
  government offices, 78, 81, 109-10
  linkages, contact patterns, 4, 15-16, 72, 74-5, 81, 109-10
  location decisions, 4, 46-7, 72-5, 78
  location patterns, 46-7, 66-82, 109-16, 124-9
  professional offices, 46-7, 147-9

redevelopment, 144-9, 166-7, 169-71
relocation, 4, 46-7, 74-5, 78, 146-7

Parking
  expansion, 157-8
  frame, 36-7
Peak land value, 13, 66-7, 83-7, 94-6, 176
Pedestrians
  flows, 27, 72, 81, 87, 94, 175-6
  conflict with vehicles, 21, 37, 42, 59, 87, 98-9, 168-9, 184
Perth City Council, 25-7, 37-8, 41-2, 57, 68, 131, 146-7, 150, 153, 166-7
Planning
  freeways, 50-9
  land use, 21, 49, 58, 87, 99-100, 149, 160-71, 181-4
  redevelopment, 21, 49, 149, 165-71
Plot ratio, 144, 147, 166-7
Polynuclear structure, 17-20, 104, 160-5, 175
Population decline, 33-4, 158-60
Prestige, 66, 72, 78, 144, 146
Professional offices, *see* Offices
Profit, 1-2, 13-15, 37, 45, 87, 116, 136, 139, 144, 146, 150, 154, 156-7, 165-7, 169, 181-2
Public facilities, 1-2, 5
  core patterns, 62, 97, 175
  frame patterns, 33, 178-9
  redevelopment, 156-8, 168-9

Quantitative analysis, 68-9, 116-123
Quantitative methods, 116-23

Redevelopment
  and central area specialization, 21, 133-42, 144-6, 149, 156-7, 160, 165-7, 181
  comprehensive, 21, 167-71
  evaluation of, 21, 167-71
  piecemeal, 144-7, 165-7, 169-71
Relocation, 4, 46-7, 74-5, 98-9, 147-50, 154, 156, 159; *see also* Decentralization
Renewal index, 151-2
Rent, *see* Land value
Residential premises
  and central function, 8, 62, 158-60
  high density, 8, 34-6, 158-60
  redevelopment, 34, 158-60
  rent-paying ability, 15, 33, 158
  single family, 34, 158-9
  transitional, 34
Retailing
  as central function, 3-4, 63

in core, 82-97, 102-11
decentralization, 4, 80, 94, 139, 149, 151
in frame, 36-8, 47-8
specialist stores, 85-9, 94-5, 109, 125-6
and land values, 82-5, 94-7
vertical location, 63-5, 83, 91, 94-7, 111-20, 124-9, 174
household-goods stores, 91-2, 109-11, 128
redevelopment, 139, 150-4
Ribbon development, 27, 37

Sector, 17-19, 146, 160
Services
  automotive, 37-9
  personal, 89-91, 47-8, 128
Site, effect of, 25
Social costs, *see* Externalities
Spatial analysis, 32-3, 68-9, 101, 116-23, 130-31
Spatial groupings, *see* Groupings
St George Terrace, Perth, 66-8, 70-1, 74, 79-82, 116, 128-9, 144-6
Stock exchange, 72, 74, 176
Subjectivity, 116-19
Suburbanization, *see* Decentralization
System
  city centre as, 99, 158, 172-5

Taxonomy, 116-23
Telecommunications, 74-5
Tertiary activity, 3-4, 142
Threshold, 95, 97, 176
Transition, 19-21, 133-42, 146; *see also* Land-use succession
  and blight, 49, 151-4, 159
  zone, *see* Frame
Transport
  effect on core, 36, 59
  effect on frame, 36, 50-8
  planning, 50-8, 166-70
  problems, 36, 59, 166-7
  to and from CBD, 4, 59, 166-7

United States cities, 5, 31-3, 36, 42, 47, 49, 59-64, 81, 87, 108, 163
Urban planning, *see* Planning
Urban region, 3
Utility (economic), 13-15, 95, 97, 153, 157, 181-2

Vacancy
  and Freeways, 32, 53-5

in core, 89-91, 111
in frame, 32, 49, 53-5
Variance, 119-21
Vertical structure
  and redevelopment, 167-71
  of core, 63-5, 72, 75, 78-9, 82-6, 89-91, 94-7,
    111-16, 124-9
  of frame, 23, 27, 29, 45

Wholesaling
  central function, 6-7
  core location patterns, 45, 97
  decentralization, 7, 44-5, 139, 153-5

frame location patterns, 44-6
redevelopment, 151, 153-5

Zone
  of assimilation, 19, 102, 123, 133, 145-7
  of discard, 19, 92, 102, 123, 133, 146, 151,
    153, 164-5
  of transition, *see* Frame
Zoning
  ordinances in Perth, 38, 137
  effects of, 37, 42, 44, 66, 144, 146-7, 151-4,
    156, 158-9, 161, 182
  inadequacy of, 166-7, 182